IF
LOVING
YOU IS
WRONG

Also by Gregg Olsen

ABANDONED PRAYERS
BITTER ALMONDS
MOCKINGBIRD
STARVATION HEIGHTS
THE CONFESSIONS OF
AN AMERICAN BLACK WIDOW

IF LOVING YOU IS WRONG

GREGG OLSEN

St. Martin's

I have elected to use pseudonyms in this book. If I have further
obscured any identities, it was through the omission of specific
details—not through the inclusion of false biographical information. Among the pseudonyms are Abby Campbell, Linda Gardner,
Kate Stewart, Natalie Bates, Patricia Watson, and Ellen Douglas.

G.O.

For June Rose Wolfe

PROLOGUE

June 19, 1996

THE NIGHT WAS a pinpricked blanket over the dull sheen of Puget Sound. Errant seagulls—feathered rats, really—teetered on the edge of a Dumpster. In an instant, they slid inside looking for food before fluttering out and sending white droppings into Jackson Pollack splatters on grungy asphalt further marked by oil stains and melted bubble gum.

Music wafted from one of the boats in the guest moorage section of the marina in Des Moines, Washington, a suburb just south of the Seattle–Tacoma Airport. In its setting and size, Des Moines, Washington, held little in common with its Midwestern counterpart. The westernmost Des Moines was on Puget Sound, facing west to the Olympic Mountains and Vashon and Maury islands. It was suburban, yet with the feel of a neighborhood place where people gathered in crime watches and fed each other's pets when vacations came.

Even the name wasn't pronounced the same in Washington as Iowa. The Washington Des Moines was pronounced with the *s* sound at the end, which gave most everybody not from there great difficulty when learning to say it so incorrectly.

That June night something very disturbing was taking place in Des Moines. And from the moment Dave Shields, 27, began his walk a very personal story started moving slowly from tragedy to the stuff of sleazy supermarket magazines and sordid tabloid television reports. In time, lawyers, writers, friends, and family of those involved would all lose sight of the one thing that had caught their concern and interest in the first place. It was a woman and a boy. *A mother, a teacher, a wife. And a boy.*

Dave Shields had never wanted to be anything but a cop. Not really. Though it was true that he had enlisted in the Coast Guard and had given most of his family and friends the impression that he had a career as a cop of the sea, he wanted nothing more than to be a police officer with his feet on dry ground. Both his grandmother and a close high school friend had died in accidents caused by drunken drivers. The idea that he could be part of a solution to a terrible and senseless problem led him to law enforcement. The former San Diegan came to Seattle with the Coast Guard in 1989; two years later he left in pursuit of his dream. It wasn't easy going. He worked his way up from a fire department job in Des Moines to the marina security job. By the spring of 1996, he was also a reserve police officer in Buckley, a town in the foothills of Mount Rainier, some forty-five minutes away. At the marina he worked graveyard, which he loved.

Even if the evening is dead, it is almost always resuscitated around one in the morning. Shields and other cops of the night knew that. The last hour before the bars shut down the exodus of the drunk begins. The hardy party folks make their woozy attempts at demonstrating sobriety—direct steps to their car, the key ready, the door pulled open without a false move. All police officers, from the parking-lot rent-a-cop to the seasoned veteran called back into late-night patrol, know that although it may be the dead of the night, things happen after one in the morning.

At the Des Moines marina, Shields was used to the after-midnight revelers who leave the bars and are drawn to the waterfront to continue the night. Sex and drugs are the usual reason. Kids come down to the water to maraud, smoke, and screw while their parents drift off to sleep in front of the soft blue glow of television sets that never seem to find a respite from use. Sticky, spent latex condoms sometimes pockmark the parking lot like the remnants of a water-balloon fight.

The tide was way out and in the warmth of the June evening Dave Shields could smell the salty, rotting mud that passes for a Puget Sound beach. He barely needed a jacket; the air was warming. His uniform was a light blue shirt, with a "City of Des Moines" patch on the shoulders. His pants were black and a duty belt dangling with a radio, flashlight, and pepper spray hung around his waist. Dave Shields looked the part of a cop.

He parked his silver and blue security-issue bike and followed the source of loud music down the ramp to the guest moorage in front of the harbormaster's office. When the tide was out, it brought the boats low and widened the beach. The music—some eighties junk—played from a stereo and bounced off the bank of condominiums that fringed the east side of the parking lot. Dave Shields knew the partiers—"old guys, some in their late thirties, even forties"—hadn't meant to be a nuisance. The sound carried across the black water and hung in the still air. They turned the volume way down and apologized and Shields headed back up the ramp to his bike.

But at the top of the ramp, something caught his attention. Bursts of red, then white. Dave Shields fixed his clear hazel eyes into the darkness, and in an instant he saw lights flash on a blue Plymouth Voyager with Alaska plates parked in one of the darker areas of the parking lot. The van was facing west. The brake lights tapped again.

Some guy's getting a blow job, he thought. It happened a lot at the marina. Shields and other officers well knew the shadowy form of a man leaned back from the wheel, touching the brakes with an errant foot, while a head popped up into view.

From the top of the moorage ramp, he watched it for a second, and the van started up, backing into a landscape island planted with junipers and Saint-John's-wort before rolling a tire up over the curb. The van rolled forward, but when it backed up once more it hit the curb and ran into the island again. The driver was a slight figure, a young boy, Shields thought, though later he was not so sure.

By now, Shields was suspicious. He watched the van, sure that it was a DUI. The van rolled forward and drove slowly, walking pace, through the parking lot. He cocked his head to his lapel microphone, called dispatch with a possible DUI, and walked along the bushes, not wanting to lose the van by returning for his bike.

The young officer continued walking in the shadows thirty or forty feet behind the van as it crawled south along the edge of the parking lot abutting the cliff of condominiums. The van turned right, followed along the docks, then turned left again, toward Anthony's Home Port. The restaurant was closed and the parking lot nearly empty. The pace of the van was odd, because it was so slow. The officer wondered how the van had enough momentum to make it over the speed bumps that interrupted the asphalt every few yards.

The van stopped for a few seconds, and went around the restaurant's waterfront eating deck before circling back around once more.

What are they doing? he thought. Did they see me?

The van pulled into a spot in front of a cyclone fence on the edge of the restaurant parking lot and its lights went dark. On the corner of the lot, just in front of the condos, Dave Shields waited for Des Moines's finest to show up.

Blond-haired, light-complected, Rich Niebush arrived first and checked in with the young security guard. Niebush was a favorite of Shields's, the kind of officer that he aspired to be: direct, professional, and even-keeled. Dave filled in the officer on what he had seen. As Rich Niebush and another officer, Bob Tschida, approached they fixed a spotlight on the van. Niebush could see a woman move from the back and slide into the driver's seat. By then Sergeant Robert Collins was there, too.

The officers pulled closer to the van and turned on their flashing lights. Niebush got out and walked toward the woman driver. A swipe of light from his flashlight also revealed the figure of a boy under a sleeping bag. The officers exchanged glances. Bob Tschida went to the driver's side to talk with the woman. Niebush stayed on the passenger side.

"Get out of the van, please," Tschida said.

Niebush went around the van to open the driver's door and called to the boy in the back. But there was no answer. The light filled the interior and the officer could see that seats were folded down as if to form a kind of bed. The boy lay motionless, feigning sleep.

"What is going on here?" the officer asked.

The blond woman offered no answer. It was as if she didn't hear his words. After some prodding, she gave her name as Mary Letourneau. She was a schoolteacher from Shorewood Elementary in the Highline School District. There was no problem; there was no reason to interrogate her.

"Why were you in the back of the van with the boy?" Sergeant Collins asked.

Mary Kay said she was watching Vili overnight because his mother worked a late shift. She told the officers that she and her husband, Steve, had had an altercation less than an hour before and she and the boy left.

"I decided to teach him a lesson," she said, "and not return until after he went to work in the morning."

She explained that Steve left at 3:30 A.M. for a job handling baggage for Alaska Airlines.

"We're just trying to get some sleep before returning home after my husband leaves for work," she said.

Sergeant Collins radioed for the Normandy Park Police to check the Letourneau residence to see if Steve Letourneau would be able to back up his wife's story. A bit later, Des Moines radioed back that no one answered the front door.

Next, the sergeant asked Mary Kay what she was wearing. His flashlight washed over her to reveal a layering of four T-shirts and a beige skirt. She had on a thin jacket, no socks, and sandals. (Later officers would differ on what the woman had on that night. Niebush thought she was only wearing a T-shirt. "I did not notice a skirt," he wrote later in his report.)

Sergeant Collins told Mary Kay that they were taking Vili into protective custody.

"You're blowing this out of proportion," she protested. She was a teacher, a friend of the family's. There was nothing improper going on in the back of the van. She told them she taught at Shorewood Elementary. She said she was thirty-two.

The officer didn't seem too concerned, telling her that her story made sense, but there was an appearance of impropriety. The woman was wearing a nightie or a T-shirt and, as far as Shields and the officers could see, nothing else.

What's she doing dressed like that coming down here? Shields wondered.

By then Dave Shields had moved closer to the van. Whatever was happening was not dangerous and, without a doubt, far more interesting than lingering back by the condos. The woman was very pretty. Even years later, Shields said he remembered thinking, "Boy, she's got great legs."

It was Tschida who spoke to the marina security guard. The cop's dark eyes appeared mystified.

"This kid's like only twelve or thirteen years old," he said, his voice trailing off. "And I think he was putting his clothes back on."

Shields shook his head. "Oh, shit," he said. *Maybe they were having sex?*

Niebush radioed for more help. Another sergeant arrived a few minutes later. Something was wrong.

"She wasn't really scared, but she seemed just a little nervous," Shields said later.

The officers pressed for answers and grew more concerned the more evasive Mary Kay became. He wondered if she was being held captive by the boy or perhaps he was being held against his will.

"Who is back there?"

Mary Kay didn't answer.

"What's his name?"

Again, no answer. Finally she said it was Vili Fualaau, a student of hers.

"How old is the boy?" Tschida asked.

Mary Kay hesitated for a moment before answering, "Eighteen."

The officer told her to wake him, but when she refused, he yelled at the boy to wake up. He wanted to talk with him, but the figure didn't stir.

What gives here?

The Des Moines officer called out again. He'd seen his share of fakers and it was clear the kid was awake. His dark eyes were open, though his head lay motionless. Finally, after another admonition, he lifted his head and climbed out from under the sleeping bag. A few moments later, Vili Fualaau told the officer that he was fourteen years old, but when asked for proof, he came up short. Of course, he had no driver's license and no Washington State ID card. He was only a kid.

Vili said he had been staying at the Letourneau house that night when a fight between Mary Kay and her husband Steve made him upset. He left the house and walked down the hill to the QFC store on Marine View Drive. It wasn't far from the Letourneau home in neighboring Normandy Park, which was on a ridge just above the shopping center. Mary Kay picked him up in the van and they drove to the marina for sleep.

Mary Kay Letourneau's story seemed odd, maybe even suspect, though it matched Vili's. She became irritated. She told them they were being too extreme, taking it too far.

When the police told Mary Kay Letourneau that they were going to take Vili to the station, she became insistent. She flat-out didn't want to leave him alone. She was, she explained, *responsible* for him.

Just before the patrol cars went back up the hill away from Puget Sound and the marina, Shields huddled with another of the officers.

"We were kind of talking behind the patrol cars. The whole thing seemed fishy, we were convinced, but our hands were tied. He's in the back trying to put his clothes back on and she's wearing this little nightie thing. She didn't look as old as she is, but I knew she was older than eighteen,'' the security cop later said.

Back at the Des Moines police station, the officers failed to reach Soona Fualaau at her home in White Center, some fifteen minutes to the north. Once more, they pressed Mary Kay and Vili for the name of the mother's place of work. Specifics were not forthcoming.

"She works for a pie-baking place in Kent," Vili finally said. Neither he nor his teacher could come up with the name.

A phone call to the Valley Comm Center turned up the name of a commercial bakery called Plush Pippin. Another call turned up Soona Fualaau.

The sergeant told Vili's mother what had transpired that night. She was unconcerned and asked to speak with the pair. After both spoke to her, Soona Fualaau instructed the police officer to leave Mary Kay Letourneau in charge of her son.

"She had said that she feels completely comfortable with him being with her and she trusts Mary and that they could release the boy back to her custody," Shields recalled.

What happened that night haunted him when all hell had broken loose and the world was introduced to Mary Kay and Vili.

"They had already had sex . . . or were about to have it," the young marina officer said later. "We all knew it."

A day later, the wife of a Des Moines police officer told the director of security for the Highline School District what had happened at the marina between Mary Letourneau and Vili Fualaau. An employee of the school district herself, the cop's wife said her husband had told her that the mother had approved the early morning excursion with the teacher. Though the officers on the scene had felt very uneasy, there wasn't enough evidence that a sex crime had been committed. With no crime—*no charges*—there would be no official action by the police. A report wouldn't be sent to the district.

Two weeks later, a lieutenant for the police department

sent the report to the city attorney for Des Moines. He too was uncomfortable with what happened at the marina. It just didn't seem right.

Evidently, nothing happened once the report got there. The Highline School District didn't hear another word about the marina, the teacher, and the boy. Not for almost another year. Not until so much had happened that it could never be undone.

PART ONE
DAUGHTER

To put it bluntly, to be free in right and natural law does not mean we are free to break the Ten Commandments . . . to lie, to covet, to steal, to dishonor father and mother, to commit adultery . . .
—John Schmitz, in his 1974 book, Stranger in the Arena

She was the most beautiful of the children and by far the most devoted to John. She was the one who sat beaming— like Nancy Reagan gazing at Ronnie—whenever her father spoke. . . .
—Randy Smith, a Schmitz political aide in a 1998 Los Angeles Times *interview*

Let's look at this with reasonable and compassionate eyes.
—Mary Kay Letourneau to a friend in a 1999 prison visit

ONE

IN REALITY IT was the tony homes of Lemon Heights perched on the scorched hills above Tustin that gave the city the nickname *The Beverly Hills of Orange County*. The majority of Tustin was Middle America with neighborhoods of mostly unpretentious tracts of stucco and tile-roofed houses filled with children freckled, tanned, or burned by the sun. The wealthy living on Lemon Heights looked down on Tustin, or rather past it, to the waters of the Pacific. When John and Mary Schmitz and their sons Johnny, Joey, and baby Jerry moved into a one-story house with a lone palm tree on Brittany Woods Drive in Tustin in the early 1960s, on the surface they were a good Catholic family with moderate means.

Yet if there was anything to distinguish the family from others in Tustin, it was the indisputable appeal of the parents. John was dark and dashing with the rigid posture of a military man. Mary, with her soft eyes and sweet smile, could play demure, but she was sure of herself in ways that few women allowed themselves at the time. John Schmitz and Mary Suehr had met at a college graduation party at Marquette University in Milwaukee, Wisconsin, where both had earned degrees. She was a chemist who set aside a promising career to support the man she loved. But it was more than love. It was also the marriage of conservative and religious ideals that made them such a good fit. John and Mary were a team in life, the afterlife, and, in time, the purgatory that was California politics.

An eight-year stint in the Marine Corps in El Toro

where John was a pilot and helicopter aviator brought them to California. Like so many others who made the military migration during the forties and fifties, they saw California as a golden hope for a life of opportunity. When John left the Marines, like his father and father-in-law, he became a teacher. He taught philosophy and government at Santa Ana College.

"I'm a good teacher," he once told a reporter. "I've always been able to make a subject interesting. No one falls asleep in my class."

Part of what made that a true statement was that the man had an undeniable charisma and wit. He was brash, brilliant, and handsome with dark hair, dark eyes, and a pencil-thin mustache. John G. Schmitz was onstage whether his audience was a single student or a roomful. He was the center of the world. In the beginning, the lightning rod for attention presided over a family that was the envy of friends and neighbors.

"They were a devoted family," said one neighbor who still keeps in touch with John and Mary. "The kids all loved each other. It was sort of like, the family that prayed together, stayed together."

Indeed, prayer was an important ritual at the Schmitz home. Visitors to the house then—or any other place the family lived—never recalled a single meal when prayer wasn't a prelude to dining. Life revolved around the church. John sang in the choir at St. Cecelia's and Mary hauled the children in their station wagon ("our Catholic Cadillac") to class each day.

To supplement his college instructor's wages, John worked part-time at Disneyland as a Cobblestone Cop.

"That made him a real hero among the kids," the neighbor said.

Although Mary Kay has memories of her father as that Disney character, she would later tell a friend she wasn't certain if she actually remembered it or had been told about it so often that she had kept it as memory. "It is a glimpse," she told a friend many years later, "when I was three years old. Like a Mary Poppins doll I had, or putting my father's hair in curlers at our first house, just a glimpse of my childhood.''

It was a lovely beginning to what everyone thought would be a wonderful life. Summer nights were filled with the laughter of the boys playing kick the can, hide-and-seek. Summer days they played baseball or football games that stretched for hours. In time, the family would get a German shepherd that John named Kaiser.

In the early 1960s there were still orange groves off Irvine Boulevard, not far from houses lined up in the sun along Brittany Woods Drive. It was a beautiful place and time. California was challenging the East Coast as the center of the universe. The Beach Boys had just released ''Surfin' Safari''—their first big hit. It was sunshine and beaches. And on January 30, 1962, Mary Katherine Schmitz was born. She would be her father's staunchest ally and, some would say later, her mother's greatest disappointment.

No one wanted to talk about it years later, and no one wanted to put much importance on the fact. What would happen later with Mary Kay was not a bonding problem. But the fact was that Mary Schmitz had an injury that made it impossible to care for her new baby daughter for several weeks. As the baby stayed with the neighbors across the street, her mother convalesced in her bedroom.

Later, the woman who cared for the Schmitzs' firstborn daughter refused to talk about the cause of Mrs. Schmitz's need for convalescence. She believed it had no influence on their daughter.

''They loved Mary Kay then, and they love her now,'' she said.

When John Schmitz returned to Brittany Woods Drive, he always made a beeline for the neighbors' to hold his daughter in his arms. Every day. Mary Kay's blond hair was but a faint downy glow around her little head. But her brown eyes were enormous. No father could have been more pleased.

''Sons are wonderful,'' said the neighbor who took care of Mary Kay. ''But to a father, a daughter is extra special.''

If mother and daughter didn't bond, as had been suggested, those closest to the family in those early years didn't see it. It appeared that the little blond-haired girl was her mother's pride. It was true that Mary Schmitz expected a lot from her children, and probably more so from her sons.

"When Mary Kay was a little girl," said the neighbor, ". . . I can still see that front bedroom fixed like she was a little princess or something. Mary always seemed to be there to help her and Mary Kay went right along with it. So she had to be very happy with her mother."

No matter how busy they became, no matter where they would live, the Schmitz children were always foremost in their parents' minds, according to the neighbor.

"They never forgot the kids," she said.

The tide was moving in the direction of conservative upstarts in Orange County—more so than just about anywhere in the country. John Schmitz, with his David Niven mustache and sharp-as-carbide-blades wit, was in the right place at the right time in 1964. It didn't matter that he was a card-carrying member of the right-wing John Birch Society, the anticommunist organization founded in 1958 to promote conservative causes. In 1964, when Mary Kay was two, her father found his arena. He was elected state senator.

None were more proud of John's victory than those in Tustin and at St. Cecelia's. He was the pride of the congregation. Choir director Richard Kulda, a conservative, though no John Bircher, admired John Schmitz as a legislator and a man. A reelection followed two years later, and by the end of the decade, a bid for the U.S. Congress. His campaign bumper sticker read: "When you're out of Schmitz, you're out of gear."

"John has a brilliant mind, witty, conscientious. Good-humored. He was not easily ruffled, a fighter pilot. In mortal combat you cannot get ruffled, you have to be thinking every instant. You've got to use every bit of brainpower you have," Richard Kulda remembered.

During his six years in the California legislature many

argued that his finest achievements were in curtailing sex education in the classroom and limiting the availability of condoms where young people might get their hands on them.

"More self-discipline is needed," he said.

By 1970, three more siblings had joined Mary Kay and her three older brothers. When Mary Kay was three, her sister Terry was born, followed by Elizabeth and, lastly, Philip, born in March 1970.

"John and Mary loved having three boys, then three girls, then a boy. It was so wonderful. And so tragic later," the close family friend and neighbor later said.

In the years of his heyday as the king of the quip, John Schmitz became beloved by reporters looking for a loose-cannon quote that could guarantee outrage and increased readership. John Schmitz became known more for what he said than what he did. Whenever he opened his mouth, John Schmitz supporters cheered and his foes wondered if he'd left enough room for his foot.

"They like to be called gays," he once said of homosexuals in search of political clout. "I prefer to call them queers."

Sometimes charm was slipped into the mix and his remarks came off as one-liners, given like a political Johnny Carson.

"I may not be Hispanic, but I'm pretty close. I'm a Catholic with a mustache," he said.

When the Schmitz family left for Sacramento or later for Washington, D.C., their good Brittany Woods Drive neighbors' joy for the family was tempered with personal sadness. Though they kept in touch and saw old friends and neighbors whenever they came to town and attended fund-raisers—for which Mary Schmitz had made her daughters' dresses—it wasn't the same.

"When we got to Washington, John took us to the White House and everything. I got to sit in Tip O'Neill's chair," said the neighbor. "We were so happy for them."

It was June 1970 when John Schmitz moved his family to Washington, D.C., to fulfill the time remaining on a

congressional seat won in a special election. Mary Kay
would later say she made the transition easily, basking in
the attention reflected from her father's admirers. There
were parties to host, Easter eggs to roll on the White House
lawn, and photographers to smile for at every turn. *Heady
stuff for an eight-year-old girl.* Her father was at the top
of his game at that time and he knew it. Things were happening for her mother, too. Mary Schmitz was more than
a wife; she was a savvy political partner. She was passionate about her political and religious beliefs and every
bit as adept—many felt more so—as her husband when it
came to tapping into the strengths of the conservative con-
stituency. She attracted a following by campaigning
against the ERA and was dubbed a "West Coast Phyllis
Schafly." Like her husband, she was a fervent right-to-
lifer who considered abortion nothing short of murder.

If John Schmitz was the leader of the band when it
came to Orange County Republican politics, as one adversary later characterized him, his wife was equally pow-
erful and accomplished. Mary Schmitz was a captivating
public speaker, and an articulate crusader for conservative
causes. She was more than just a woman standing behind
her man—though she espoused the ideal that that's where
women belonged.

Some friends of the family felt sorry for Mary Kay, and
her sisters Terry and Elizabeth. The emphasis in that
household was always on the sons. It was a man's world
and John and Mary Schmitz made no bones about it and
the fact that they wanted to *keep* it that way. When the
Equal Rights Amendment died, Mary Schmitz had a card-
board tombstone put up in her front yard as a cheeky reminder of her greatest achievement.

"Their prejudice extended down to the women in their
family," said a friend and political adversary of the
Schmitzes many years later. "Women were low on the
social scale. Here was this woman espousing antiwoman
values. Her own daughter, who was as bright as hell, could
have gone to Stanford like her brother did, but didn't."

It wasn't the money, though most people knew that the
Schmitz family wasn't rich. The truth was that John

Schmitz, political gadfly extraordinare, could have gotten his daughters into any school in the country. If he had wanted to. If his wife had wanted to.

But Mary Kay was a girl.

"What was she going to do?" the friend asked. "Go off and get married and have kids."

TWO

IT HAD BEEN foggy every morning for a week before the sun burned off the milky haze to reveal the sparkling waters of the Orange County coastline. In the afternoon the temperatures would rise near eighty degrees and air mattresses were rolled out, beach balls pumped up. But half the summer was gone before the new house at 10 Mission Bay Drive in Corona del Mar would be Southern California—complete with a swimming pool. A pool was as necessary on Spyglass Hill as orthodontics for a perfect smile, a shiny new car, and a pretty wife who made weekly visits to the hair salon. It was *de rigueur*. When the Schmitz family moved back to California from Washington, D.C., they did not return to Tustin. Instead, they moved up. *Way up.* Just south of Newport Beach, Corona del Mar was an area of affluence and power. It was hibiscus and bird-of-paradise. John and Mary built a beautiful new home in the hills high above the Pacific. While it was true that only one room in the house had an ocean view— Mary Kay's—they could see the blue when they drove toward town and the coast highway.

On Saturday, August 11, 1973, John and Mary hosted a barbecue party to celebrate summer and the completion of the pool just two days before. It was a pleasant mix of a few political cronies and friends, including the family from the old Brittany Woods neighborhood in Tustin. It was the year after John Schmitz ran for president of the United States on the American Independent Party ticket. He didn't win, of course. He hadn't expected to. He ran to keep the dream alive.

Mary Kay, eleven, and her baby brother, Philip, three, joined the other Schmitz children—John, eighteen, Joe, sixteen, Jerry, fourteen, Terry, seven, and Elizabeth, five—and kids from the neighborhood in the water as the adults enjoyed cold drinks and the perfect vision of a California summer day: the blue water of the pool, the orange of the sun, and the sound of happy children. Nothing could be lovelier. Those who were there that day recalled the event as being a typical Schmitz affair—devoted friends presided over by the charming John and, of course, Mary, the mother of his children, the soldier for her husband's dreams.

By Monday afternoon all of the joy of the pool would be drained forever. Its blue shimmering surface would always be a backyard reminder, silent and still, of a family tragedy. Just after three-thirty that afternoon, Mary Schmitz removed the plastic life preserver from her toddler son's slender body and sent him to the bathroom. She went inside to work in her office while Mary Kay and her brother Jerry played in the shallow end.

A few minutes later—maybe a half hour, no one could pinpoint how much time had passed—someone noticed that the three-year-old was missing. It took only an instant to find him at the bottom of the swimming pool. Somehow, though Mary Kay and Jerry were in the same waters, neither had seen Philip slip into the water and splash.

No one saw him struggle. He just slipped under and was gone.

Hurd Armstrong, a thirty-two-year-old Newport Beach motorcycle cop, was the first on the scene. A distraught Mary Schmitz, who kept repeating the same sentence, met him.

"I only left him for a minute. Just a minute."

She led him through the house to the pool where he found little Philip, who was as blue as the water, tiny and lifeless, lying in the sun on the edge of the pool. Water matted his dark blond hair to his small head. His eyes were closed. The other Schmitz children watched from the inside of the house as their mother and the motorcycle cop hovered over the baby. Everything was spinning. Everything was happening so fast.

Newport Beach firemen arrived moments later and tried to revive him with oxygen and heart massage, but the effort appeared futile. Seconds later, a tornado of helicopter blades fanned the brush in the vacant land behind 10 Mission Bay Drive. A police helicopter landed. Hurd Armstrong cradled the little boy in his arms and handed him over the fence that cordoned off the wild of the hills from the groomed yard. The hospital was only four or five miles away. No one said whether the boy would make it or not, but most already knew that it was bad.

"That night when I got home my wife knew that my day had involved a tragedy with a child. She always knew," Hurd Armstrong said many years later. "Whenever something happened with a child it lingered for days. I wasn't myself."

The doctors at the intensive care unit at Hoag Memorial in Newport Beach couldn't save the baby. He was pronounced dead eighteen hours later.

"We were all there," Mary Schmitz said to a reporter. "I don't know how it could have happened."

The headline on Tuesday in the Corona del Mar *Pilot* was marked in letters more than an inch high:

JOHN SCHMITZ' SON DIES IN NEWPORT

Those who knew him then—and later—would all agree that it was the most devastating time John Schmitz would find his name on the front page, though there were many, many times when the press was less than kind or when scandal would riddle his image, his world.

Richard Kulda, the choir director from St. Cecelia in Tustin, was devastated by the news of the drowning. His wife and Mary Schmitz had been pregnant at the same time with their last babies. He prayed for the Schmitz family, but he knew that they'd be able to get through the tragedy because their Catholic faith was so strong.

"Mary and John were good troupers," Richard said later. "They have to carry on. You have a duty. Mary's face was so drawn she obviously suffered just horribly when he died. When you have a lot of children it is a comfort.''

Philip James Schmitz was buried in a little white casket in a grave in Ascension Cemetery near El Toro. Tourists now tromp past the child's grave to pay their respects to Nicole Brown Simpson and to remember her tragic life. They know nothing of the boy buried in the same cemetery and the impact of his death on another woman, a sister.

Years later, people would look back at Philip's drowning to search for answers as to its possible effect on his oldest sister and what happened to her more than twenty years later. How did it weigh on Mary Kay's mind? Did she feel responsible? Was she?

Willard Voit, a family friend and a political supporter of John Schmitz's, understood through his conversations with the family that Mary Kay had, in fact, been in charge of watching Philip.

"I don't know if it triggered what [mental illness] she got. I know it had to be a very heavy item.'' Willard stumbled for words. "I'm saying it could be related,'' he said. "I know that the event could be the source of some of Mary Kay's disorder. Jerry might have been there at the same time,'' he said later. "But I know that Mary Kay had been given the responsibility of watching Philip. It was horrible. Horrible.''

It was shortly after the drowning that a girl named Michelle Rhinehart met Mary Kay Schmitz. Over the years the subject would come up and there was no doubt that Mary Kay's heart was broken when Philip died that August afternoon, but she never told Michelle that she felt responsible.

"She adored her little brother. She said he had more life at three than most people have . . . he was really a bright spirit. It wasn't her fault. She had nothing to do with it.''

Even so, Michelle would later admit that the three-year-old's death did have a profound impact on Mary Kay. There were times when Mary Kay didn't want her children near the water, especially a pool; she was even reluctant to let her kids take lessons. The drowning was a piece of the puzzle that, when put together with other traumas, explained how Mary Kay ended up where she did.

"The thing that is so phenomenally amazing is how she continues to deny that any of these things had any impact on her," Michelle said later.

The drowning also had an impact of incredible consequence to John Schmitz.

"That's when we feel that John really lost it," said a neighbor from Tustin, alluding to events that would take place a decade later.

Mary Schmitz was stoic about the loss of her baby. It wasn't her style to make a scene, to toss her body on the casket, or even to shed a tear. Not in public, anyway.

"They took it better than most people. I would have been very emotional," said a friend.

It was a family tragedy, the kind many families must deal with. The Schmitzes were the kind that could deal with it. Years later Mary Kay would tell a friend that her family never blamed her for the drowning. The whole idea of blaming someone for an accident was an unnecessary hurt.

"I am upset if anyone blamed anyone," Mary Kay said. "It is such a sacred, private tragedy. No blame should be put on anyone and none ever was. Not on me. Not on my mother."

The day before Philip drowned Mary Kay was out by the pool. Her baby brother, fearless and determined, wanted to show his sister that he could swim. As she watched, the three-year-old stepped to the edge of the pool and jumped in. He sank to the bottom like a stone and Mary Kay went to get him.

"It wasn't but a second, but I looked through the water at him. He was standing on the bottom of the pool looking up at me. I can still see his eyes. Looking at me and saying so much. *I thought I could, but I guess I can't. Save me.*

And I did. It wasn't but a second when I reached down for him and pulled him from the water. His eyes had said so much to me then. And they speak to me now. His eyes haunt me now.''

THREE

IT DIDN'T HAPPEN every time, but sometimes when Michelle Rhinehart Jarvis drove her white VW convertible ''Lamby'' up the hills above the ocean near Corona del Mar, she'd catch a whiff of a fragrance that would send her back, way back to the time when she and Mary Kay Schmitz were young girls. When a little moisture from the Pacific mixed with the fragrance of the wildflowers, the bougainvillea, and the eucalyptus, it would come back to her. It was 1998 and like Mary Kay, Michelle was a mother. She had two little girls—Danielle and Kylie—and a son, Michael, named for her husband, a multi-media developer and designer. Michelle's life in Southern California was the busy-working-mother-with-never-enough-time routine she had once imagined Mary Kay's life had been up in Seattle.

She pulled her car to the side of a canyon road and looked around.

Bleached white condominiums and gated communities of pink stucco had obliterated much of the visual beauty of a raw landscape. There had been a time when hawks circled and coyotes sometimes made it down to where the houses lined up in glistening rows on Spyglass Hill. There had been a time when two girls slid down the hills on paper bags, or spent all day following a coyote's trail. Time had marched on and all of that was gone now.

But even all of the progress couldn't mask the scent that brought back memories. The sweet, salty smell of ocean and canyon. The smell of summertime and youth.

In a moment, Michelle could feel the wind blowing through the open windows of Mary Kay's bedroom on the nights when she'd sleep over on the floor next to her friend. She could hear the water of the swimming pool splashing against its tiled walls while the two of them pretended to flee from sharks.

"Jaws is coming!"

Years later when everyone in the world would have an opinion about her friend, Michelle would sometimes roll down her window and breathe it all in and remember. And she'd think how far Mary Kay had tumbled from Spyglass Hill and how inevitable she believed it all had been.

Mary Schmitz had priorities and none of her children felt the need to make excuses for it. It was the way they lived. The enormous house at 10 Mission Bay on Spyglass Hill had marble floors and carpeting that cost more than forty dollars a yard. The furnishings on the main level were exquisite. Years later, Mary Kay still marveled over a couch her mother had selected and how stunning the silk organza fabric covering its cushions had been. To be sure, upstairs was another world. There was no matching furniture, no gorgeous crystal, and no exquisite figurines. No family photos lined the walls. The children's bedrooms were spare in their furnishings to say the least. Mary Kay's bed had no frame. Her windows went without curtains or screens. Facing west, her corner bedroom would fill with the hot air of the California sun. Some of the Schmitz children used drawers set on the floor to hold their underwear and socks.

"There was so much mold and mildew in the bathroom that I couldn't even use it," Michelle Jarvis recalled.

But downstairs everything was picture perfect.

Mary Kay would later say that it didn't bother her. She was happy to sprawl out on the forty-dollar-a-yard carpet or flop on a beanbag chair when she watched TV.

"What do those kinds of things matter?" she asked later. "My mother's priorities were elsewhere. We were in private school. She entertained downstairs. We weren't put upon. So what if our couch in the TV room was given to us? We were very happy indeed."

Michelle and Mary Kay met through their mothers, who were casual acquaintances and played tennis together.

With Mary Kay's school friends in Costa Mesa at St. John the Baptist, she was isolated from kids outside of her siblings. Michelle lived in East Bluff just down the road from Spyglass.

Mary Schmitz was the one who suggested getting the girls together. They were in grade school at the time. It seemed a good idea to have a friend close by. It was an idea, however, some would later suggest, that Mrs. Schmitz would have liked to reconsider. Mary Kay and Michelle became inseparable.

"I practically lived there. I annoyed her mother to no end," Michelle said later. "She always called me *that* Michelle. She was dismissive to anyone whose last name wasn't Schmitz and who couldn't help her husband's political career. I couldn't help her in her quest to be mother of the year or whatever her pet project was that time."

Michelle and Mary Kay's mother didn't hit it off because as far as Michelle could tell, Mary Schmitz cared more about herself and her husband's career. The kids appeared to be window dressing.

"A Rose Kennedy wannabe," Michelle said later.

While that could have been true, it was also true that Mary Schmitz was not interested in any of Mary Kay's friends, especially Michelle, whom Mary Kay said her mother found "abrupt and crass." Mary Schmitz was a righteous and busy woman with no time for children that weren't her own. She was the type of woman who would look past a kid in a room and address her own child: "Don't you think it is time for Michelle to go home?" She didn't say, "Michelle, we have some things we need to do. Do you need a ride home?"

It was something they didn't talk about at first. But in time it was the basis for the bond that only strengthened over time. From the darkness of a shared childhood trauma came the light of their friendship. Michelle and Mary Kay shared a common experience that ensured a unique closeness. Both had been molested by a relative.

"I think back on when we first talked about it," Michelle later said. "[One of her brothers] molested her, but I don't think he actually had sex with her. I think for her it was the fear and the betrayal from somebody that she loved. It happened. I knew about it. I was ten or eleven years old and dealing with my own.''

Mary Kay told Michelle how as a nine- and ten-year-old she used to search for new places in which she could hide when their parents were away.

"Can you imagine her cowering in some closet praying to God that her brother didn't find her?" Michelle asked later. "And nobody there to protect her! Where the hell were her parents?"

On the campaign trail. Accepting an award. Appearing on television.

Michelle didn't fault John Schmitz as much as she blamed Mary Schmitz. A daughter needs a mother to talk to. John Schmitz was running around Washington, D.C., or Sacramento trying to change the world. Mary Schmitz was yammering on television about the virtues of taking care of children and keeping the home fires burning. The hypocrisy of it all still angered Michelle more than two decades later.

"She's never been accepted by her mother. *Never.* Mary Kay couldn't even tell her mother what her brother had done at that age. She knew how her mother would react. She knew her mother would probably blame her.''

Mary Kay would later describe Michelle's recollections as an "exaggeration" and dismissed the sexual abuse as nothing more than "fondling."

"I don't even feel I was violated. Not my body. I was not forced into anything, but when I decided it was wrong, I said no. And guess what? It stopped."

John Schmitz wasn't home much. But when he was, he always gave the girls a hug and a kiss. He joked with his sons. He made them laugh. He had a way of taking a song and twisting it around and making it his own and his children loved him for it. But no one in the family would argue that he didn't have a favorite. His first daughter, all blond and brown-eyed, was the apple of her father's eye from the first moment he held her. She could sit for hours still and quiet as he read, just to be near him. He called his adoring and most beautiful daughter Mary O'Cake, Mary Cake, finally just Cake. No one else in the family adopted the nickname.

"No one dared to," Mary Kay said later. "It was something only for my father to say."

In Mary Kay's eyes, her dad could do no wrong. Her mother was always in the way; always the killjoy.

When John Schmitz became interested in learning more about his genealogical background, he made several trips to Europe. An excited Mary Kay told Michelle one time that through her father's research, he'd discovered that he was related to the Romanian royal family through an illegitimate son of one of the kings.

"Mary Schmitz did not want the story out because it was too embarrassing to the family," Michelle said later. "She forbade them to talk about it."

Mary Schmitz was not a demonstrative mother. She was not hovering in the kitchen with a pan of brownies in the oven and a piñata to be finished on the table—not like her eldest daughter would grow up to be before her world would crash. Yet Mary Kay, like any young girl, coveted the attention of her mother. But few saw any.

"I never ever in all those years saw her mother hug or kiss her or show her any type of affection in any way. *Ever.* I never heard her say I love you. Nothing," Michelle said later.

To the outside world, the family was golden. John, the oldest, was the all-American, smart and good looking. Joe was overshadowed a bit by John, but he was also bright and political-brochure–ready. Jerry was intelligent, sensitive, and certainly the most caring and protective of Mary Kay. The girls—Mary Kay, Terri, and Liz—were cute, quiet, and relegated to the background.

According to Michelle it was all by design. The girls were raised to be homemakers. The boys were going to be lawyers and politicians and the dynasty that Mary Schmitz had nurtured in Orange County would prosper.

From the time that she was a girl, Mary Kay was raised to smile and wave. To look good. To be polite. To be "on." All the time. Political families are always onstage. Every weekend during a campaign, there was a parade, a fund-raiser, and a dinner. No one could deny that the Schmitzes were a gorgeous family. Handsome boys and adorable little girls all lined up around their charismatic father and perfectly coiffed mother.

"They were a façade family," said an adult friend of the family. "A Hollywood set."

Years later some would wonder if Mary Kay Letourneau had paid a price for the deception that was her idyllic California childhood. How had being a public family affected her? How had it affected her to have to smile even when she didn't want to because being "public" was the way her father made his living?

"Maybe she had a mental breakdown? Maybe living that life wasn't healthy? I can just imagine the conversations in that household," said the friend. " *'We're not rich people, but we have values . . . God has entrusted us with this.'* "

Even as a young girl, Mary Kay Schmitz loved the mirror. No one could really fault her for it. She was, without a doubt, beautiful. The only blonde in her family, when she practiced piano in the normally off-limits living room, she often stopped to dance in front of a large mirror. She dreamed of studying music at Juilliard. She could dance, sing, and act. Maybe a career in musical theater? She was disciplined and enjoyed the control she had over her body.

And because her mother taught her that a girl must always look her best, Mary Kay took the lesson to heart and made certain that she always looked put together.

Primping was one thing, but as they grew into adolescence, Michelle began to find it excessive. As Mary Kay grew older, it seemed to border on the obsessive. There were times when Michelle wanted to take a baseball bat to Mary Kay's head to put her out of the misery of standing in front of the mirror.

"It took her at least two and half hours to get ready to go anywhere. She would mess with one curl on her head for a good twenty minutes before she got it exactly the way she wanted it to be," Michelle recalled.

After a while, when they were teens, Michelle couldn't take it anymore.

"Why is that one curl so important? How long does it take to get ready?" she asked.

Cake never had an answer. It just *was*.

FOUR

MARY KAY SCHMITZ and Michelle Rhinehart were two hot girls and they knew it. They had it all. Any guy, any boyfriend. They had yacht clubs and champagne. They had trips to Palm Springs, Catalina, and Mexico. They partied with the heirs to the May Company and Heinz Ketchup fortunes. Although the two best friends never attended the same schools, they were inseparable. Mary Kay went to St. John the Baptist in Costa Mesa and the Roman Catholic prep Cornelia Connelly School in Anaheim. Michelle attended Our Lady Queen of Angels and the local high school in Corona del Mar.

At Cornelia Connelly, Mary Kay made her name by being on the varsity cheerleading squad for three years in a row. Cheerleaders from three Orange County Catholic girls' schools vied for spots on the squad that cheered for Servite, the boys' Catholic school. By her own estimation, Mary Kay was good at cheerleading not only because she knew the routines, but because she actually followed the game. She was nominated at one point for a spot on a national cheerleading team, but dropped the ball on the paperwork and never got her rightful place on the team. Her high school grades, she later said, were as good as she wanted them to be. The classes weren't easy and she gave just enough to keep her grades halfway decent. She had other priorities.

"We just played," Michelle said years later. "That's all we did. We just had a great time. We didn't care much about school. We didn't have to."

In fact, Southern California was made for girls who

looked like Mary Kay and Michelle—beautiful girls who
could put on a pair of shorts over a swimsuit and slip into
sandals and look like a million bucks. In cars with the top
down, hair tousled by the warm, moist air of the ocean,
they were girls who could catch all the looks that came
their way. Michelle had blond hair, fine features, and gray-
blue eyes. She looked like Mary Kay's sister. Many
thought so. And if Mary Kay with her feathered Farrah
Fawcett hairdo was a good Catholic schoolgirl by day, she
was a completely different sort when she stashed her
cheerleading skirt and pom-poms ("She never had any
books, never did any homework that I ever saw," said a
friend of Mary Kay's).

Mary Kay liked to party, and she liked boys. And with
a few exceptions, boyfriends didn't last long. Even so, they
were kept on a string of steel and shoved aside when something better came along. Something better was someone
cuter, or richer. Moving on was easy. A broken heart was
the price of admission. As far as Michelle could determine,
those were talents Mary Kay honed to perfection.

"We knew the power we had over men and we were
very aware of it and we used it," Michelle recalled of their
high school days.

Sometimes the pair got in the car and just headed south
where they'd end up partying for the weekend in Mexico.
Ensenada was a favorite destination. So was Catalina Island. The two best friends were lovely and blond and that
meant they didn't need money. Guys were always willing
to shell out for a pretty girl. It didn't matter that they were
high school students or supposedly had a curfew. Mary
Kay didn't seem to worry about much beyond having a
good time. While others might have been concerned about
their school work or their jobs, Mary Kay focussed on her
hair and getting to the next party to meet the next guy.
There were no obstacles. She was invincible. It was never
too late, too far, too expensive. She lived for the moment.

"Mary Kay always liked to live on the edge and do
dangerous things," Michelle said later.

During that period Mary Kay held a succession of jobs,
working the counter at the Snack Shack in Corona del Mar

or hostessing and waitressing at restaurants Casa Maria, Gulliver's, or the Good Earth. At most of those jobs, Michelle worked alongside Mary Kay. When it was time to quit for greener pastures or because they couldn't get the time off they needed to party, they quit together.

They were then, as they always imagined, friends forever.

Greek Row at the University of Southern California campus was only a short drive from Corona del Mar, and it became a magnet for Mary Kay and Michelle. When they were sixteen, the pair was on campus every week partying. Sometimes things got out of hand. On one occasion a friend of Michelle's told her that Mary Kay's party-girl antics got her mentioned in the *Row Run,* the newspaper for fraternity boys and sorority girls.

"It was just well-known that she was the girl to party with. 'For a good time, call Mary Kay.' It's sad. I don't know that my reputation was much better, but I never read about myself in the *Row Run,* that's for sure."

Michelle worried about Mary Kay when she went out to party. It seemed Mary Kay lived to tally the number of boyfriends she had. She measured her worth by how many guys had *wanted* her. Popularity was everything. She made the same mistakes over and over, and if she had been looking for love, it was like the words in the country song: She was looking for love in all the wrong places.

"There were some very traumatic things that happened in her high school and college years," Michelle said later. "The promiscuity is a classic symptom of somebody who has been molested. She was sexually used by men she dated, too. She was physically hurt. I know that she was. As much as she keeps denying it by saying that it doesn't matter, I know that it does."

Mary Kay had an on-and-off-again boyfriend during much of her teen years, but Michelle never considered that relationship exclusive or really that important. Mary Kay seemed to feed off the guy's adulation. It was almost as if he were starstruck by the girl from Spyglass Hill and she liked that aspect more than she liked him. The relationship was based on how he viewed her.

"We had way more power than we should have had. We basically did what we wanted to do. Our life was basically whatever we wanted it to be. We worked when we wanted to work, where we wanted to work. We played where we wanted to play and when we wanted to play," recalled Michelle.

When Mary Kay was seventeen, her mother pushed her into running for Miss Newport Beach, even though she wasn't old enough to enter. The headstrong eldest Schmitz daughter thought the whole thing was a big joke, almost an embarrassment. But she did what was asked. For the good of the family name. It turned out later that the joke was on John and Mary Schmitz. Mary Kay told Michelle that a man associated with the pageant was doing everything he could to get into her pants.

"He was a dog," Michelle said of the man. "It would have been really fun to see how her parents would have reacted if they could see what he was all about."

Mary Kay didn't win, but one of the sponsors told her that she placed "in the top five."

The response was classic Mary Schmitz. Jerry Schmitz announced he was getting married to another Scientologist, and his ultra-Catholic mother refused to support the wedding with her attendance. That also meant none of her children or her husband could attend. Mary Kay was the only one to break ranks. She loved her brother, and no matter what her mother said, she was going to be at the wedding in San Francisco. She and Michelle drove north in the Schmitz family's Oldsmobile. The engine blew in Bakersfield.

The teenage girls had no money, nowhere to stay. Mary Kay called her father and he said he'd drive up and trade cars in the morning. He still wouldn't go to the wedding. Mary Schmitz had laid down the law. The girls ended up talking a trucker out of his truck for the night and they curled up in the cab.

"She gets herself into trouble, she manages to weasel
out of it. No matter what happens," Michelle said later.

Years later, when the world would hear of their classmate,
a small group of women from Cornelia Connelly gathered
after the connection was made between Mary Kay Letourneau and Mary Kay Schmitz. One who knew her from the
Catholic school in Anaheim had never considered the former classmate a mental giant, calling her "simple-
minded." It was an opinion that held up when they met
again when Mary Kay was grown and the mother of four.
She was a sad, tragic figure. The former classmate wondered if she was a victim of her childhood.

"She never really got the love she needed," a friend
recalled.

FIVE

KNBC, THE LOS Angeles NBC affiliate, had a locally
produced issues show that was not only a ratings winner,
it provided fodder for water-cooler commentary. Among
the panelists were Mary Schmitz, lawyer Gloria Allred,
and the president of United Teachers of Los Angeles, Hank
Springer. *Free for All*, with its roundtable format, was
taped on Friday nights and aired on Saturday afternoons.
It was at the height of its popularity in the mid- to late
1970s.

Sometimes after the taping, Mary Schmitz would join
the others for a drink or a meal at a Mexican restaurant
off Olive in Burbank. Hank Springer was surprised that
Mary would go out with them; she seemed so uptight on
the show.

A fuckin' right-wing cunt, Hank thought at first.

But somehow Mary Schmitz, "to the right of Attila the
Hun," and Hank Springer, "to the left of Jane Fonda,"
developed respect and a friendship.

"Mary Schmitz was elegant," he said later when he
thought of the wife of the California state senator. "Very

beautifully dressed. Never a hair out of place. I wouldn't call her strident, but next to strident. She didn't let her hair down much. On camera she was very, very professional."

And predictable, too.

"Almost like she was a cookie cutter," Hank said of her on-camera persona and her defense of her causes, the anti-ERA, antiabortion movements. "You stamp her out, like a Stepford wife."

Hank Springer found things to like about Mary Schmitz outside of her politics, which he loathed. But he found little tolerance for her husband. Mary was alone a lot during those years. Her husband was in Sacramento most of the week. If Mary could relax a little and be a person, John Schmitz could not. At least, Hank didn't think so. Once in a great while John—always on, always in a suit and tie—would join the group after the tapings.

"A very uptight man, so self-righteous. He believes in his ideas so virulently—to me it's a virus—horribly negative, homophobic, antiunion, antiabortion. Everything that had to do with people, he was against it. His homophobia was almost off the Richter scale," Hank recalled later.

Mary Schmitz worked the same political agenda. Although she never held an elected office, she was named to a number of panels and committees and carried considerable clout. She was always at the ready to present her views. Sometimes getting the message out was all that seemed to matter.

One night Lois Lundberg, Orange County Republican Party chairwoman, invited Mary Schmitz to speak at a meeting. Mary was highly regarded as a knowledgeable speaker, articulate and quick. Though sometimes, her critics felt, she would go off on a tangent. She was a good speaker, though not as humorous or as warm as John Schmitz. The same night, the party secretary informed Lois that a local Brownie troop would be attending.

Later, Lois wished she would have asked Mary Schmitz the topic of her talk. As the little fresh faces of the Brownies looked on, Mary proceeded with a graphic discussion against abortion. A frantic Lois tried to get the speaker to modulate her message, or even better, to get her off the stage. But Mary Schmitz wouldn't budge. She was there for the night.

"She gave a long and detailed speech, talking about every form of abortion. The vacuum cleaner was the one where I had a heart attack. I was hopeful the kids were small enough that they didn't know what she was talking about."

Los Angeles lawyer Gloria Allred not only worked alongside Mary Schmitz on the weekly television show, she worked tirelessly in the support of feminist and human rights causes. That meant she was in frequent and direct opposition to John Schmitz and his right-wing agenda. Whether stumping on television's *Merv Griffin Show* or presenting Schmitz with a "chastity belt" when she fought him on prochoice issues, she was a woman of undeniable power. John Schmitz knew it, and as some would later suggest, it irritated him. He joked about her surname: All-Red.

In December of 1981, State Senator Schmitz issued a press release entitled: "Attack of the Bulldykes." The release described an audience of prochoice supporters as "a sea of hard, Jewish, and (arguably) female faces." He called Gloria Allred a "slick butch lawyeress."

His comments touched off a firestorm of publicity that culminated in his being stripped of committee chairmanships, and receiving the censure of the Republican Party. Gloria Allred filed a $10 million libel suit that would fester for years.

Throughout the publicity, Mary Kay stood up for her father like no one else in the family. One time at lunch with a boyfriend at the Good Earth restaurant, Mary Kay overheard a party at an adjacent table engaged in a lively and very nasty debate about her father and the Allred fracas. It was too much for her to bear. Later she recalled how she stood up and walked over to the group.

"You don't have all the facts," she told them. "You are talking about John Schmitz and his character in such personal terms and you don't even know him. I know him. He's my father."

The diners set their forks down and looked embarrassed.

"You're right," one said. "We don't know him."

"Yes," she said before turning away, "and you attacked his character!"

The charges of anti-Semitism were fueled by demonstrations staged by members of the Jewish Defense League in front of the Schmitz home on Spyglass Hill. As always, Mary Kay, then a nineteen-year-old student at Orange Coast College living at home, backed her father to the hilt. Later, some would insist, blindly so. And if her brothers and sisters were less demonstrative in their devotion, she didn't care. She and her father had a special relationship. She went upstairs and cranked up the stereo, releasing ear-splitting German marching music from an open window. *That'll teach them.* Cake didn't like anyone messing with her father.

SIX

CARLA VERNE BOSTROM Stuckle's home in Tustin was on a quiet street nearly out of earshot of the ocean waves of sound that is the Garden Grove/Santa Ana freeway that snakes past her subdivision. It was a California ranch-style house with a pool in the backyard that featured a little waterfall. Inside, over a brown linoleum floor, a white couch with red pillows and a piano dominated their respective corners of the house. Carla Stuckle had a library overflowing with books by Taylor Caldwell and Stephen King. She also had a secret. For years she had been carrying on with a married man. A very important, very married, man.

At one time, the Swedish-born Carla Stuckle had been a beautiful woman, but diabetes, too much work, and poor judgment cost her her youth before her time. She had botched two marriages by the time she found herself in the glare of the spotlight. Her first to a Marine officer ended in divorce when the husband returned from a tour

of duty to learn from his daughters that their mother had
been sharing a bedroom with "Uncle Pete." Their father
raised her two little girls, the oldest named Carla for her
mother, born in 1959, and Amy, two years later.

"My mother was the kind of woman who couldn't be
without companionship," said Carla Larson, Carla Stuckle's daughter, many years later. "So she . . . she got kind
of wild, I don't know if it was the times. There were lots
of men in the house, my aunt told me she did drugs . . .
but I don't know. My father never confirmed that."

By 1966, their mother was in California, chasing after
"Uncle Pete" and starting over. The two little girls would
grow up with scarcely any contact with their mother over
the years. Neither really knew if their mother, who took a
job at the Marine base in El Toro, missed them.

The only gift they ever received for birthdays or Christmas was a pair of Hollywood star nighties and gold plastic
high-heeled shoes.

That was the first year their mother was gone.

A dozen years and a thousand tears later, with only
sporadic contact, Carla Larson got a call from her mother.
The abandoned daughter had graduated from high school
by then and was living in a trailer in Tucson and working
as a bookkeeper for a tire store. Her younger sister, Amy,
was at a convent school in Indiana. Their mother wanted
to reconnect. There were apologies and promises of a better relationship.

Not long after that, Carla Larson bought a 1964 station
wagon for $200 and drove west.

There was someone her mother wanted her to meet. It
was the late 1970s.

Carla Stuckle insisted that her daughter should meet John
Schmitz, her good friend and former community college
instructor. She indicated that she and the well-known politician shared ideology and commitment to the conservative cause. Carla Stuckle simply told her eldest daughter
that it would be a good idea for the two to get together,
and if she was interested, she could enroll in one of his
political science classes someday.

Carla Larson had no idea what had been going on, though later she gathered from things her mother told her that she and John Schmitz had been "involved" for quite some time.

An early clue was the ringing of the telephone.

"Sometimes the phone would ring and it would only ring once and my mother would say, 'Don't answer it! Don't ever answer the phone unless it rings more than once or twice!' " Carla Larson recalled many years later.

It was only after things were more out in the open between the politician and his "favorite campaign worker" that her mother told her what the single rings meant to her.

"It was his code to let her know that he was thinking of her, when he couldn't talk—like when he was at home. It worked. But I was really annoyed by it. She knew that it was him. He told her that when he couldn't talk he'd let her know," she said.

Carla Larson told her mother that she objected because John had a family and a wife.

"My mother never cared if anyone was married or not. Not a big issue with her," she said.

John Schmitz often visited Carla Stuckle's home on Drayton Way in Tustin. So often that Carla Larson's suspicions increased. He spent so much time with her mother, something had to be going on. The young woman noticed how they talked to each other in ways that seemed more intimate than a mere friendship. The suspicions were confirmed one afternoon when she arrived home and went inside her mother's bedroom to find her in bed with the state senator.

"My mother told me that they weren't having sex. They just liked to lie there naked together," she remembered later.

Carla told her daughter how she had become involved in politics, mostly behind the scenes, though she did make a losing bid for a seat on the Tustin School Board. She was one of John Schmitz's most ardent supporters and considered him of tremendous intellect and ability. She invited her daughter to get involved in John's latest campaign and she agreed. She stuffed envelopes, made phone calls, ran errands, and watched her mother get closer and closer to her candidate.

Young Carla liked Schmitz, but she knew that politics was a sham. His brochure showed pictures of his wife and children—and yet he was sleeping with Carla's mother.

"It just confirmed my belief that all politicians were liars," she said.

Carla Stuckle had a dream, a plan. She was going to be Mrs. John G. Schmitz, because she had a right to be. She saw herself as smarter, more beautiful, and certainly more of a political asset than Mary Schmitz. Once she had stolen the handsome dark-eyed politician's heart, once she had him in her bed, she was determined to get the rest of him.

All of him. She would not be denied what she had coveted, her ego would not allow it.

"My mother liked to be the center of attention," Carla Larson said many years later. "I think in her fantasy world John was going to leave Mary for her, marry my mother, and she was going to be Mrs. Senator John Schmitz."

Whenever the relationship seemed strained and Carla Stuckle thought she might be losing her lover, she did whatever she could to keep him.

"He would tell my mother, 'I can't see you anymore, Carla. We need to distance ourselves. That's where I belong—with my family. I'm not with my kids, I'm here with you. This is wrong.' And she would manipulate him back into it."

One time Carla told her daughter that she swallowed a bottle of sleeping pills in a mock suicide attempt to keep John from leaving. She called the doctor right after she made the attempt. She wanted to keep John, she didn't intend to die.

John Schmitz came back to her. He couldn't let go.

There were numerous times when Carla Stuckle threatened to tell Mary Schmitz the truth. She threatened to expose him during the campaign. Her mother's tactics disgusted her daughter. As much as she wanted to love her, it turned her stomach to think that her mother could be so evil to the man she purportedly loved.

"She blackmailed him. She taped their phone conversations. She had one of those little suction-cup things and a tape recorder. I saw her do it. And I listened to the tapes. Typical lovers' talk. 'I miss you. I wish I was with you . . .' "

Carla Larson considered John a victim of his own mistakes and of his involvement with her conniving mother. She saw how he had tried to break it off several times. Carla told her how John said he was violating his marital vows, he was putting his political future at great risk. But Carla wouldn't let him go.

Carla also taunted John. She'd show up at the Catholic church in Costa Mesa where the Schmitz family celebrated Mass. She'd run into him at fund-raisers and walk up to him and his wife simply to unnerve him. It was a kind of game for her. And maybe for him, too. *Maybe the risk of being found out was as exciting to him as it was to her?*

Carla Larson even joined her mother on a couple of visits to the Schmitz home on Spyglass Hill. The outside was beautiful, she thought, but the inside of the residence was cold. She saw how it matched her mother's description of John Schmitz's wife.

"It lacked any personality, charm. It lacked familyness. It was formal, cold. Wintry, icy. Mary was a cold woman."

Going there was extremely uncomfortable for Carla Larson.

"I didn't want to betray my mother, and I liked John, but it didn't feel right. I wasn't comfortable being around Mary, because I knew."

Years later, when reporters would once again search the archives for tidbits about John Schmitz and his affair with Carla Stuckle, the daughter she left behind when she was just a little girl would consider once more if it had been a love affair or a convenience.

At least on her mother's side, Carla Larson concluded, it hadn't been about love.

"She admired him, respected him, was drawn to his power. I don't think my mother's capable of truly loving anyone. It is not in her nature. She's too selfish a person."

* * *

It was the oldest trick in the book. Carla Stuckle became pregnant to hang on to her man. She gave birth to a son in June 1981. One afternoon at her home in Drayton Way, Carla Stuckle sucked on a More menthol and flatly stated to her daughter she had become pregnant on purpose.

"To replace Philip," she said.

Getting pregnant and having a son was something that Carla Stuckle wanted to do for John Schmitz. She told her daughter of how she had been visiting at the Schmitzes' home in Corona del Mar when she passed out.

"In the exact spot where Philip fell into the pool," she said.

Carla Larson found her mother's story suspect. As she understood it, Mary Schmitz was inside and Mary Kay and an older brother were in the water playing. No one had seen where the little one had gone in. Carla Stuckle told her daughter that if Mary Schmitz had been more mindful of her children, the little boy would never have drowned.

John Schmitz's mistress also confided that she had had an amniocentesis performed during her pregnancy. She had done so not because she was concerned that giving birth in her forties would have jeopardized her chances for a healthy baby. She did it because if it had been a girl she would have aborted the baby.

"It has to be a perfect boy," she said.

She was giving him the son he lost.

She chose the name—*John George* Bostrom—to irritate Mary Schmitz, if she ever found out.

"John was not real thrilled that I put his name on the birth certificate, but I'm not going to lie," she told her daughter.

"Birth certificates are public record, Mother."

The older woman smoked and sighed. "Oh, well."

SEVEN

BY THE SUMMER of 1982, things had changed dramatically for both Carlas, mother and daughter. At age forty-three, Carla Stuckle had given birth to her second child by John Schmitz, a baby girl she named Eugenie or Genie. She told no one at El Toro who the father was, nor did she reveal it to the women she worked with at the Santa Ana answering service where she took messages on the weekend.

Carla Stuckle's daughter, Carla Larson, had a child of her own by then, a son, the same age as John George Bostrom. For a time, the twenty-three-year-old cared for her half brother and half sister in her base housing, but it became too much and she told her mother she needed to make child-care arrangements. Her mother was angry at first, complaining bitterly that baby-sitter's fees would send her to the poorhouse. She was already late on her mortgage and other bills were piling up.

One afternoon in late July, Carla Larson got a phone call from her mother, who was crying and saying something about her son's penis being injured.

"What? How in the hell did that happen?" the younger woman asked. She was in shock. "Did it get caught in something?"

Carla Stuckle didn't have any answers. She sobbed some words into the phone and told her daughter that the baby was in microsurgery to repair the damage.

"Mother, tell me what happened," the younger woman asked once more, this time using more soothing tones in an attempt to calm her mother.

"I took him to the doctor," Carla Stuckle said. "He said the baby has a hair wrapped around his penis and it had been there for some time."

"Oh, my God. Don't you ever bathe him? How could this have happened?"

Carla didn't have an answer. She muttered a quiet, "I don't know."

Carla Larson hung up the phone and made quick plans to go see her baby brother at Children's Hospital. When she arrived she found the boy asleep in a little crib, unaware of the problem that had brought him there. He was bandaged. Carla Larson couldn't get a look at him to see what in the world her mother was talking about. The nurses said nothing.

Back home, she got another call from her mother.

"They aren't going to let me take him home," she said.

"What are you talking about?"

"They're saying I did something to him."

"What do you mean?"

"That I wrapped hair around his penis."

Carla Stuckle told her daughter that she had done nothing wrong, but was in big trouble. She had no idea what would happen to her or her son. She was tired and upset.

Sadly, suspected child abuse calls were commonplace in Orange County, and indeed in every jurisdiction in America. But a doctor calling from the Children's Hospital reported a most unusual injury—a hair had been wound around and tied so tightly to a little boy's penis that the member had nearly been severed. Tustin police detective Jim Hein answered the call and immediately went to the hospital.

The doctor explained that such injuries were not completely unknown. Human hair or similar fibers can work themselves into the folds of skin in a baby's diaper area, causing ulceration and infection. But this was quite severe.

The boy's penis had been so damaged that he urinated out a gash in the side of it.

"What was unusual here, the doctor told me," the detective said many years later, "was that the hair had been tied in a square knot. It had been deliberate."

He wanted the hair as evidence, but it had been discarded during the reattachment surgery.

"You've got to do something," the doctor said.

"Well, you sure didn't help me by disposing of the hair."

Doctor and detective were mortified at the extent of the injury. Although the surgery appeared to be a success, both men couldn't help but worry about the boy's future.

Who was the boy's father? Neither Carla Stuckle nor her daughter and reluctant protector would say. Custody issues were at stake. The detective was convinced that Carla had injured her son, that it was not a freak accident. Jim Hein returned to her house at Drayton Way for an answer.

It was a square knot, for crying out loud!

Carla Stuckle, looking a bit worn and weary, let him inside and offered him a seat. Under suspicion for child abuse, Carla didn't seem too concerned. She almost seemed relieved that her son was at the Albert Sitton Home, getting care, while she went on with the business of taking care of her baby daughter, Eugenie. She wasn't evasive, either. She just seemed to be slow, speaking in a cadence all her own.

Detective Hein figured there wasn't much chalk on that blackboard.

Even so, he wanted her to talk. He needed to know who the baby's father was. That might lead to an answer. He pressed the point and even threatened her.

"Until we find out and get this thing all done, you're going to jail. Chances are you'll never see your son again. Tell me who the father is so I can help place the boy back with the father . . . Tell me."

Carla looked blank. She stared past the cop as if there were something of great interest on the wall behind him. Finally, she moved her thin lips.

"Well, it's John Schmitz."

"John Schmitz?"

"John Schmitz, the senator."

Jim Hein was dumbfounded. He repeated the name and Carla Stuckle nodded. He figured the woman was out to lunch, a nut, a troublemaker, *certifiable*. She had made it up to make trouble or get money from the politician. He didn't think it even close to true, but she went on. She said they had been lovers for years, that both her son and daughter were John Schmitz's progeny. Carla Stuckle told the detective how she and the senator would rendezvous at various hotels when he was traveling.

"He told me that wherever he was that I was to meet him there," she said.

She talked about his family, how his wife and children didn't know. It would be a big shock to so many. And though she protested the release of his name, her demeanor suggested otherwise.

She wants the information out. She wants the world to know.

Jim Hein had a hard time believing it. The woman was so haggard, why in the world would John Schmitz want to meet up with her at some hotel?

"Political people normally have the pick of the litter, so to speak. They want to go out and play games, they don't have any problem finding someone to play with. Why he would pick something like that I can never figure out," Hein said later.

"The only thing that occurred to me was that she had to be a demon in bed."

The Tustin police detective drove away to find John Schmitz. He left messages all over town, his office, his home, anywhere he could imagine. But Schmitz never called back.

The case brought the inevitable headlines in papers all over the country. The senator who espoused family values was a phony, a hypocrite. Even the little *Tustin News* weighed in:

MOTHER ARRESTED FOR CHILD NEGLECT
THIRTEEN-MONTH-OLD VICTIM ALLEGEDLY SON
OF SEN. SCHMITZ

Mary Kay Schmitz was a twenty-year-old student at Orange Coast College just down the road from Corona del Mar when the scandal first broke. The seriousness of the allegations did not hit her right away. She didn't see it for what it was.

"It never crossed my mind," she said later of her father having an affair with Carla Stuckle. *Even when she first saw it on the news.* "I thought, my father is such a good man. She's having some legal problems and he's helping her out. That's all it is."

But it was more than that, of course. And no one in the family knew it had been going on for so long. Who could conceive of such subterfuge? Surprisingly, not Cake, who as "the girl most likely to . . ." had become adept at preserving a perfect image. Not even Mary Schmitz, who went on TV as Queen of Family Values, and the champion of brightly burning home fires.

No one.

EIGHT

IT WAS AT a John Birch Society meeting out in Orange County that Detective Hein cornered the politician with the paternity problem. The detective wanted to know if John Schmitz really was the father, and more importantly as far as the child abuse investigation was concerned, whether he knew anything about the injury. He identified himself and told the state senator what Carla Stuckle had said.

"She's in trouble," the cop said. "The boy is in the hospital."

For all his well-known charisma, John Schmitz was oddly flat in his response. "Yes, I know."

"Well, is it your son?"

"Yes, he is, but I do not and will not support him financially. It is her responsibility to take care of them."

John Schmitz said he didn't know anything about the hair on the baby's penis. And that was that. The detective didn't let on, but he couldn't believe his ears. Here was this man, the ultraconservative politician who told everyone to take responsibility for their families . . . and he had two children by some woman in a tract home in Tustin.

For Carla Stuckle, at least according to her eldest daughter, the fact that her children's father had been ex-

posed brought relief. She thought that John Schmitz would
be forced into a decision. He had to choose her or Mary.
She, after all, was the one with the little babies.

"She was gleeful," Carla Larson recalled. "She said,
'Well, now he won't be able to get out of it, will he?' "

It irritated Carla Stuckle that John Schmitz hadn't been
man enough to acknowledge his children. Even after they
were born, he refused to tell his wife that he had been
unfaithful.

The media crush was torturous. Cameras were everywhere; reporters hid in the bushes. Only once did Carla
Larson speak to the press.

"I'm very upset at Senator Schmitz for not showing his
face and standing by my mother. They are his children,
too," she said later.

Detective Hein drove up from the beach to Spyglass Hill.
He had a few more things to ask John Schmitz about the
potential child abuse against little John, but the man who
loved the spotlight had made himself scarce. Mary Schmitz
was home, however.

Mary was cool and polite. She reacted in a way that
suggested the events had no impact on her. She said as
much.

"I love him and I'm standing by him," she said.

She said she knew he had a mistress, but that was no
concern of hers. In fact, all of it was John's problem.

"She was rather indignant that she was brought into it
at all. It was something her husband did and this other
woman . . . it was their affair," the detective recalled later.

He left Spyglass and drove down toward the ocean
highway thinking that Mary and John Schmitz had some
kind of bizarre understanding. It appeared to the detective
that Mrs. Schmitz had known about the affair and didn't
care.

If any in his inner circle knew that he had been carrying
on with Carla Stuckle for all of those years, they never let
on. Then or years later. Tom Rogers, close friend and one-
time campaign finance manger, had no inkling that John

Schmitz had played that kind of game. He'd been around politicians for twenty years and had seen dozens who played the field when their wives were back home taking care of the family. Politicians, by their nature, tend to be flirtatious and charming, feeding on the adulation of the people around them. John had an ego the size of California, but he wasn't any bed-hopper.

Though it was never an area they discussed, Tom Rogers tried to figure how it could have happened with John Schmitz.

"Maybe somebody who's egotistical has this kind of admiration, or adoration of a woman. She took night classes. She thought he was everything. John was susceptible to that because he thought really everyone ought to figure he's that good," Rogers recalled.

Some wondered how he had time for *two* families. It was true he had twice as much energy as most and seemed tireless on the campaign trail or hammering out a deal in the legislature late into the night. *But two families?* How could he have kept it so secret?

Though they did not talk about the Stuckle affair, St. Cecilia choir director Richard Kulda was struck by how John Schmitz exhibited no shame or repentance over what happened. He was the same charming person as always.

"There's something that he did a marvelous job of hiding from all the rest of us, possibly even from himself for many years," he said later.

As the choir director from St. Cecilia considered it, there was no question John Schmitz had lied with the same facility as he employed when he told the truth. He didn't want to put the label "pathological liar" on the man he had admired for so many years, but Richard Kulda thought it might be within the realm of the man's personality.

"It is possible there is some of that in John. It is possible that Mary Kay could be that way, too," he said.

NINE

EVEN WHEN THE newspaper and television reporters made her out to be a child abuser, the perpetrator of an unspeakable act—"she tied a hair around her son's penis"—Carla Stuckle continued to put the blame for the affair on Mary Schmitz. Mary hadn't been giving her husband what he needed at home. Carla had a deep hatred for Mary Schmitz. They had carried on the affair for so long, for so many years, that the woman had to be an idiot or completely blind to have missed it. Where had she thought her husband was when she was in bed in the little house on Drayton Way?

Carla Larson, through her own observations and through what her mother told her, didn't get a sense that Mary Schmitz cared one way or another. She had seen Mr. and Mrs. Schmitz at gatherings in public and at their home in Corona del Mar.

"I never got the sense that Mary truly loved John. I saw them together a lot at political fund-raisers. Have you ever watched Hillary Clinton looking at Bill Clinton? That gaze. Mary never ever demonstrated that gaze. She was always looking elsewhere to see who was looking at her."

Carla thought her mother was wrong to think that Mary didn't know about the affair. The woman wasn't stupid, just pragmatic.

"I think Mary knew. Maybe she didn't want to give up what she had and her position and social status? It was very important for her to be the wife of a senator," she said later.

John Schmitz had a lot of friends, and most stood by him during the Stuckle affair in 1982. Some figured that he wasn't getting what he needed from Mary and it didn't surprise them that he went out looking for it elsewhere. What did raise a few eyebrows was his woman of choice.

Most considered Carla Stuckle a step down from what he could have been sleeping with.

Carla Larson, bitter over her mother's abandonment, would find her already tenuous loyalty wearing thin. At times, she felt sorry for Schmitz.

"He was trapped. He was trapped from the first time they went to coffee after class. When she stuck around to have a conversation with him and he suggested they go somewhere to talk outside the classroom, he was trapped," she said later.

Yet the young woman also found room to blame John a little, too. Several times she thought of confronting him and telling him that it takes two to make such a mess.

You were the idiot that didn't learn from the first mistake. You kept coming around. You didn't have to. You could have said, "This is enough, woman," she thought.

The media had a field day with the two-timing politician. Camera crews staked out 10 Mission Bay Drive and didn't leave. John Schmitz never commented on the affair and his wife did little more than laugh it off as her husband's problem.

For those who knew them, and those who thought they knew John, there were broken hearts all over Orange County.

"I could just see what they were doing. They were all holding hands praying for God's deliverance from this plague on their house. And John's leading the sermon," said Hank Springer, the liberal ying to Mary Schmitz's conservative yang on their TV show, *Free for All.* "I felt so sorry for Mary. She didn't deserve this. Look at the hell he brought down on his family."

Hank Springer later saw great relevance in the scandal, almost a foreshadowing of what would happen to John Schmitz's oldest daughter a decade and a half later. It was in her genes. It was a lesson learned. Somewhere there was meaning for Mary Kay in what happened with her father and Carla Stuckle.

"They came from a family that whatever they did, didn't matter. It was okay. That God would find a way. They could be purified in this fervor they had, this self-righteousness. The rules are not for them, not for him.''

Hank Springer couldn't recall seeing Mary Schmitz after the scandal. He doubted that she taped another *Free for All*. Eventually, they put the Spyglass Hill house on the market and they slipped out of town for Washington. It was the final chapter. Mary started a career selling real estate for psychic and broker Jeanne Dixon in Washington, D.C., and John moved into a trailer in a Tustin trailer park to finish out the time he needed for his teaching pension. His political days were over and his wife's star had been extinguished.

"She would have been the grande dame of Orange County," said a friend of Mary Schmitz's. "She would have been."

Mary Kay felt sorry for her mother, father, and Carla Stuckle and the invasive publicity that came with the scandal.

"My father has a human side, an intimate side, to him, too. That does not belong in the public. It should be kept private. He has needs—and I don't mean *sexual*—that are no one's business. I never asked about it and it wasn't my place to ask about it. It was none of my business."

Carla Stuckle was living a hand-to-mouth existence and wanted child support for her two children. John Schmitz had given his mistress a few dollars on an occasional basis, but it wasn't enough and Carla made no bones about it.

"John offered me the magnificent sum of two hundred dollars a month for them," she told a reporter when she was threatening to sue. She thought $500 was more reasonable. For God's sake, she was living in a modest home in Tustin while his other kids had been raised in the splendor of Spyglass Hill. She wasn't being greedy, she said. She didn't want to have to work a second job at the answering service in Santa Ana.

John Schmitz had always told Carla that a formal agreement hadn't been possible because Mary Schmitz controlled the purse strings. But with their relationship out in the open, Carla saw no reason why she had to beg for money.

Mary Schmitz reportedly held her ground.

"She was unwilling to change her lifestyle to help him pay," Carla Stuckle said.

In the end, however, John Schmitz was ordered by the court to pay $275 a month.

The Schmitz family's downward spiral continued after Carla Stuckle's name faded from the headlines. The family focused its attention on Mary Kay's favorite brother, Jerry, a twenty-three-year-old Scientologist living in San Francisco. The gentlest of the boys, the Schmitz attack against him appeared as nothing more than bullying.

In January 1983, Mary Schmitz and her two oldest sons had drawn a line in the sand with a bulldozer, with the Church of Scientology and son Jerry Schmitz on the other side. They said they thought Jerry had been brainwashed by the church. He wouldn't listen to reason. He wouldn't forsake Scientology for Catholicism. He wouldn't leave his staff job for the church in San Francisco.

What was wrong with him? Why won't he come to his senses? they thought.

Mary Schmitz threatened to sue the church and asked political crony Jesse Helms to launch a congressional probe. Her son was a victim. He barely slept and worked all the time on Scientology activities.

"I'd like to get him out of the clutches of this beast. Jerry can't be himself. He seems to be wholly unproductive," she told a reporter.

Son Joe, then a twenty-six-year-old Navy officer, weighed in, too. He characterized his younger brother's responses to criticism as angry and irrational.

It was clear to those who knew the family that it was Mary Schmitz who led the charge. She just didn't get it. Her son was happy. He wasn't a zombie. Of all the boys, he marched to a drummer none could comprehend. He wasn't like the high-powered John and Joe. He was *Jerry*. Couldn't she see the difference?

During the Scientology ordeal Mary Kay had been kept in the dark. Her brother, the family member she was closest to—the one she would later say was second in importance in her life only to the boy who would change her life—never mentioned their mother's crusade. Neither did their parents.

"It is something we just never talked about," she said later.

The "felony child neglect" charges against Carla Stuckle were eventually dropped, and she was put on six months of social-service agency supervision, but the indignities continued. The Schmitz boys and their father had a meeting at Carla's home after the dust had settled and there was no longer any media interest in the case. One of the boys proposed to Carla that the best thing for everyone would be to put the children up for adoption.

"Best for who?" Carla Larson, the oldest daughter, later said when she learned of the plan. "Can you imagine the gall? As if my mother didn't love those children?"

And if that was the Schmitz style, to sweep the mess under the rug and avoid any further embarrassment, it was insulting to the woman John Schmitz had said he loved.

"I nearly threw him out of my house," Carla Stuckle told her daughter. "John didn't say anything then but later told me he didn't like that idea and knew I wouldn't go for it."

TEN

BOTH MARY KAY Schmitz Letourneau and Carla Bostrom Stuckle would feel abandoned by John Schmitz at critical times of their lives. Mary Kay needed her father by her side when her world was unraveling and her own personal scandal was sucking her down like a whirlpool; Carla needed John's support when she had the gall to let the world know she'd borne his children, children he ignored. Carla and Mary Kay had barely talked in their entire lives, but they shared something very deep. They both had been hurt by the man they loved more than any other. In little more than ten years' time their lives would end up in devastating tragedy.

Carla Stuckle did her best to hang on to all she had: her children. Despite working two jobs, she was nearly destitute; her beige stucco house was being foreclosed. Her gas service for her water heater had been shut off so she resorted to heating water on the stove for bathing. Her swimming pool had been drained because her pump was broken and she couldn't afford to repair it. She was gaunt, alone, and bitter. The children hadn't received as much as a card or a phone call from their father for months. Not even at Christmas or on their birthdays.

She told a reporter in early 1984 that "long after I'm gone, we'll know the reason these children were born. I didn't go through all of this for nothing."

For the rest of her life, Carla Stuckle was a tragic figure. Though she was seen at the Tustin trailer park where John Schmitz lived while finishing up his remaining time for his pension, she eventually dropped off the face of the earth. Ailing with the diabetes that ravaged her in her forties, Carla Verne Stuckle had reclaimed her maiden name by the time she came to live in a Midwestern Catholic care community with her children, then twelve and ten, in 1993.

She was at the end of the line. Carla was found dead a year later in her apartment. She was only 56. No family other than her son and youngest daughter attended her funeral. And while one would have hoped John Schmitz would have taken in John and Genie, he did not. Oddly, it was Mary Schmitz's close friend Jeanne Dixon who assumed guardianship of the boy and girl. When the famed astrologer died in 1997, Carla's children were made wards of the state. They now live in an orphange.

The contact with their half-siblings has been sporadic at best. Mary Kay, for one, never visited John or Genie.

"Some of the Schmitz children—the younger ones—have come out to see the kids, but Mary Schmitz has forbidden it. I don't think she knows about it," said the spokesman. "Gifts have been sent."

May Kay's childhood friend Michelle Jarvis often wondered what happened to John and Genie Bostrom. Not long after the affair between John Schmitz and Carla Stuckle hit the papers, it seemed that the mother and her babies simply disappeared. But John and Genie were half siblings to the Schmitz kids, after all, and in many families that was good enough to called brother and sister. When she asked Mary Kay about it, the answer came through loud and clear. Mary Schmitz had forbidden any relationship with those children. Mary Kay, in fact, had never laid eyes on the children, with the exception of seeing John in his mother's arms at church.

"Mary Kay told me that they had been back East for Christmas and her mother basically said that none of them could contact those children or have anything to do with them."

Michelle thought Mary Kay's mother's edict was "sick" and told her friend so.

"If it was my family," she said later, "I'd tell my mother to, you know, go you-know-what herself and I would go and help those children. They're in an orphanage and they've got family! That's sickening. What does John do? Nothing. His kids are in an orphanage . . . and he does nothing."

Those who joined in making the "apple doesn't fall far from the tree" analysis of Mary Kay Letourneau's behavior weren't that far off the mark, according to friends of the teacher in trouble.

"Look at the parallels with her father," college roommate Kate Stewart said in the living room of her Chicago home one afternoon in the fall of 1998. "I think that Mary Kay probably has her father's personality. The risk-taking. And his ideals. Here she is in prison and she's not going to be defeated and she still turns around and says to the people there, 'Screw it, I'm not doing that.' "

It didn't matter to Mary Kay if her defiance only made things worse for her first in jail, and later in prison. She was the type who had to prove a point.

"Listen," Kate once said, trying to get her college friend to make things easier on herself. "It's not going to get you anywhere there."

*   *   *

Carla Larson, Carla Stuckle's daughter, had some hard times in her life—marriages that didn't work out, periods of poverty during which she and her son, Carl, lived with her father in Montana. There were times when she and her son lived on peanut butter sandwiches and kept their fingers crossed that times would get better. And they did. By 1994, Carla Larson had purchased a little house in Hamilton, Montana, just south of Victor where her relatives lived. The house was nothing special, except that it was hers. It had a view of the Hardees restaurant where her son worked until heading off for the Navy. Though things were better, it had been more than a decade since the younger woman had heard of anything of her mother—an estrangement that had been Carla Stuckle's choice. By 1998, when she first learned her mother was dead and her brother and sister were wards of a Midwestern state, she was a civilian officer for the sheriff and worked nights and weekends at a family restaurant, the 4Bs. Never more would she feel sorry for herself.

But for years after the affair with John Schmitz left her mother a broken and pathetic woman, Carla Larson always believed that her youngest brother and sister were living somewhere, happily, in California. She had no idea John and Genie were in an orphanage and the thought of it brought anguish and a flood of tears.

"They have a sister who would have taken them in a heartbeat. If someone had called me when our mother died four years ago, I would have been there. We would have found a way to take them into our home. I was living here in Montana . . . I would have found some way. They are my brother and sister. They have a father and they have two sisters—and the Schmitz kids, too."

She wondered why John Schmitz didn't contact her when her mother died. Carla Larson knew John Schmitz. It wasn't as if he had no knowledge of her.

Then it hit her.

She blamed Mary Schmitz. Mary hadn't wanted to take the children in or acknowledge their link to her husband.

"Why would she take the proof of her husband's infidelity into her own home? That was not Mary's way. That

would be asking too much of a woman like her," Carla
said later.

But John Schmitz, what was his excuse? She couldn't
figure out why he didn't stand up for those children when
they really needed it. It blew her mind that those children
had to live like that when they had a father.

*"Why are those kids in an orphanage?" she asked over
and over in 1998. "Those poor kids must think their sister
doesn't care about them. They must wonder why their own
sister didn't come after them."*

ELEVEN

CALIFORNIA WAS FAR away, the shimmer of the ocean
from her bedroom window was a cherished memory.
Never more would there be phone calls from friends all
over Orange County.

*"Hey, Mary Kay, look outside and tell us what the
beach is doing!"*

The Carla Stuckle scandal was not relevant anymore,
because her father had told her it was not important. And
Mary Kay Schmitz was enrolled in classes at Arizona State
University, far from it all.

All of Mary Kay Schmitz's friends were beautiful. That
had been true with Michelle in Corona del Mar and it was
true of a fine-boned blond named Kate Stewart at Arizona
State University where she met Mary Kay in the late fall
of 1982. Kate was a political science major and Mary Kay
was dabbling in the arts, talking about teaching. And while
they were at Arizona State to get their college degrees,
both knew that meeting the right man was a possibility,
too. The young women dumped their roommates and
moved in together when the best apartment in the complex
where they both lived became available.

Mary Kay had just broken up with a man that friends
thought was the love of her life—long before a Samoan
boy named Vili Fualaau, of course. Mary Kay had entertained the idea that she might marry the guy, though he

hadn't asked her. And, she said later, she hadn't gone to bed with him. It was a long time since she'd been a virgin, of course, but for this man she was saving herself for the honeymoon.

"I'd seen [Mary Kay and the college man] together a few times when Mary Kay was at the apartment," Kate Stewart recalled. "Then it was over, and I wasn't paying too much attention that he was such a big deal to her. When we got closer she described the whole thing for me. I read the letters and I thought, *How could this guy undo this . . . it shouldn't have happened.* I wouldn't say it devastated her. It would take a lot to devastate her. I wouldn't say she's devastated *now.* You can't break this girl."

Kate and Mary Kay never had any classes together. At the time they met, Kate had left her sorority, tired of being told what to do and when to do it. Mary Kay was looking into pledging and, in time, would choose Pi Fi. Their friendship remained strong. Between classes at the university and hostess and waitress jobs at Mother Tuckers Restaurant or the Paradise Bar and Grill, the two were party companions, driving to and from hot spots in Mary Kay's Ford Fiesta without any brakes.

Mary Kay loved to party.

"She lives on the edge," Kate said later of her friend. "She's one of those personalities. She's very outgoing, very nonmainstream. She has her own mind, her own way, and I've accepted that."

Wearing miniskirts they had just made—hemmed with tape because there hadn't been time to finish them before heading out one night—Kate and Mary Kay went out to party. That night at a frat party at Pi Kappa Alpha, Kate ran into friends from Chicago and Mary Kay was partying and dancing with a nice-looking guy, blond and buff, a fraternity boy from Alaska named Steve Letourneau. When Kate wanted to move on to the next hot spot, she couldn't get Mary Kay to shake the new guy. Steve even followed them out to Mary Kay's car. Kate got into the driver's seat.

"They were talking and talking. *Come on, let's go.*

Then I thought, *Well, maybe she's really interested in him.*"

As the weeks flew by, Mary Kay and Steve were always together. For Mary Kay, coming out of the breakup that had crushed her, it seemed like a nice diversion. Nothing more. Mary Kay said that Steve Letourneau was fun. And with that, Kate shrugged off the relationship. It was nothing serious and it certainly wasn't going anywhere. Mary Kay was more than the boy from the Pacific Northwest could handle.

"He was very average-looking. She liked him. So that was fine. They clicked. They enjoyed each other's company. I don't think it was any more than that. He certainly was not a perfect pick for her," Kate said later.

But as Kate observed Mary Kay and the new boyfriend, she could see some changes in Steve. He was dressing better, for one. Kate wondered if Mary Kay was performing some kind of male makeover. Some women, she knew, were drawn to men they could mold and transform. Steve could have been that kind of a project for her friend. Looking back on those days at Arizona State and the years that followed, Kate Stewart could never say that Mary Kay ever really loved Steve.

"She certainly never, never loved him. When I use the word 'love' I'm talking about the bonded-at-the-hip love. Certainly not. If she would have had the opportunity to get back together with her old boyfriend, I think she would have. It would have hurt her to tell Steve that she was going back, but I don't think she'd have thought twice."

Mary Kay never planned on marrying Steve Letourneau.

"In fact she said, 'I'll *never* marry him,'" Kate recalled years later.

But at twenty-two, Mary Kay became pregnant.

"I wanted someone to tell me, 'It's okay to have the baby by yourself. You'll be able to take care of it. You'll be okay. You can still finish school. Your baby will be loved.' But no one said that," she said later.

*   *   *

Confusion and worry was all over her face. Mary Kay Schmitz told Kate Stewart that she was pregnant as they stood outside in front of Kate's town house next to her convertible.

"What are you going to do? I know you don't love him," she said.

Before Mary Kay could respond, Kate pushed the point harder.

"You're not going to marry him, are you?" she asked.

Mary Kay was uncertain. "I know I shouldn't," she said finally. "I don't want to. It's not my choice. I'm not sure what I'm going to do."

Not long after Mary Kay told Kate that she was pregnant by Steve Letourneau, tragedy struck on campus and she miscarried. She hadn't had time to come up with an answer about marrying Steve; she hadn't told her family she was pregnant. As Mary Kay later recounted to Kate, she had been in class when she started to bleed. The blood flow worsened and she was taken to the hospital.

"Okay, now I have to tell my mother," she told Kate. "Now I'm in the hospital, now it's serious. Something's going on. Now, it's just not we're in college and I'm pregnant. It's now, what are we going to do?"

She called her mother.

Mary Schmitz was very right wing, a right-to-lifer for whom abortion was always murder. From her home in Washington, D.C., Mary Kay's mother talked to the Arizona doctors and told them that absolutely under no circumstances would a D & C be performed on her daughter. It was possible, she said, that there could be another baby. As it turned out, Mary Schmitz was right. Her daughter had lost a twin, but the other baby would survive.

Kate parts company with Michelle when it comes to the relationship between mother and daughter and she considers the support Mary Schmitz gave her daughter when she was miscarrying the baby as the perfect illustration. Kate saw something that Michelle never saw. When Mary Kay really needed her, her mother was there.

"I think her mother has always been there for her but she hides behind her spirituality. I think her mom *wants* to be there for her, but Mary's always been the high-roller, live-on-the-edge member of the family. It's hard for Mom. *'You're not my straitlaced daughter, but you're probably my most capable if you'd go that route and it pisses me off when you haven't.' "*

There would be no D & C. But, Mary Schmitz pointed out, there would be a wedding. Her daughter would be marrying Steve Letourneau after all.

Maybe I can learn to love him. I owe it to my child to give it a try, Mary Kay thought.

When her best friend left Orange County for Tempe, Arizona, Michelle felt lost and abandoned. She hadn't bothered to make any other close friends because Mary Kay had been more than enough. Michelle dropped in and out of community college trying to figure out what she wanted to do and where her life would take her.

Mary Kay was off at college and seemed so happy. She was in love with a wonderful man. But suddenly, the relationship fell apart. Mary Kay was crushed by the breakup with the man she dreamed of marrying—before Steve Letourneau came into her life. Depression gripped her for weeks, months.

"She was almost suicidal when that ended," Michelle said later of the relationship before Steve Letourneau. "She was as low as I've ever heard her. I remember talking to her on the phone and I was really worried about her. *Really worried.* This was serious."

And then she starting talking about Steve Letourneau.

"Try to imagine where her heart and mind was when Steve came along. She needed someone safe. Someone she knew wouldn't hurt her. Someone she could manipulate."

Michelle had no doubts that Steve was a rebound relationship, the change had been so sudden. Mary Kay had gone from the depths of depression to the joy of a new love. And then she was pregnant and married. Lickety-split. It was too swift.

Michelle would never forget her first impression of Steve Letourneau. He was nice enough, she thought, but

Mary Kay could have done much better. She was way out of his league.

"He reminded me of a puppy. Following her around licking her hand."

Michelle knew that her friend's upcoming marriage meant an end to their friendship as they had envisioned it. The closeness they shared would never be the same. She only wished that Mary Kay would be happy. That Mary Kay's deal with her family to marry her baby's father would be worth it. That her dreams wouldn't die because she had to settle for a man she didn't love.

TWELVE

WHATEVER STEVE LETOURNEAU'S role in what happened with his wife—and what drove Mary Kay to do what she did with her student—his background was no Norman Rockwell ideal, either. When he was a boy, his parents, Sharon and Dick Letourneau, moved to Anchorage, Alaska, from Puyallup, near Tacoma, Washington, located near the base of Mount Rainier. Dick Letourneau had a job as a salesman for a food products company and the move was a step up. The Letourneaus' shaky marriage didn't survive long after the move. Steve was thirteen and his sister, Stacey, was nine when their parents divorced.

Grandma Nadine, Sharon's mother, was heartbroken, not only because of the divorce, but because the children ended up staying with their father. She said it was their choice, not their mother's wish.

"Sharon *didn't* abandon them. She lived close to them. She kept track of them every day. She stayed in their living quarters until the kids adjusted to their being apart," Nadine said later. Sharon stayed nearby and never missed one of her son's baseball games. In time, Steve's mother married a younger man.

Grandma Nadine understood why Steve was resentful of the divorce, but she felt that her daughter Sharon had been made out to be the cause of everything. Years later, the hurt was not completely absent from her words. Grandma Nadine had to admit that though Steve and Stacey loved their mother, they worshiped their dad.

"They had every right to," she said. "He did everything with them. He was a great father, still is."

Steve Letourneau returned to the Seattle area for Thanksgiving 1983. His grandmother Nadine had hosted the family gathering in her mobile home in a Puyallup, Washington, trailer court for as many years as most could remember. The guest list included Steve's sister, Stacey, and his father, Dick—Nadine's former son-in-law who had not yet remarried. Among the topics of conversation was the woman Steve had been dating at Arizona State. The pair were having a fling, but Steve wasn't serious about her.

Grandma Nadine later recounted the new relationship in terms very different from Michelle or Kate's versions. It wasn't Steve who was the hanger-on. "She was on his back constantly. Every place he goes she's there and he can't get rid of her. She had her eye on him. He was very preppy-looking, very good looking.

" 'She just won't leave me alone,' Steve said."

Grandma Nadine never minced words. "Steven," she said, looking him straight in the eye and with convincing authority. "If you don't want her around come right out and tell her, 'Look, buzz off.' "

Later, the grandmother would regret how her grandson had ignored her words.

A few months later, Nadine heard some startling news. Steve and the girl were getting married. Her name was Mary Kay Schmitz, the daughter of a highfalutin senator or something. Nadine was surprised because the last she heard, Steve had wanted to get away from the girl.

Arizona State University was part of the past. The college degrees they had sought would have to wait. Suntanned sorority girls and fraternity boys joined the Schmitz family as they celebrated the hurry-up wedding of Steve Letourneau and almost four-months-pregnant Mary Kay Schmitz on June 30, 1984. Dolgren Chapel at Georgetown University, where John Schmitz had been on sabbatical, was the venue. It was by any estimation a lovely and very Catholic wedding. Leaving no detail unplanned, the bride paid special attention to the music. She had three trumpeters *and* a vocalist.

"If you ask any of my relatives which was the most beautiful wedding, they would say mine," Mary Kay later told a friend.

Steve's maternal relatives didn't have the funds or couldn't take time off from work to attend the ceremony. Dick Letourneau and his second wife made it, though. It was just as well. It wasn't the wedding of anyone's dreams, anyway. For Mary Kay, everything was perfect with the exception of a groom that she didn't love.

Back in Puyallup, Washington, Grandma Nadine had worked her fingers to the bone at a local drugstore chain; she had raised her children with love and a firm hand. She was the kind of woman who refused to take any guff from anyone. She didn't like the phoniness that came with money and social standing. Steve was her grandson and when he and his new bride returned from the wedding in Washington, D.C., after dropping out of college, she insisted on holding a reception for her side of the family, since only the money side—the Letourneaus—had been able to travel back East for the wedding. Steve's mother, Sharon, had yet to meet her son's bride. Nadine cooked day and night, spruced up her mobile home, and set a pretty table.

Mary Kay was polite and demure and very beautiful and Nadine took an instant dislike to her. A few minutes after they met, the sixty-something woman with glasses that pinched her nose excused herself and went to the kitchen where her daughters were working.

"Well, wonder when she's due?" Nadine asked.

"Mother!" one of the daughters said.

"Okay, bet me. I didn't have six kids for nothing."

The younger women laughed it off.

But, of course, their mother was right.

A few weeks later, Steve confirmed that his new wife

was pregnant. His grandmother was satisfied that she had been correct.

"It takes two to tango," she said. "If a girl's gonna lay down with a guy, a guy's gonna take it. I don't care who it is—could be the Pope."

"She trapped him," Nadine said several years later, still furious over the situation. "She thought she was getting into a wanna-be Kennedy-type situation because he was the preppy-type kid that was going to Arizona State."

Her perspective possibly skewed by bitterness, Grandma Nadine would later shake her head at the memory of her first impression of Mary Kay Letourneau. She was uneasy about Steve's girlish and wide-eyed bride with the upper-crust pedigree, and wasn't afraid to say so. Nadine was the type of woman who arrived at instant and ironclad conclusions when it came to sizing up a person's character.

"I knew there was going to be trouble," she said later.

A few months after Nadine's reception in Puyallup, Steven, Jr., was born at a hospital in Anchorage, Alaska. When Mary Kay and Steve brought their first baby home from the hospital the new mother put him in a family-heirloom bassinet that she had lined with fabric she had ordered from the Paris specialty retailer, Descamps.

"It was just perfect," she said later of the fabric. "It was a pattern of soft delicate hearts, classic, not the Valentine's hearts, but a more classic look."

THIRTEEN

SOUTH OF SEATTLE and not far from the airport, Kent, Washington, had been in a growth spurt for much of the 1980s. The suburban city was a bland mix of old and new. Ticky-tacky apartments along I-5 and view homes overlooking the Kent Valley and Mount Rainier were at the extremes. It was by far middle and working class.

Traffic had been increasing steadily. Making a left turn down into the valley was becoming more difficult for the folks who lived in the condominium complex called Carriage Row and worked in the basin that had become a sprawl of nondescript aerospace offices where truck farms once flourished. In 1985 Steve, Mary Kay, and their toddler son, Steven, moved into unit 109 of the town-house-style complex done up in theme more akin to Boston than Seattle. The family moved down from Anchorage; Steve had been transferred to the SeaTac hub of Alaska Airlines where he worked handling baggage. Mary Kay was gearing up for classes at Seattle University where she would complete what she had started at Arizona State. She was going to be a teacher.

One sunny afternoon when Joe Bendix was pruning some shrubbery in front of his condominium, he was interrupted by Mary Letourneau. A very casual Mary.

"Have you seen my son, Steven?" she asked.

Joe said he hadn't. He put down his tools.

"I haven't seen him in a while," she said. "Wonder where he is . . ."

Her tone was flat. She was so casual about it.

Hadn't seen him in a while.

Joe Bendix knew the drill. There were plenty of times when Mary would get busy doing something, lose track of the time and her barely-out-of-diapers son. More than once Joe would call over to another neighbor and the pair would canvas the parking lot, the greenbelt, and the edge of the property abutting the apartment construction site in search of little Steven.

Mary's lack of urgency mystified the man.

She's a sweet lady, but only by the grace of God has that little boy made it as far as he has, Joe thought.

Years later he still wondered about it. Oddly enough, he never doubted that Mary loved Steven or her other children. She was a good mother, except for losing track of her progeny.

"This kid was three or so and running around this complex," Joe recalled. "My next-door neighbor and I would freak out. There was a busy street and they were building some apartments. We'd find him watching the heavy

equipment on the edge of the construction site. They could
have squashed him like a bug. It really shocked me.''

If ever someone needed a new beginning, it was Teri Simmons. The daughter of Fran Bendix, who lived across the
Carriage Row complex from the Letourneaus, was fighting
a secret disease that in time would nearly take her life.
Bulimia had been her secret hell since her parents split up
when she was just twelve. Fran went off to flight attendant
school and eventually married Joe Bendix, also a flight
attendant. The two worked at Alaska Airlines with Steve
Letourneau. Teri, a soft-voiced young woman from Texas
with a little bit of the Lone Star State in her accent, came
to Seattle to start over, finish her degree at the University
of Washington, reconnect with her mother, and, God willing, get better.

Almost immediately, the young woman across the complex caught her eye.

"When you first see her she is so stylish, so striking,
and such a beautiful woman and so precious that I was a
little put off," Teri Simmons said later. "I thought maybe
she was a little, for lack of a better term, snobby. I got to
know her a little bit at a time, then all of a sudden we
were great friends. Once you get past that façade."

Though Mary Kay was a mother and wife, she and Teri
were at similar places in their professional lives. Mary Kay
was trying to finish up her degree at Seattle University,
following it with a student teaching stint at a Catholic
school in Seattle. Teri was enrolled at the University of
Washington. Both women had let things slow them in their
plans to complete their education. For Mary Kay, it was
motherhood. For Teri, it was her bulimia.

"We were like those little fishin' bobbers," Teri remembered some time later. "We were all by ourselves and
we happened to bump into each other and we stuck. Neither one of us had any other friends. We were very for-
tunate to have found each other."

The Letourneaus were a family that was focused on the
future. There didn't seem to be much affection between
Mary Kay and Steve Letourneau. Their lives were a rou-

tine. A marriage more like a business deal than an affair of the heart. The love between them barely showed. But, Teri and others wondered, how could it? Mary Kay was going to school and Steve was always working or taking the odd classes at Highline Community College. Steve was hardly ever home.

"He worked his ass off," Teri said later. "He worked so hard for that family. They were a family that had a mission that was bent on both of them getting their education and doing what they wanted to do."

Years later, when his supporters would be few and far between, Teri Simmons would stand up for her old friend and neighbor, Steve Letourneau.

"He never got to finish [his education]. He never got to do what he wanted to do. And Mary Kay did. She got what she wanted and she blew it. If I were Steve I would feel so badly about that."

The weeks and months flew by. Mary Kay and Teri carpooled to class with little Steven in tow. They clipped coupons for grocery shopping at Albertson's and they hung around the town house, joking and laughing like a couple of teenagers, and sharing their dreams for the future sprawled out on towels at Seattle's Alki Beach. Throughout all of it, Mary Kay had a singular focus.

Now pregnant with her second child, Mary Kay told Teri that she had wanted nothing more in her life than to be a teacher. And she gave the endeavor her all. It was not uncommon to look across the way late at night to see the lights still on at the Letourneau town house. At two, three, four, five A.M. the lights would shine. Somehow Mary Kay could tap into energy sources unknown to most as she cut pieces of construction paper into pretty shapes for her classroom assignments. She was determined to be the best.

In the summer of 1987, Mary Kay, twenty-five, delivered her first daughter at Seattle's Swedish Hospital. The blond-haired baby resembled Steve's side of the family. When Mary Kay held her infant, she looked down on the most beautiful baby girl in the world. In keeping with eight generations of Irish tradition, like her mother before her, she named her first baby girl Mary—Mary Claire. She cuddled her little one as though she wanted the moment to last forever, as though she couldn't let her go. She wanted a closeness with her babies.

"My mother just wasn't that way," Mary Kay said later. "When I'm with my children, they are in my arms and I'm with them. I sat at my mother's side. That was the way she was. She was the queen, and I was just her daughter. That we're not close doesn't mean that I don't love her and that she doesn't love me."

Teri Simmons wasn't just off the turnip truck. She had been raised in Dallas, for goodness' sake. But the woman across the way from Corona del Mar had a sense of style that took her breath away. No matter how scant funds were, Mary Kay Letourneau always looked like a million bucks. Even with her hair up in a simple ponytail and her lips tinted with bright pink lipstick, there was no one lovelier. Teri admired that style so much, for a while she even emulated Mary Kay. When they were taken for sisters it was the greatest compliment Teri had ever known.

Mary Kay was a firm believer in the idea that it was better to have one fine thing than a half-dozen average items. Quality over quantity. Clothes were a key example. She'd save up her money and splurge on a garment from Ann Taylor or I. Magnin and wear it until it disintegrated. A green wool short skirt was a particular favorite during the early days at Carriage Row.

"I'll never forget it. It must have cost a fortune. She wore it all the time. It was better to wear something that was perfect and nice, than trash," Teri recalled.

Her husband was not that way—at least at that time.

"Steve would rather have three pairs of blue jeans from Target than one pair of chinos from the Gap."

The Letourneaus' town house also demonstrated Mary Kay's ideal that a little of the best was better than a lot of the mundane. The furniture was ratty, but some of the accessories were exquisite. Crystal and porcelain befitting a family of wealth, not a young couple just starting out in life. Appliances were first-rate, too. The vacuum cleaner in particular impressed Teri.

"You could ride that sucker, it was so neat. It was top of the line. Had every attachment."

And so in the world according to Mary Kay, there was a lesson that Teri Simmons would take to heart and retain for the rest of her life.

"You don't have to have *everything* the best. You can take one piece, one item and it sort of uplifts everything around it. It was sort of like her. She could walk into a room and the elegance level would sort of rise."

It was the cruelest kind of payback that Teri Simmons could have imagined. Why hadn't the Schmitz family—Mary Schmitz in particular—stepped in to help? Mary Kay and Steve Letourneau weren't starving to death, but things were so tight that Mary Kay went most of the winter in a windbreaker because she couldn't afford a warmer coat.

Her parents could probably do a little more than they are now, with this struggling family. It's awful, Teri thought. They have the money.

But as Mary Kay explained it, though she certainly didn't whine about it, her family, some thought, had written her off after she married Steve. Her family had expected better things of her. A better husband. Someone more in line with their socioeconomic status.

"They were sort of punishing her," Teri said later. "I don't know what they hoped to gain from that."

Teri would never forget the time when Mary Kay got a notice that the post office was holding a package for her. The two went together to get the parcel, addressed to Mary Kay by astrologer and close Schmitz family friend Jeanne Dixon. Opened at the Carriage Row town house, the box held a gorgeous brown wool coat with a trim of sleek black fur. Enclosed was a touching letter from Jeanne.

"Mary Kay was so excited," Teri recalled. "I don't think it was the coat, I think it was that somebody had mothered her. She loved Jeanne. Jeanne Dixon was the only connection she had with anyone on a parental level."

Years later people went looking for answers to why

things had turned out as they had. For some, like friend
Teri Simmons, it was easy to point to the Schmitz family.
She viewed Mary Kay as the tragic product of a family
that largely ignored their daughter because she disappointed them by settling for Steve Letourneau. In time,
something dire was bound to emerge.

"I'm surprised it took this long for something to happen," Teri said.

With the exception of her brothers and the mention of
her estrangement with her mother, Mary Kay seldom discussed the Schmitzes. Tears came when she spoke about
Philip and how the family "never got over" his death. But
she *never* talked about her sisters. Most peculiar of all was
Mary Kay's representation of her father.

"I could swear that she told me he was dead," Teri
said later, puzzled because by then she knew it was not
true. "She would tell me how close they were when she
was little. But for some reason, I had it in my head that
he was gone. I don't think I would have made it up. I
thought in my head all this time that he was dead."

Mary Kay never referred to him in the present tense.

"Maybe if he had shunned her it was almost easier to
say he was dead?" Teri speculated.

And despite the turmoil of her past and the estrangement
from her family, Mary Kay found time for generosity. One
gift that she gave Teri Simmons will never be forgotten.
It was a beautiful writing journal, with a black leather
binding accented by red corners, made in France. Mary
Kay presented Teri with the journal between classes at the
university during one of their carpooling days. It was the
perfect gift for the troubled young woman who liked to
write and who had a need to pour out the hurt in her heart
on pages of paper. Though the gift probably took her last
dollar, Mary Kay didn't care.

"She wanted to make sure everyone around her that
she cared about had the tools they needed to be free, to be
liberated," Teri said later.

That was Mary Kay Letourneau. Free. Encouraging. *A
giver.*

FOURTEEN

CIRCUMSTANCES WOULD LATER change perceptions and alter memories, but no one at Gregory Heights Elementary in Burien, Washington, could deny that the pretty young teacher started her career in public education with the kind of brilliance that ensured a remarkable career. Colleagues could easily tick off a list of attributes: creative, enthusiastic, artistic, thoughtful, patient. She was everything any parent would want for their child in a classroom setting. Mary Kay Letourneau, twenty-six, came to the Highline School District 401 in September 1988—it was the third of her student-teaching internships.

Master teacher Mary Newby saw a great future for Mary Letourneau and would later tell friends that she had benefited from the experience of working with her in her sixth-grade class.

"I loved working with her because I could say something and she'd add a level to it, then I'd add a level to it. It was a great experience. It expanded my teaching and my thinking."

Part of Mary Kay's gift was her enthusiasm. Though in her mid-twenties and the mother of two, she had not lost the sense of wonder and excitement of the learning process. Somehow she had been able to retain it.

"We'd talk about something we needed to do and she'd have fresh ideas and ways of looking at ways to approach it, versus the same old stuff."

Mary Kay was always prepared, always went the extra mile. She was at ease with the students and they liked her. Only once did Mary Newby see any cause for concern.

"One time when she was being observed by her college professor. She was very, very nervous, very tired. It was the one time when her lessons didn't seem as thought-out. It was still okay, but not as outstanding as she had done [before]."

"Is there something going on?" she asked her.

Mary admitted she'd been up very late. She said Steve had been working graveyard at Alaska Airlines and he wanted her to keep the kids up as late as possible so that they'd sleep for him in the morning. She couldn't start her schoolwork until after they went to bed.

"It didn't happen again," Mary Newby said later. "She didn't offer much more. It was a sleep issue. She was very . . . now I use the word 'driven'; back then, I thought very 'committed' to doing an outstanding job."

Mary Newby knew that her student teacher was pressed for money. Steve Letourneau didn't have a terrific job. Tossing baggage at SeaTac couldn't have paid that much and Mary Kay indicated that her husband had been pressuring her to do whatever it took to get her teaching certificate so that she could "go out and earn some money."

No matter what pressures she had from husband Steve, Mary Kay somehow fueled her ambition to do what she wanted, to shift the priorities of the day to suit her sense of importance. Often that meant setting the bills and worry aside for the fun stuff. With Halloween at hand came the quest for the perfect costume for little Steven. Mary Kay had decided her little boy would be the quintessential dragon. She outfitted her son in colored hightops, a little green tail, and a pullover. She even attached felt triangles to the back of the pullover. But something was missing. Something kept the costume from perfection. She recruited Teri Simmons to help in the search for the right fabric to finish it off.

"She wanted his chest area to be covered with green shimmery stuff to look like scales," Teri recalled many years later. "We must have gone to thirty different stores! But we found it and she did it. At the last minute we had this perfect little dragon."

When the hunt was on there was no stopping Mary Kay. If it meant driving around all day with a car running on empty, it didn't matter to her. If it required circling the globe in the quest of something she envisioned, she'd do it. Making do with something less than that was never an option.

FIFTEEN

NATALIE BATES WAS one of those who came to celebrate Mary Letourneau's graduation from Seattle University. Mary told her neighbor that it was an "informal" get-together. The word "informal" was important to Natalie, who considered herself "a jeans and sweats" kind of person. To Natalie's surprise, the spring 1989 gathering included Mary Kay's mother and father, just in from Washington, D.C. Natalie wasn't the type to party with strangers, but she was so fond of and so proud of the young woman's accomplishment that she decided to pop over for cake and coffee. It was the only time she'd known Mary Kay's parents to make the trek from back East for a visit. Years later, Natalie couldn't deny that she was a little bit curious about John and Mary Schmitz. Mary had told Natalie that she was not close to her mother.

"It was really strange. I couldn't believe the mother. She was a nice-looking lady with sort of reddish-brown hair, slender and well dressed. But I didn't see anything in the way of love over there. It just didn't seem like a family affair. It was like somebody came to tea . . . and then she was gone," she said later.

A lack of interaction between John and Mary Schmitz also struck Natalie Bates as odd. It almost seemed like they weren't connected to each other, bonded like a longtime married couple.

"No closeness," Natalie recalled.

It was years later that Natalie Bates began to wonder what, if anything, could have caused the tragic turn of events that would ruin lives, make people rich, and send a woman to prison. She remembered the graduation party and the cold vibes she picked up from the parents.

Then one day the answer came to her. It was so obvious, she thought. It must be a lack of love. Mary didn't get any love. Not from her parents. Not from her husband.

"If she had had some love from somebody else, maybe

Steve ... this would never have happened," Natalie said many years later.

The relationship with Mary Kay and her parents was complicated, and after a time Steve's maternal grandmother, Nadine, didn't even try to figure it out. Mary Kay acted like she couldn't stand her mother and that her mother didn't care about her. Her father was wonderful and could do no wrong. Such descriptions were at odds with what Steve's grandmother heard from Steve or saw for herself.

Steve had told his grandmother that his in-laws didn't have the best marriage; in fact, John Schmitz had fathered two illegitimate children with a campaign worker.

"This was her Prince Charming father?" Nadine wondered.

Whenever Mary Kay had a baby, Nadine and her daughters would show up with a gift. One time when they were over there, Mary Kay made mention of a present her mother had sent for the new baby.

"I got a box from my mom today," she said, looking disgusted. "I wish she'd mind her own business. It was something I wouldn't put on my child."

As far as Nadine could see, it was an absolutely beautiful outfit.

"How's your dad?" Nadine asked one time.

"I don't know," she said. "I talked to my mom, but I didn't ask her."

Years later Nadine would wonder how much Mary Kay's parents knew about her daughter's life in Kent. Mary Kay put on such a pretty face about everything. But it wasn't pretty from where Nadine sat.

"It was a big front. It was too nicey-nice. You've got kids running wild, and you'd say, 'Honey, will you take care of the children? Honey, would you see what they are doing now?' "

Their financial situation was perpetually in dire straits, too.

"They were always sending home for money. Sharon said it was constant. Two hundred dollars. Three hundred dollars. Telephone service would be cut off. Didn't have food on the table. Where was the money going? They were making over sixty thousand dollars a year. Where was it going? They had nothing to show for it.''

Steve and Mary Kay's chronic lateness was no joke to Steve Letourneau's grandmother. She was the opposite. When she was required to be at work at five-thirty, she'd show up at the drug and variety store at five just to be safe. But that was her and she did her best not to fault people for running a little late. But not two or three hours, as had been the case with Steve and Mary Kay. *And not at Christmas.*

She blamed Mary Kay for the tardiness.

"That was her. *Control.* That was her way of controlling. That's like a kid pooping his pants when he's five. Because he's got the control. That's the way Mary was,'' she said later.

But being late for a Christmas celebration and gift exchange, however, would not be tolerated by Steve's grandmother.

"They knew what time we started. I got the table all set. The little kids are running around wanting to open presents. How do you explain to a three-year-old that we can't start yet [because] Mary Kay's not here?'' Nadine said later.

Everyone was needed on time because the children had drawn names and if everyone was not there someone wouldn't get their present. Finally, Nadine couldn't hold it inside and have another Christmas ruined. She confronted Mary Kay over the phone.

"No more! I've had it up to my eyebrows! If you want to exchange gifts, you bring the gifts the day before. I don't care if you come from Timbuktu, bring the gifts over here. At least we will have the gifts for the kids,'' she said.

If Mary Kay was an outsider in Steve's family it didn't matter much to her and she dealt with it when she had to. Individually, she considered them all right, salt-of-the-earth types. But all of them together in a group was something else. She thought that they carried gigantic chips on their shoulders.

"I don't know what it is all about," she told a friend later, "but Steve's family—his mother's side—spend every minute of the day thinking that the world owes them something. It is as if they aren't good enough. There is so much negativity there."

When Gregory Heights sixth-grade teacher Mary Newby picked up the phone in the late summer of 1989, it was her former student teacher Mary Kay Letourneau calling with a good news / bad news scenario. She had been offered a job teaching second grade at Shorewood Elementary, but she didn't know if she wanted to teach that grade level. She had preferred teaching older kids. The principal, she said, was pressuring her.

"Well, you know," the veteran teacher said, "I've taught every grade and there are wonderful things about each one of them. You'll do fine with second-graders . . . you'll have your foot in the door."

Mary Kay said she'd think about it.

SIXTEEN

JUST BEYOND A church sits Shorewood Elementary School at 2725 SW 116th Avenue S., down the hill from the trouble and traffic of Ambaum Boulevard, one of the SeaTac Airport area's busiest streets. The neighborhood is older, with lots of "Grandma Houses"—small, single-story homes with mature camellias and driveways without oil stains. In the past few years, some have been torn down to make way for newer, bigger, not nearly as charming homes for a younger crowd of Boeing workers and professionals just trying to get a toehold in a tough Seattle housing market.

The neighborhood surrounding the brick- and glass-block-faced school hasn't changed all that much since the 1950s when the school was a bastion of middle-class homogeneity. The homes are tidy and the yards clean. No autos growing moss on blocks in the front yards. Shorewood remains far enough from White Center and Burien to feel safe at night, though not as many would walk its streets as they did in the past. Today, the school draws students from a larger area, going far to the east to pick up children who live in low-income housing and fixer-uppers-in-waiting. Almost a third of the children enrolled at Shorewood are eligible for the free-lunch program.

The building is unremarkable in a way that makes one wonder if anything, or anyone, of any particular interest could come from such a place. Inside, the school is antiquated, though clean; a victim of failing funding levies. One teacher's father once inquired if the building was condemned. A seagull is the school mascot. Glazed terra-cotta tiles made by students over the years are inset into the hallway walls. The gymnasium walls are painted with college football-team logos from Washington State and the University of Washington.

All teachers are white, which belies the ethnic diversity that has taken root over the years. More than forty languages and dialects are spoken in the Highline School District. At Shorewood, twenty percent of the students are Asian and Pacific Islander; six percent black; four percent Hispanic; and the other two thirds, white. Five hundred students attend the school. Twenty-four teachers stand up in front of their classrooms each day to provide the foundation for the education that will carry their students through the rest of their lives.

But in the end, that world would only focus on two. *One teacher and one student.*

When Mary Kay Letourneau arrived to teach second grade in 1989 she brought with her an undeniable and welcome burst of enthusiasm. For the shiny new students in her class, she was Mary Poppins and the tooth fairy all rolled into one. The children adored her because she was pretty, young, and probably most important of all, fun to be around. She invited the children to participate in the process of learning.

One teacher who observed her classroom during those early days noticed that Mrs. Letourneau gave her children nearly an unprecedented amount of personal choice when it came to curriculum. Whatever the kids wanted, she allowed.

"She would constantly rearrange things; she never had a lesson plan book. Well, she did, but it was hardly filled in and she never followed it because things would change minute by minute or hour by hour," the observing teacher said later, though she admitted, "It seems like when the class had big projects to do they did get done."

Mary Letourneau seemed to thrive on her own chaos, a deliberate chaos in which she was planted firmly in the center of the storm, ready to sort it all out in the end. No matter how long she had to stay up into the night, she could handle it. It suited her personality. The kids liked it. And as time went on, she became known as a creative teacher, one who didn't line things up in neat rows with all the dots connected. For many, that was her charm.

It started from Day One and escalated only slightly until 1996 when Mary's chaos became a typhoon.

"I think there was always that disorganization, that comfort level, of being able to tolerate more volume than some teachers can. Personally, I think that's one of the reasons some children really adored being in her room. There was not a lot of structure. They got to do a whole lot of things in a different way than they did in a more structured classroom. They were given a lot of different choices," said one friend from the school.

There was a price for the charm and personality that made Mrs. Letourneau's reputation as a "fun and creative" teacher. It was a price paid by other teachers. Mary Kay almost never made it to a meeting on time—from the very beginning of her tenure at Shorewood. When she'd arrive late for class, she'd shrug it off with a laugh and the look that all harried mothers know. . . . *Day care problems, you know!*

It was nothing for Mary to phone a staff member after eleven in the evening to check on something related to an event or project. In truth, few minded. They understood that with two, three, then four children, she had her hands full at home. From what her colleagues could tell, Steve almost always worked nights and often on the weekends, leaving his wife with the lion's share of the day-to-day family responsibilities. She had to feed the children, put them to bed and get them ready for school the next day. If she was at wit's end getting everything done, then she was like a million other working mothers.

Mary had a reputation for staying up all night working on report cards for conferences and barely finishing them as the parents walked into the classroom. Receipts turned into the office for reimbursement were noted not because of their requested sums, but for the time noted on the bottom: "Kinko's copies, 2 A.M." According to Mary, late-night hours had been a way of life for her even as young girl. It was the Schmitz way. And later in life, she said, it was nothing for her to call her mother or sister after midnight to find out they were just clearing the dinner dishes. Mary Kay was from a family of night owls.

"But Steve was never a part of that life, that late-night rhythm," she said later. "Partly because of his work, but also because he just didn't function the way the rest of us did. The kids understood it. We all did."

One teacher who taught some of Mary's former students noticed that every other paper was wrinkled, and had coffee and food stains spilled onto them. The stack of papers looked more like garbage than a sheaf of schoolwork.

But in time, over the years of missed meetings and unfulfilled staff responsibilities, there was the feeling that Mary Letourneau was given special privileges. She was given more slack than just about anyone at Shorewood. One time when she was scheduled to give a portion of a presentation at a staff meeting, she did not arrive.

"Oh, you know Mary, she's on Mary's time," said the principal as if being on time was not important. Others had families, too. Others had places to go. It was irritating and unfair. But even so, for the most part, the staff liked her. She was so very likable.

When his wife made the move from one classroom to another, Steve Letourneau came to Shorewood to help. Her room was overloaded with stuff another teacher wouldn't imagine saving.

"There were papers that she had from kids two and

three years prior. These kids are fifth-graders now, why do you want to hang on to that? It was something tangible she wanted to keep," said a teacher who was there the day of a classroom move.

It was also a sign of a woman so on the go she didn't have time for the most rudimentary of housekeeping chores. A cat box in the corner of the classroom was fetid with feces. The cat Mary had adopted to help illustrate a story she was reading with the class had been gone for more than a year.

SEVENTEEN

IDENTICAL TWINS AMBER and Angie Fish and their mother Joy, and older sister Lisa, were making a fresh start at Carriage Row when they moved into condominium unit 108 in 1990. The Letourneaus, in 109, were their next-door neighbors. That first day, when the twins returned a naked three-year-old Mary Claire home after the little girl went calling for the neighbors that had just vacated the Fish condo, they met Mary Kay. She was pretty and sweet and in need of some help. Too young for mall jobs, too young for boyfriends, and stuck in the south Seattle suburbs, Amber and Angie answered yes in unison when Mary Kay asked if they wanted to baby-sit. And from that day forward, the dark-haired, dark-eyed look-alikes would come to view Mary Kay, Steve, and their growing brood as close as family. But for the twins, the jewel of 109 was Mary Kay. It was more than that she was beautiful and blond, though most preteens would have held her in high regard for the physical perfection she exemplified. For the Fish twins their love of Mary Kay came from how she treated them and the way she showed a personal interest in them. She was more like a friend than some grown-up.

"I thought she was really young," Amber Fish recalled some years later. "I always thought she was really young in how she looked and acted. She always made us feel older when we talked to her. She respected us. She talked to us all the time. We always felt like we were on a real communicative level with her.''

Angie agreed with her twin.

''She would go down to our level. She made me feel like an adult when I was thirteen or fourteen. I think it was because she asked our opinions about the kids. She didn't just say, 'You need to do this and this...' She asked for our input. When we were there she had us interact with the family so we felt more superior, on her level.''

The Fish girls also adored Steve Letourneau. At twenty-eight, the handsome man was in perfect shape, outgoing, and fun to be around. Their adoration went deeper. With their father out of the picture, the girls' only male role model was Steve. He was the other half of the perfect family that had been missing in their own lives. Steve spent time with his children, worked in the garage, and redid the kitchen cabinets.

Amber Fish later wondered if what she had seen in those early days was an illusion.

''I thought they were the perfect family. That's what was so shocking about it. We knew there were arguments and disagreements, but they were beautiful, all-American people. I really thought they were honestly the perfect family. They were bustin' ass,'' she said.

The condition of the Letourneau household was the opposite of the Fish family's condo. If Joy Fish kept a stable, spotless, and orderly home for her three daughters, Mary Kay's house was utter chaos. All day; all night. Nothing happened on schedule. Dinner was served at ten P.M. so often that the twins thought nothing of smelling the barbecue smoke wafting into their bedroom at that late hour.

Steve's making dinner again.

Piles of school papers, toys, and books grew in every place possible, from the kitchen to the living room to the bathroom to the risers leading upstairs. Sometimes Mary Kay asked the girls to come over to help her get organized. While the house was cluttered, Mary Kay was positively fanatical about cleanliness at that time.

"She hated dirt and dust. If there were crumbs on the table, the minute she walked into the house she grabbed a sponge to wipe up any crumbs," Angie said later.

When Mary Kay needed help grading papers, she sometimes turned to the neighbor girls and the three would be up until two A.M. carefully reviewing student papers. A few times the Fish girls stayed the night because it was just too late to go home.

The girls chalked up the perpetual chaos to the different schedules of a two-income family. Steve worked a late shift at Alaska Airlines and Mary Kay was a schoolteacher with work that was carted home because there was not enough time in the day to get it done.

And throughout the maelstrom of their lives, it was clear that Mary Kay had the upper hand. Steve was a follower.

"It was Mary Kay's way or no way, basically," Amber said later. "They did what Mary Kay wanted to do."

Only once did the girls see Steve lay down the law. When Mary Kay cut her finger and wanted to go to the emergency room, Steve told her no.

"They fought about it forever. I remember she got so pissed. She was bleeding and bleeding and bleeding. And Steve was, like, 'You're not going to the emergency room for that!' "

The Fish girls figured it was a money thing. Money always seemed to be tight—at least cash was hard to come by. Whenever it came time to pay the girls for baby-sitting Mary Kay would say Steve would pay them. Steve would say Mary Kay would pay them. It was the old "check's in the mail" without the need to involve the postal service.

The girls didn't care. Whenever they were paid they were paid well, but the money didn't matter. The Letourneau condo was a hangout, a place to gather with the all-American family and share their dreams or problems. Mary Kay was always willing to engage in long discussions with the girls.

"We used to talk to her all the time, and she'd get so sidetracked," Angie recalled. "We'd talk about one thing and five minutes later a whole new subject would come up. We spent a lot of time over there.''

To hear Steve's grandmother tell it, Mary Kay was a selfish girl who would stop at nothing to get what she wanted. What she wanted most, besides attention, was money. Grandma Nadine would never forget the time Mary Kay told her and her other daughter that Sharon should fork over the bucks she "should have paid for child support" when Sharon and Dick Letourneau split up.

Nadine bristled. Sharon had paid for plenty, and Steve and Stacy Letourneau never went without anything because she didn't support them. Besides, it wasn't any concern of Mary's.

"But she wanted to make it her business. She wanted the money," Nadine said later.

"It was money that she should have paid for Steve to go to college," Mary insisted.

Nadine looked at her and snapped, "Look, Steven is married. What do you mean?"

"She should be paying for his college education."

"She doesn't owe him anything. For your information, you've got it all wrong. Who paid for yours?"

"Grants, student loans," Mary Kay said.

"Which Steven is still paying for! Loans after loans!"

"Well, I differ," Mary Kay said.

Nadine had had it with her grandson's wife.

"You can differ all you want, little girl, but I really don't care," she said.

By the spring of 1991, Mary Kay was twenty-nine and expecting her third baby. She loved being pregnant. She was not one of those complainers about morning sickness, feeling bloated or fat. In fact, she seemed to thrive on the pregnancies.

"She was cute pregnant," Angie Fish recalled. "She had all these cool maternity outfits."

Amber corrected her sister. Those weren't maternity clothes at all.

"*All* the clothes she wore could be worn as maternity

clothes. A lot of the time she would wear Steve's T-shirt with pants. She wore her 'maternity clothes' even when she wasn't pregnant, like a red jumper. She could pull it off.''

EIGHTEEN

MANY OF THE neighbors at Carriage Row would agree that Mary Kay and Steve Letourneau and their children were nothing short of a beautiful family, all golden. Even so, no one could deny that the Letourneau children were allowed to run around the complex with little supervision. It wasn't that Mary Kay really lost track of her kids. As one neighbor put it, "They were in different directions." Life at the Letourneaus' was tumultuous. It would become even more so in September of 1991 when Mary Kay and Steve prepared to welcome their third child. As always, there was never enough time to get everything done. Mary Kay even worked the morning she went into labor.

"Steve," said Shorewood's principal at the time, when she reached him on the phone, "you better get in here and get Mary and get her to the hospital. If you don't, she's going to have the baby in the classroom."

At ten pounds, Nicholas was Mary Kay's biggest baby.

Mary Kay told all her sitters that she had some rules. The kids didn't get any junk food. No one could chew mint gum in the house ("I hate the smell!") No soda pop. For snacks, she preferred graham crackers, honey, and lots of cheese. In fact, the Letourneaus often made the trek to Costco to buy a mammoth brick of cheddar and a stack of tortillas for quesadillas—a family standby. Halloween candy was rationed for more than a month. And the kids seldom had McDonald's or other fast food, unless someone other than their parents took them.

There were plenty more "Letourneauisms," according to the Fish twins. "Bum" was used for "butt" or "bottom." Rules were posted on the fridge and children were marched over to the refrigerator for refresher courses in how to get along. Art was loved. Music was played. And fun always ruled.

Amber Fish defended Mary Kay later when people questioned her parenting skills.

"I still think she was an awesome mother, but as far as running the house it was really hectic."

The family tried having pets a few times, but given the way the Letourneaus ran the house, they couldn't make a go of taking care of anything. It was hard enough to take care of themselves. A pair of rabbits lasted a few months, before going over to live at the Fish condo.

But more than anything, the biggest factor in their lives was their inability to make it anywhere on time. Mary Kay, friends used to joke, would be a day late to her own funeral. Like others who would come in and out of their lives, the twins learned Letourneau Time. No one bore the brunt of the tardiness more than the baby-sitters. They learned to add an hour or two to Steve and Mary Kay's estimated return time, but even that usually wasn't enough. And most annoying of all, there was never a call to say they were running late.

Amber blew it off and accepted the tardiness as "just the way they were," but Angie let it get to her.

No one else's time seemed to matter.

"Mary Kay would come home after being two hours late and sit in her car for a half hour and go through mail and papers, and I'd be just sitting there waiting to go home. After the kids were sleeping . . . I was just sitting there. She would irritate me."

The lateness was in the coming *and* going. Often, the twins would get an urgent call asking them to hurry over to help get the Letourneaus out the door for church or a party or a family gathering at Grandma Nadine's in Puyallup. The chronic tardiness was as puzzling as it was irritating. It wasn't that Mary Kay and Steve were running late because they'd overslept or had forgotten the time of the event. It seemed like pure disorganization. A gift was being wrapped in one corner by Mary Kay while she was doing her hair; at the same time, one of the little ones was instructed where to hunt for a missing shoe. Steve was helping iron a shirt while making a snack because one of the kids was hungry.

Throughout all of it, Mary Kay remained in charge.

"She was always focused, now you need to do this, I need to do this . . . She knew what was happening, but things were lost. And everything had to be perfect before she went out. Ironed, clean. Everyone had to be just right," Amber recalled.

Every once in a while Mary Kay would settle down on the ratty sofa or at the table and talk about her past. Sometimes she pulled out pictures of her family, her parents, and her siblings and compared them to snapshots of her own children. She told the Fish twins that she and her mother weren't close, that her father had run for president, and that "Steven was special because he had a twin in heaven." She kept a portrait of her parents near her kitchen stove.

She also told the teens next door that she had barely graduated from high school because she was a nonstop party girl. The revelation shocked Amber because it was so different from what she had imagined of Mary Kay's pool-perfect life in California.

She was a cheerleader, a perfect student . . .

And though she spoke of her family now and then, Mary Kay rarely spoke about Steve's family—with the exception of his sister, whom she did not like. In fact, she used Stacy as a weapon whenever she and Steve got into an argument. Mary Kay considered Stacy a pleasant enough girl, but not particularly bright.

"If I've ever needed to get at him in a fight," she told Amber one day, when they were hanging around the condo, "I'd say, 'you're just like Stacy,' and that would really get him."

It happens in nearly every family and the reasons vary. But Mary Claire was Daddy's little girl and Steven was Mary Kay's pride and joy. Parents and children often pair off and special bonds are formed. In the Letourneau household it was clear to just about everybody that Mary Kay and her daughter didn't get along. They were always at odds. Steven, however, idolized his mother and she idolized him, too.

"Mary Kay and Mary Claire butted heads a lot. Mary Claire was stubborn and she didn't put up with anything. Steven was Mary Kay's prodigy. That kid could do no wrong. Mary Kay wanted him to be the boy genius and worked at it really hard. A lot harder than she worked with Mary Claire," Amber Fish recalled.

And from where one observer sat, the relationship between mother and son was detrimental to Mary Kay's oldest daughter.

"Mary Claire was most jealous of their relationship, I think that's why she leaned toward Steve so much."

There were other factors at work, too. Mary Kay wanted her daughter to slim down, though to any observer the little girl looked just fine.

She was a child, for goodness' sake, not a fashion model.

"I know she was very concerned about Mary Claire's weight," Angie Fish said later. "I remember when we first moved in there and she was three and they were watching what she ate: *'Mary Claire's not allowed to have any cheese.'* "

Steven was everything to his mother. Although the twins felt Mary Kay loved all of her children, she was closest to Steven. The Fish girls remembered "Mommy and Steven Days," when Mary Kay and her son would go out and do things together, while Steve played with Mary Claire. When Steven got a little older, Mary Kay would take him shopping. They'd return from their outings with tired feet and bulging Nordstrom bags.

The twins later talked about the shopping habits of their favorite neighbor.

"She had really expensive tastes—more expensive than anyone I'd ever known—" Amber recalled.

"And that she could not afford," cut in Angie.

"She was way out of her range," Amber continued. "She brought home bags and bags from Nordstrom when we knew they could not afford it. Shoes for the kids, a two-hundred-dollar dress for herself.''

Her best friend from her days at Arizona State, Kate Stewart, understood Mary Kay's quandary and her *modus operandi*. So what if she over-shopped? Who didn't max out a credit card from time to time? Kate always considered Mary Kay a ''loves life'' kind of woman, one who lived each minute to the fullest. She knew what she wanted and went after it with the kind of gusto that few could emulate. And, more than anything, she wanted to be surrounded by people who lived life the same way. That included her friends, her children, and her husband. Mary Kay was a woman who wanted a lot from the world, a woman who *required* a lot out of life. Yet there she was, trapped. Trapped in a dull, mundane existence in a crummy condo in Kent, Washington, with a husband she didn't really love.

Her emotions quietly fraying like blue jeans, Mary Kay deserved more.

PART TWO
TEACHER

Mary Letourneau is not only a gift to Shorewood Elementary School, but a gift to the entire Highline School District.

—A teaching colleague quoting the Shorewood principal's last evaluation of the teacher headed for disaster

The school is suffering. The teachers certainly suffered tremendously from this. Teachers walk in those classrooms . . . [and ask,] "what has this done with my standing in my classroom? Are they [the students] going to worry about me?" It chokes me up to think of the impact on them and the students.

—Gary Roe, grandfather of a Shorewood student

This is not a case questioning our educational system or the delivery of curriculum.

—Mary Kay Letourneau in a press release, November 1997

Before students left, I made sure I gave them a choice of a high-five, handshake, or a hug. H.H.H. I got it from a teacher at Seattle U. and I did it every day with every student since my first second-grade class. It was a way of touching base, ensuring contact.

—Mary Kay Letourneau on a teaching technique, 1999

PART TWO

TEACHER

NINETEEN

IN NEARLY EVERY way, White Center couldn't be farther from Corona del Mar, California. *White Center*. The name is a big joke among Seattlelites who don't live there. Toss a rock, they say, and you couldn't hit a white person if your life depended on it. Nearby Top Hat is another with a moniker that doesn't fit the ambience of the place for which it is named. Those who live there shrug and acknowledge the obvious.

"You'd think a place like Top Hat would be a little classier," said one resident, aware of the irony.

Though White Center's name is a joke, its nickname is worse. The slogan the chamber of commerce would like to forget is Rat City, from an infestation that local boosters claim has been annihilated, although most know rodents rule the basements and back bedrooms of some of the Seattle area's worst housing. The projects appear tidy and nondescript, and some think they are a cut above some housing in Vili's neighborhood, a world of jacked-up cars, liquor bottles, and water-stained curtains. This is not Compton or Watts, but it is Seattle's version of the 'hood. Rap and hip-hop pulse in headsets and from boom boxes. Country, Top 40 radio, *classical*, be damned.

If other Seattle neighborhoods are more defined by money, cars, and lawn services, White Center is defined by the people and cultures that claim it. Cambodians, Russians, Samoans, and African-Americans run the restaurants, go to the storefront churches, and their children stake out the Taco Time and Dairy Queen on Ambaum Boule-

vard. When drizzle doesn't send them for cover, some kids
hang around the shores of a pond behind Evergreen High
School where drug use is so common deals are done in
the light of day.

This is the neighborhood of a boy who would be the
catalyst for unbelievable change and dire consequences for
Mary Kay Letourneau. This is the neighborhood that
would become the home of her youngest children.

Enrollment at the Highline School District had declined
since the 1970s. After Boeing went nearly bankrupt and
laid off most of its workforce ("Will the last person leaving Seattle please turn out the lights?" read a famous bill-
board) enrollment dropped from 40,000 to just less than
half that in the mid-1990s. Perhaps understandably so,
those who were left behind to hold down the fort at Burien
and White Center in many cases could not afford to move
elsewhere. To the south of the Highline School District
boundary in Des Moines and Normandy Park and north to
Shorewood and Seahurst, however, are the Gold Coast
homes of the more affluent.

"This is the land that time forgot," said Nick Latham,
public relations flack for the district. "Progress jumped
over the area and not much has changed." When the former television reporter first came to work for the district
one aspect fascinated him above many others: the people
who lived in the area *never* left it. White Center, Burien,
Roxbury—whatever the address, it was their town.

"They are living within minutes of one of the most
vital, exciting cities in the country, if not the world, and
they may never, ever come here. It might as well be New
York City. Nothing in Seattle interests them. They do not
cross that First Avenue South Bridge."

In the center of the district is SeaTac International Airport, one of the nation's busiest, and the source of many
jobs and, without a doubt, the starting point for nearly all
who live in the area. But it is more than that. Ironically,
the airport is the area's biggest impediment to communication and traffic. It is also noisy. And as the airport has
grown, nearby property values have plummeted and people

have departed for quieter environs to the north or east.

For those coming and going, the airport is conveniently located between Seattle and Tacoma. For those who live close by—especially directly in its flight path—it is a disaster. Some schools have been so impacted by the noise that teachers have to stop lessons to wait for passing planes to go by. Families have turned up the volume on their televisions to ear-splitting decibels and learned to live with it.

The Port of Seattle is public enemy number one in those neighborhoods, filled with people who are tired of the promises for noise abatement and the reminder that they "knew what they were getting into when they moved there." The truth is, many didn't know. Airport traffic has grown steadily over the past quarter century and many of those complaining have been doing so for years.

Nick Latham saw the impact the airport had on the people of the Highline School District. The Port of Seattle, he said, was to blame.

"My allegiance has changed since I took the job down there. So much power. They [the politicians] don't care about the communities, and they don't care about our kids. Should they have to suffer?"

If White Center and the surrounding areas seem a bit hopeless, despite a proliferation of the glitzy-cheap signs of fast food franchises, Burien has retained its small-town feel. It even has a feed store. Like most of suburbia, it isn't a pretty place, but it is home to thousands who sleep there at night and drive to jobs in Seattle or farther out. In her early years at the district, Mary Kay Letourneau did a reverse commute. In the fall of 1989, she came from outside the community to teach second grade in room 20 at Shorewood Elementary. She was admired and loved by nearly everyone in those early years. Her energy was unequaled; her ability to reach into a child's soul to pull out the dreams that she could foster was a gift. There wasn't a parent who didn't want their child in her class; there wasn't a little girl who didn't want to be just like the pretty teacher with the somewhat spiky, gelled hair. *Hip hair.*

Patricia Watson was Mary Letourneau's principal for

four of the teacher's first five years at Shorewood. She
considered Mary Kay to be one of her top teachers, a nur-
turing presence in the classroom where some students
needed that kind of caring in addition to their lessons.
Mary was the type of teacher who looked for the best way
to reach a student and she would make the effort to find
the way.

She was also an excellent mother. Patricia would never
forget the day Mary Kay brought her son and daughter to
the office to meet her. Mary Kay was so proud of them.
And it showed. Steven and Mary Claire were groomed to
perfection; shoes shined, hair combed and parted. Over the
course of several years, the Letourneau children would frequently come to Shorewood to wait for their mother. Steve
would drop them off to be with Mary Kay, and they ended
up in the principal's office coloring pictures.

"I still have some of the little treasures they made me,"
Patricia said later.

TWENTY

BY 1992, MARY Kay Letourneau had really wanted to
sell the condo. She wanted to live in Normandy Park, one
of the south-end-of-Seattle's more exclusive areas. She and
the children had found the dream home when out on a
drive before mass at St. Philamena, the Des Moines Catholic church the family attended and where the older two
children attended school. It was on a quiet street that
looped around to commanding views of Puget Sound,
Vashon Island, and the Des Moines marina. The 1960s-era
olive-green house didn't have a view of the sound, but it
was on the edge of a lovely, wooded ravine. At the condo,
Mary Kay organized their belongings into boxes, cleaned
like a fiend, printed five hundred flyers, and served lasagna
dinners to real estate agents. When the unit sold, she was
elated. The family was moving up. But even so, Mary Kay
emphasized to the Fish twins that although the new residence might have a better address than the condo in Kent,

the house itself was nearly a fixer-upper. It also tested their budget, already strained beyond repair. Even with the proceeds from the sale of the condo, some of the down payment was coming from Steve's family, Mary Kay told the girls.

"It's going to be tight for a while," she said cheerfully. "And it will be a long time before we can fix it up, but it's going to happen."

As she spoke of the move she was upbeat, animated, and very excited. So much so, that Amber and Angie didn't want to reveal their own sadness. The Letourneaus were their dream family. Little Nicky was "their" baby. Steven. Mary Claire. All of them had meant so much.

The Letourneaus promised the twins they could continue baby-sitting. Steve said he'd take care of driving them back and forth from Kent to Normandy Park. It made the girls feel as though it wasn't over between them, really. Mary Kay continued to do her part in keeping the relationship alive. She phoned Amber and Angie more often than either phoned her. Sometimes she called when she needed a sitter. Other times she dialed their number when she only wanted to chat.

Despite the warnings that the place needed a handyman's touch, the house surprised Angie and Amber.

"I thought it was going to be a lot nicer," Amber later said.

Angie, as usual, was more direct.

"It wasn't even built right. The front door was on the wrong side of the house."

If the house in Normandy Park was meant to bring happiness to the Letourneau family, Amber and Angie Fish wondered if it had been a flop. Even as teenagers, the girls could see that both Mary Kay and Steve were more harried and pressed for time than ever.

"Steve didn't seem happy," Amber said later. "In the condo he did seem happier. In the house he was more cold, withdrawn."

Mary Kay was working longer hours then, too. And though the sisters kept up with her on the phone, they didn't see her much. The days of hanging out were over and Amber and Angie missed them terribly. Whenever Mary Kay called out of desperation for a sitter, Amber or Angie—or both—would come right over. They spent the night a few times at the Letourneaus' new place, but by the following year, those kinds of visits had dropped off. Even so, they kept in touch by taking the kids out for ice cream or McDonald's every four months or so.

The little enclave of forty-some homes that made up the Letourneaus' Normandy Park neighborhood was a surprisingly tight group, even in the days of whirlwind careers and ever-evaporating time. What brought much of the cohesiveness was the network of children, and the connection they gave to the adults who raised them. Ellen and Daniel Douglas had two children, Scott and Jennifer, the same ages as Mary and Steve Letourneau's two oldest. So it was inevitable that the Douglas family would get to know the Letourneaus, though they lived at opposite ends of the neighborhood.

That Mary Kay and both Daniel and Ellen Douglas were teachers was merely a bonus. The children were always the primary connection. And while the kids shared many similarities, there was one difference. The Letourneaus were enrolled in Catholic school at St. Philomena and the Douglas kids went to public school in the Highline District where all three teachers taught.

"I'm not sure why they did it. Maybe they wanted the stricter values of the church? Ironic, isn't it?" Ellen asked later.

The Douglas home was on a stunning piece of view property once owned by Ellen's grandmother. At one time Ellen's older brother and his childhood buddy, lawyer David Gehrke, rented the little house. Years later, when the grandmother died, the property was divided and the north half sold to the Gehrkes for a much-dreamed-about home that he would build one day—"when the money comes in."

In time the four children were inseparable. There were lessons together, bicycle rides, trips to the grungy shores of Puget Sound, and for Scott, Little League baseball with Steve Letourneau as coach.

"A really young, active family," is how Ellen described the Letourneau brood years later. "Very involved with the kids, busy with the church. They were always busy, always hectic, and always late—for school, meetings, parties, picnics, and life. Life was busy. They were overbooked, maybe not too organized."

There were times when Mary Kay would drop off her children at neighborhood birthday parties, leave and go to the store to pick up a gift, wrap it in the car, and return to the party. Even though the invitation had been posted on the refrigerator for weeks.

When Ellen Douglas figured out the frazzled ways of the Letourneau household she made sure she was designated car-pool mom for Steven and Scott's Cub Scout meetings. That way they would not be stuck waiting for Mary Kay and Ellen would be able to get the two boys to where they needed to be on time.

Several years later, Ellen dismissed the lateness as inconsequential.

"Nobody was ever hurt by it," she said.

When the quicksand of a scandal enveloped the blond-headed family with the four beautiful children, Ellen Douglas wanted the world to know one thing: At one time the home had appeared happy and Steve and Mary Kay Letourneau were devoted to their children. At least, she thought so.

As much as Steve and Mary Kay sought a brand-name, status-soaked lifestyle, it was no secret among friends in the neighborhood that they had money troubles. One time Ellen Douglas watched the Letourneau children when their parents went downtown to meet with the Internal Revenue Service over some back taxes that they owed in order to get approval on some refinancing.

Another time a neighbor listened as Mary Kay complained that St. Philomena wanted to send the kids packing for public school because she hadn't kept current on their tuition. It had reached the crisis point, and a letter had been sent home and overlooked.

"It was about three inches down in the pile on the kitchen counter," the friend said with a sigh.

Ellen Douglas even hated to bring it up later, but she couldn't understand Steve and Mary Kay's choices. Both made okay money. Both worked steadily. Yet, they were struggling beyond belief. But they had the best clothes. Steven had the coolest new bike. They even had a landscape service.

"They had no money, but they paid for lawn care. But if you're broke, you mow it and just let it go brown and you don't care," Ellen said later. "We knew all along they weren't good at handling whatever money they did make."

To a few, it still seemed that Mary Kay and Steve Letourneau were a team. The focus appeared to be on their family. Steve worked nights so that he could be home when Mary Kay was teaching at school. When she returned to work after her babies were born, she'd pump her breast milk in the classroom and Steve would make milk runs throughout the day.

"Steve was her best friend," Principal Patricia Watson said later.

At times, the principal worried about Mary Letourneau, the person. Mary the teacher always gave one hundred percent and more—but that was a problem.

"Even before I left Shorewood," Patricia Watson said years later, "I had some concerns about her stability."

She talked with Mary about focusing her priorities. She was staying up too late, and running herself ragged. The principal worried that the teacher's own children were not getting enough of their mother's time.

"Mary," Patricia said more than once, "you need to get some things in control. You got to set your priorities because you can't do it all."

Mary would promise to give it consideration, come up with a plan, a compromise that allowed her to be the best teacher and the best mother she could be. She'd come back to Patricia and they'd talk some more. She was sincere in her understanding that something wasn't working.

"She was just really a perfectionist," Patricia recalled. "When you are a perfectionist you see every place that is not working for you. She could look at her children and figure out what wasn't right and beat herself up about it."

In the fall of 1993, Mary Kay Letourneau moved into the annex, a cluster of Shorewood classrooms joined to the main part of the school by a narrow covered walkway, to teach sixth grade—at her request. She was pregnant with her fourth child, and after Christmas she delivered another beautiful daughter, Jacqueline. Mary Kay Letourneau was doing what she was born to do, being a mother and a teacher.

In time, toddler Jackie would join her mother and big sister as they sang the songs from the Bette Midler movie *Beaches*, and danced around the house. Like her father, Mary Kay would twist the lyrics and make them her own. She sang "Happy Sunshine" instead of "You Are My Sunshine." Her children loved it.

TWENTY-ONE

IN SAD REALITY, the Steve and Mary Kay Letourneau marriage was a gorgeous package with nothing inside. They seemed to want the world to see them for what they had a right to be—pretty, handsome, and with money to spare. Flight benefits from Steve's job at Alaska Airlines allowed for a big part of the charade by giving them next-to-nothing airfare to anywhere they desired. Nordstrom credit cards and creative bookkeeping did the rest. Steve would later say he didn't want to know that he was in so deep and that his wife was a spendthrift extraordinare. He didn't want anyone to know how bad it was.

It was true. One of Steve's relatives recalled a cousin's wedding and how Steve and Mary arrived late, though not as late as usual. They looked beautiful. *Better than the bride and groom.* Their children were equally well decked out.

"The kids were all dressed like Little Lord Fauntleroy, you know, *knickers*. They dressed like they thought they were the Kennedys or something," the relative said later.

Steve and Mary were the gorgeous golden couple. She was the California girl with the stylish hair and the figure of a model. He was the square-jawed Dudley Do-Right; all blond and broad shouldered. Mary Kay even called him Dudley Do-Right and teasingly gave him a bathtub toy depicting the cartoon Canadian Mountie. Their children were perfect, too. *A balanced grouping for the family Christmas card.*

But as Steve and other family members learned, it was not so lovely after all. The Letourneaus' money problems escalated after they moved to Normandy Park. Even with family help, things were speeding from bad to worse. They were behind in their payments for the van given to them by Steve's father in Alaska. Even the money given by a wealthy aunt and uncle for part of the down payment on the house in Normandy Park had not been enough to provide a cushion in their overwhelmed checking account. The mortgage payments had been too high and the house was headed for foreclosure. The month before Steve and Mary Kay celebrated their tenth wedding anniversary, they filed Chapter 13 bankruptcy. Student loans of more than $27,000, medical bills, and assorted credit cards had overwhelmed them. They still owed the IRS more than $10,000. The total unsecured debt was almost $50,000. For assets, they listed a 1985 VW Jetta and a 1969 Buick. Steve had $25 cash on hand.

The couple's difficulty with money brought the inevitable problems among the family lenders.

"Sharon and Mary Kay didn't get along at all," said a relative. "They were always calling Sharon for money to pay the power bill, money for food."

But they kept up the lovely front. Mary Kay flew off to California to visit Michelle or just to get her hair done. When they lived in Alaska when they first got married, Steve would come down to Seattle for his hair appointments. From the outside, it looked like they were glamorous and rich.

"They were trying to be somebody they weren't," the relative said later. "They didn't care. They knew that someone would bail them out. They knew Steve's mom would give them money. She's not going to let her grand-kids go hungry."

Steve knew it was true and it made him feel terrible.

"It was all a big façade. It always was," he admitted years later to a family member.

In August of 1995, Stacey Letourneau was getting married in Alaska, and despite the fact that Mary Kay didn't care much for her sister-in-law, she was named matron of honor. She also insisted on helping with wedding decora-tions. She even spent a week working on a collage for Stacey—"something that she would keep for the rest of her life, it was that beautiful." The bride's colors were a blue tone and an apricotlike color that was hard to de-scribe. Nadine and her older daughter, Sandra, went shop-ping for balloons for the reception decorations but when they returned, Mary Kay said they had made a terrible mistake.

"Those are not the colors! Those are orange! Take them back. They won't work. They'll *never* work," she said.

Bullied into it, the women, led by Grandma Nadine, returned to the balloon store, only to learn they had the closest thing to apricot that could be found in all of Alaska. Nadine thought the whole fuss was ridiculous.

"Who in God's name is going to match those balloons with the bows and ribbons, anyway? Who cares?" she asked.

They all knew: *Mary Kay.*

That evening Mary Kay took the kids in the motor home Dick Letourneau had rented for extra sleeping quar-ters and drove twenty miles out to Eagle River to the re-ception hall. She worked all night making sure everything was just so. It was after three A.M. the next day when she returned.

Her way or no way. That was understood by everyone who knew Mary Kay, but most saw it as a sign of perfec-tionism. Mary Kay had experience with the finer things—

and those pep-rally-colored balloons were not going to
work. But there was nothing she could do about it. No
balloons of the right color could be had in all of Alaska.

Sharon's older sister, Sandra, was on hand to help. In
order to keep a clear path for the caterer's comings and
goings, Sandra put a plant on a table and placed it in front
of one of the doorways to block people from using it.

Mary Kay moved the table and Nadine watched as Sandra told her off.

"I've had it with you, Mary Kay," she recalled her
daughter saying. "I've taken all the shit I'm going to take
off of you. You are dealing with the wrong person."

During one of the Letourneau family visits to Anchorage,
Sharon Hume took her granddaughter Mary Claire shopping to pick out an outfit for her birthday. She found a
little denim shirt and vest at Lamonts, a mid-priced retailer,
and fell in love with it. The little girl couldn't wait for her
mother and father to see her wearing it. Steve praised his
daughter for her good taste and told her how lovely she
looked.

"She was so proud of that outfit that she wore it for
three days," recalled Nadine, who was up in Anchorage
visiting at the time.

When Mary Kay arrived from Seattle later, Mary Claire
put on the outfit as a surprise. The next thing the adults
knew, Mary Claire burst into the living room in tears.
Steve and his grandmother asked her what was the matter.
Mary Claire said her mother hated her new outfit. " 'That
just makes you look fat,' " she quoted her mother as saying.

Sharon was very upset. So was Nadine. With Mary
Kay, nothing was ever good enough.

Steve told his mom to let go of it and he'd clear it up
with his wife later.

"Clear it up later?" Sharon repeated. "You know you
are not ever going to bring the subject up! You're not ever
going to ask her why! Is it because Grandma Sharon
bought it for her? Or is it not good enough?"

"Mom," Steve said, "just let it ride."

Nadine jumped right into the fray.

"Who in the hell wears the pants in the family?" she asked her grandson. "You or Mary Kay? Yet I've never seen Mary Kay in a pair of pants."

Steve didn't say anything back to his grandmother and the old woman just shook her head. Mary Kay was a piece of work.

You never win with her. She is that manipulative. And where did she learn it? she thought.

Steve's grandmother was a forthright woman who never let a chance go by to speak her mind. Her family loved her for it, though there were times when they probably wished Grandma would just shut up. One of those times took place in Alaska in Sharon Hume's kitchen when the family was enjoying a salmon dinner.

The "boys"—Steve, his childhood buddy Mike Mason, and his cousin, Mike Gardner—talked about heading up north to stay in Mason's father's cabin. It would be a couple of days of hanging out, just like they used to do before wives and children.

Everyone was up for it, but Steve was reluctant. He hemmed and hawed and just couldn't commit.

"Well," he said, "I don't know. I'll have to check with Mary Kay—"

Nadine blew up. "God," she said, "are you so damned pussy-whipped?"

Everyone laughed and Steve turned red. Later, his grandmother told him she was sorry.

"But I think you are. She's got the upper hand and she knows how to use it," the old woman said.

Steve just shook his head.

TWENTY-TWO

TURNING NORTH ON Thirty-fifth Avenue SW from Roxbury is a straight shot from White Center and the problems that come with that territory. With each block toward the central business district, "the Junction," of West Seattle, come better homes, nicer yards, and that elusive pride of ownership. Thirty-fifth Avenue is lined with trees; rows of green-dipped paintbrushes in spring, yellow flames in fall. The houses are older, some approaching a century old. Little Northwest bungalows sit up high off the street in yards with lawns that drop perpendicular to the sidewalk. So steep are the yards that some homeowners hitch a rope to their mowers to drop them down and reel them up. No person could walk the edge.

The Hogden house was a pretty lemony shade of yellow that brought cheer in the winter and complemented the turning leaves that marched up the avenue in the fall. The home of Lee and Judy Hogden and their twelve-year-old daughter, Katie, sat like the others high up off the street. It was a house full of love with no shortage of pets.

The heart of their home was the kitchen, a wonderful room of clutter and computers. A kitchen island inset with a slab of marble dominated the center of the room; above the island was a canopy of pots and pans. A row of family photos mingled with eight-by-ten glossies of film and television stars—a gift from a movie director friend of Judy's. The prize of the gallery was the signed photo of Bette Davis; the River Phoenix image had never been taken from the envelope.

Someday, Judy, an accountant, would get around to it. But in September of 1995 she was focused on her daughter and her education, as she had been since kindergarten. She didn't know it then, but Katie's sixth-grade teacher, Mary Letourneau, would have a profound impact on her daughter—in ways she couldn't have imagined, or wanted.

Up a narrow staircase was Katie's bedroom, a small space made larger by the high ceilings of a vintage home. Hers was the room of a young girl with deep emotions. Framed photos of her friends, classmates, Mary Letourneau, and Vili Fualaau were pinned above the dresser. CDs filled a shelf. Candles topped a nightstand.

Classroom 39 was never neat. It held the clutter of a woman too busy to be bothered with housekeeping when there were projects to be created and lessons to be learned.

An ancient map of Washington State flanked by green chalkboards and bulletin boards that never went unadorned hung in the front of the room. A sink and soap dispenser got plenty of use in that classroom. Tempera paint splattered the wall and sponges were stained the color of the rainbows. Beams were painted with the hues of the Seattle football team, the Seahawks. The gridiron theme was the legacy of a previous teacher from days when teachers were able to give rooms a personal touch.

The annex was isolated from the rest of the school and Mary Kay's room was on the western-most end of the building. Two fifty-year-old cedars blocked the view to the courtyard area and the classrooms across the way. The setting suited the teacher's style. She was a hands-on educator who believed that experiences count as much, if not more, than what can be found on the pages of a book. If that meant noise, that was just part of the deal.

In the 1995–96 school year, as in other years, Mary Kay had a table set up where a group of kids could sit and work together. The kids at the "Round Table" were an exclusive lot. They were the *chosen*. Mary Letourneau had a warm word for all of the children in the class, but Vili Fualaau, Katie Hogden, and one of Vili's cousins, Tony, were a little bit more special. As Katie saw it, Mary did her best to make the other kids "feel like they were close to her." But there was a slight distance in those relationships. Those kids wanted to be close with their teacher, but she didn't allow it. Not in the same way that she did with Katie and the two boys. Katie didn't see the relationship between Mary Letourneau and the kids outside of the Round Table as "friendships."

"She called me to talk, she wouldn't call them to talk. *They'd* call her. She would always be there for them, always have time for them. Besides me and Tony and Vili, I don't think she called them [the other kids in the class]."

Years later, Judy Hogden smiled with the memory of Mary Letourneau and the attention she paid her "special" students.

"One thing that I noticed was that there was a handful of kids in that class that Mary saw something special in.

After Katie graduated from sixth grade, Mary put her arm around me and said, 'Katie is truly a gift from God, a very special young lady.' She taught to those kids and the other kids came along for the ride. Mary had her special kids and she focused in on them. I think a lot of the other kids were just there.''

Of course, not every child in the classroom made it to the Round Table, but whenever Mary saw a child with talent—art was always the most precious gift—she did what she could to foster emerging abilities. Mary thought nothing of reaching into her own purse to pay for art supplies for a child who came from a financially strapped family. Other teachers did it, too. But in some of the schools in the Highline School District, such supplementation would have proved costly.

One child, a quiet and sensitive girl, was adept at creating sculpted forms and Mary Kay went out of her way to see that she had supplies. It wasn't only Vili Fualaau who seemed to benefit from the extra attention.

"She was an excellent teacher," Katie remembered, "but our school couldn't really provide everything she needed to teach every student the way she could have. She kind of like nurtured the ones that had like gifts that could be helped, because she knew that if she didn't do it they'd go on to Evergreen or whatever school and probably wouldn't have thought of taking care of those gifts themselves."

For the most part, students loved her for it. Said one: "She went out of her way to help kids when she saw something that interested them when it seemed like they didn't have a lot of joy in other parts of their lives. There were a lot of troubled kids in my class. It was an interesting year."

If Vili was the artist, Katie was the writer. It was her love of writing that she thought first bonded her to Mrs. Letourneau. Be it poetry, short stories, even more typical reports, Katie infused her work with originality and a sense of fun that her teacher enjoyed, and to some degree, identified with.

"I always showed mine [work] to her and she was

amazed, because it was so much like how she writes. It was the same perspective. We used to make jokes about being left-handed and being divergent. That was the thing of the year," she said.

As the weeks of the school year flew by, Katie found herself redefining the relationship with Mary Letourneau. Mary Kay told her how inspiring she found her student's writing, the control she had of the language, the freshness of her perspective. They'd talk for hours about their thoughts and feelings and how to capture it all on the blank page of a tablet.

"There was a lot of trust," Katie said later. "She was somebody that I could look up to as an adult and she was also somebody I was equal with at the same time."

TWENTY-THREE

THE LEAVES DROPPED into a heavy pile along Thirty-fifth Avenue SW when parent/teacher conferences rolled around in early November 1995. Judy and Lee Hogden had looked forward to the meeting with Katie's teacher. By then, Mary Letourneau's phone calls had become frequent and the Hogdens knew that the teacher viewed their daughter as "special." They arrived at Shorewood Elementary a few minutes early for their five-thirty appointment—the last one of the day. They had been told the conference would last about fifteen minutes, maybe half an hour.

More than two hours passed. Two hours of hearing a teacher praise their daughter's brilliance, talent, and friendship.

"She just sat there and talked and talked about Katie. Her writing. Her future. How much they had in common. Time just went by. Lee and I looked at the clock," Judy remembered.

"We left Katie home alone and I'm sure she's wondering where we are," Lee said. "Mary, I'm sure you need to get home."

Mary Kay was in no hurry. It was clear that despite four children and a husband at home, she'd rather be sitting there with the Hogdens than anywhere else. "Oh, no, that's okay," the teacher said. "If I wasn't here, I'd have to be at a sixth-grade teachers' meeting. I'd much rather talk to you than the other sixth-grade teachers."

The teacher went on for a while longer and the Hogdens thanked her for all they had done for Katie.

Their daughter was waiting at home.

So were Mary Kay's children.

Judy Hogden was a sensible, well-read woman who along with her husband, Lee, had long known that their daughter was "born an adult." She was a girl who had no trouble talking eye to eye with older people. Katie once teasingly told her mother that she felt like she had to read *Seventeen* to learn how to act like the typical teen. She just didn't relate as easily to kids her own age, though no one would have said she was a nerd or a recluse. The phone always rang in their house, and Katie was usually the one to get on the line.

As Mary Letourneau's phone calls increased over the school year, the thought did cross Judy's mind that it was a little out of the ordinary. It didn't alarm her in any way; it just made an impression that the teacher had found something special in her daughter and both were benefiting from the mentoring.

"I knew she was a lot older, but she always struck me as the big sister Katie never had. I never felt the age thing was odd. I did wonder how a mother of four had so much time to spend on the phone with her students. Mary always struck me as young and fun-loving. It was great that she was young and loved the sixth-graders," Judy said.

The lights in room 39 were almost always the last ones to dim at Shorewood Elementary. For a time, some wondered if Mary Letourneau was so disorganized that she couldn't get her work done in the manner of most other elementary school teachers. It was true that there was never enough planning and correcting time, but *ten* P.M.? Others who knew her better thought disorganization could be a factor, but also weighed the idea that Mary just didn't want to go home. Maybe she didn't have much reason to go? Her marriage was in deep trouble and she frequently hinted at that. At one point, three teachers cornered Mary Kay to tell her that she shouldn't be so vocal about her problems with Steve. They understood she wasn't happy and didn't want to go home, but why didn't she want to get home to her children? What was so terrible about home that kept her from her own babies?

She called on Katie Hogden a number of times to bail her out of her mental disarray.

"Katie, please! Let me go photocopy this . . . fax that. Please!"

Katie was happy to help. She'd sit at Mrs. Letourneau's desk for hours using the answer key and marking paper after paper while Mary ran off to take care of an errand.

"She always had a gazillion things to do," Katie said later.

At the end of the day when darkness fell, Katie would help her teacher load up her bags with projects and papers that would never get finished. She'd carry them back and forth each day, unloading and reloading. Blanketing her desk in an avalanche of paperwork, she always said she was going get it done, *that night*. But there was always more to do. The distractions of daily life piled up and, in time, would bury her.

Danelle Johnson was a magna cum laude graduate of the school of hard knocks. She'd had it rougher than most, but pulled herself up from the abyss of living on welfare to cleaning toilets to a job with her own office at a community college. Her laugh was always ready, masking the realities of a life that sometimes seemed too hard, or just plain unfair. Her voice was deep, the result of cigarettes and the decibel level sometimes required of a mother of six. At forty-six, Danelle Johnson was doing the best that a single mother could. She had a good job, a nice house. Food stamps and welfare were a distant, but never fully forgotten, memory.

Her youngest were boy-girl twins, Drew and Molly, two sandy-haired kids with the push-me, pull-me relationship typical of brothers or sisters of similar age. They hated each other. They loved each other. They were close. They couldn't stand the sight of the other. They were Shorewood Elementary students from kindergarten to sixth grade. And they struggled every step of the way, forcing their mother to make herself known at the school office whenever the twins were having difficulty.

"I was famous at Shorewood," Danelle said later. "All I had to do was call down there and say 'This is Danelle' and they knew exactly who I was and why I was calling."

Danelle's job of nearly two decades had provided stability for her children, allowing them to start and finish in the same school—a not-so-common feat in a district that draws from the apartments and projects of the poor.

And even though Danelle and her own grown children formed an extended family, the focus on the school remained paramount. School, she hoped, would be their chance to do something better, as it had been for her when she hit rock bottom.

Their lives revolved around Shorewood.

"That's why what happened is so sad. Sad and disgusting," Danelle would say later.

When sixth grade came in the 1995–96 school year, daughter Molly was enrolled in Mrs. Letourneau's class and her twin brother, Drew, was assigned to a teacher across the hall. Drew's best friend was Vili Fualaau. For a time, everything looked all right. Danelle Johnson hoped against hope that her children would get through sixth grade with enough knowledge to make the transition to junior high.

When Danelle showed up for her son's and daughter's parent-teacher conferences in November, she was looking forward to talking with Mrs. Letourneau. Molly thought so highly of her teacher, but her grades were still below average and Danelle considered school more than a popularity contest.

Mrs. Letourneau was rushed. She barely had five minutes to discuss her troubled student. She told Danelle that she needed to get more involved with her daughter's homework. She wasn't encouraging and she didn't seem particularly interested in talking about Molly at all. Danelle was mystified. The woman she had seen around school in the past was outgoing, friendly, *and perky,* and above all, interested in connecting with parents and students. This lady wasn't interested in that at all. At least not on that day.

"She seemed a little strange," she said later.

TWENTY-FOUR

AT THIRTY-EIGHT, SOONA Fualaau had plenty of problems. With an ex-husband in prison, and bills and eviction notices in the mail, the heavyset woman with long black hair streaked in gray lived stoically in a burdensome world. She'd worked dead-end jobs at everything from taking orders at a Taco Bell to cashiering at the Roxbury Texaco. But she wasn't alone. The school was a valued link in her life on the level of the church where her father was a founding member and she, naturally, was a devoted part of the Samoan congregation. When the Fualaau house caught on fire it was Shorewood teachers and students who collected clothing to get the family of five going again. Soona was poor, but her sons and daughter could transcend all of that because they were stellar in different ways. The teachers at Shorewood saw their potential very clearly.

"Every single child in that family had promise, were gifted in one area. Vili's was his art, Perry with his voice, Leni was the athlete, Favaae was a mathematician," said one teacher.

As is often the case in places like White Center, when personal ambition does not exist and parental support is not there, promises go unfulfilled. Though Leni, the sole daughter of the family, did earn an athletic scholarship, she didn't make it to college.

Vili was Soona's last chance. And teachers at Shorewood knew that if he could develop his talent, he'd have something to hold on to. He had the opportunity to develop a passion and a talent that would carry him through high school.

"Every teacher tried to help him out and be a mentor. It wasn't just Mary who recognized the artistic ability in him and was trying to look outside to try to find help. She might have been the most successful at doing that because she drove him to his art class," said one who knew the situation well.

As early as first grade and certainly by second grade, Vili Fualaau was seen as a child with undeniable artistic talent. One teacher saw it then and inquired at the YMCA to see if they could help an underprivileged kid. He could benefit from extra attention in an area in which he clearly excelled.

"If you could see his work in first grade it is about like it is now. It was that unbelievable," a teacher said.

Whether Vili Fualaau was the Second Coming of Picasso or not was a topic of debate. Some considered the boy's artwork provocative and developed beyond his years. Mary Letourneau would nearly bring herself to tears as she thought of Vili's creative genius. Others didn't see it that way at all. They saw his creations as no better or worse than the high school artist who later pumped gas for a living and painted houses on the side.

But to Katie Hogden, her friend's talent was without limit. She noticed it in fourth grade, and two years later it was even more clear to her. Mary Letourneau had seen it two years before Katie when she taught him in second grade. With her love of art and the creative process, Mary had found her perfect student.

Certainly there were reading, writing, and math lessons, but it seemed to some observers that time in Mary Letourneau's room was filled with mask-making, drawing, and painting. When one volunteer parent brought in copies of Monet's water lily series, it was Vili who created the most stunning replica.

"It was amazing to watch him draw," Katie said later. "It was like he took a picture with his eyes and copied it."

The only thing Vili seemed to have trouble with was self-portraiture. Though he captured much of his physical appearance, his eyes, his mouth, Vili always made his nose two sizes too small—a kind of Michael Jackson makeover that Katie found both amusing and touching. She teased him in the way sisters or very good friends often do.

"You're Samoan," she said. "You can't help your nose. It adds character to you."

Vili would laugh and tease her right back, telling her she was a roly-poly.

"We both knew the other didn't mean it," she said later.

Of course later media appearances would prove that Vili Fualauu was more a typical teenager than a great intellectual, as Mary and the lawyers would eventually proclaim to the world. Teachers at Shorewood didn't know what Mary was talking about when she carried on about the intelligence and maturity of the boy. They never thought Vili was any more grown-up than other sixth- or seventh-graders.

"He was a boy. He looked like a boy," said one teacher.

And if Vili wasn't all that Mary made him out to be— though he might have thought so—he certainly had his following within the classrooms of Shorewood Elementary. Said one who knew him at the time: "Everyone knew him. Not everyone liked him."

Yet when the yearbooks were distributed at the end of the year, no one would have a longer line for signatures than Vili.

There was another side to twelve-year-old Vili.

Said one close friend: "I never knew quite what was going on with him, either. He has two very distinct personalities, and they are completely different from each other. One side you know everything about him, and the other side you don't know anything about him.''

One side was Vili, the other had the nickname Buddha.

Katie Hogden saw through it: "He has one side," she said, " 'I'm a little thug, I'm a G [gangster], I'm hard, I know how to take care of myself,' and he'll talk to you for five minutes and he'll pick the personality you like best about him and he'll stick to that personality. Just to impress you, to make that imprint in your mind that you'll remember him now.''

That Vili was the manipulator.

"He'll pay attention to the expression on your face when he starts his personality . . . I know he uses it for inspiration . . . The reason we were friends was because I saw right through him."

Don't play these games, I know you're not like this, she thought.

Katie felt sorry for the Vili that Mary Letourneau would later say she fell in love with—the artist.

"The side where he knew what he wants out of life, but he's kind of scared to let it happen because he thought with his family—his money situation—he'd never get to have it come true anyway. He didn't share that with a lot of people."

Vili could charm and cajole to get what he wanted.

"New shoes!" he called out to Katie Hogden one morning when she walked in wearing a pair of Nikes right out of the box.

"You can't have them," she shot back.

But Vili didn't give up. He told her how much he wanted a new pair of shoes, but his mom didn't have enough money to buy them for him. Katie felt sorry for him. Vili must have seen it because he continued to press the point in a niggling way that elicited more sympathy than annoyance.

"I traded him for his sister's Champions that were too small for him so he could have my designer Nike shoes," Katie said later. "One day I just took them off and gave them to him. He was so happy. Just thrilled."

*   *   *

For those who knew Vili, it was plain that no matter what had gone on in his life, no matter what troubles his mother and sister and brothers had endured—and the list was long—nothing hurt like the subject of his father, a convict named Luaiva Fualaau.

Most who knew Vili considered Luaiva Fualaau, a former auto mechanic, preacher, and purported father of eighteen, off-limits. If Vili wanted to talk about him, fine. But smarter kids knew never to bring his name up first. The fact that his father was in prison and the reason for it worried the twelve-year-old, who hadn't seen much of his father since he was two. Luaiva had assaulted his wife, and later another woman. Vili would sometimes describe some of the attacks against his mother when they lived in Hawaii. Violence scared him.

Katie remembered some time later: "He just wanted to make sure that his family was not going to end up like [his father] ended up. He never looked down on his mom for that, I don't think he ever did. He had a lot of hate in his heart for his dad. A lot."

TWENTY-FIVE

THOUGH SHE DIDN'T bring up her family often, kids from the class knew that Mrs. Letourneau had grown up in a sunny world far from White Center.

"She was brought up to be Miss Prissy, Miss Perfect," said one student who remembered the teacher talking about her past.

Kids from the Round Table also knew her father was somehow involved in government affairs, maybe a senator or something. Mary Kay told the group that she adored her father.

"But she never agreed with any of his morals," Katie Hogden recalled later.

Mary's mother was another matter.

"My mom gave birth to me and she raised my brothers and sisters, but it was never anything more than that," she told Katie, who asked about her mother a number of times. After a while she stopped asking. She wished Mary had a close relationship with her mom, like she did with hers.

Mary's children were occasional visitors to her school-room throughout her teaching career at Shorewood. Although Mary professed great love for her children—and Katie Hogden, for one, never doubted it—there was something different about their relationship. It was not the same as how Mary treated the kids of the Round Table.

Katie wondered about that later.

"I know she loved her kids, just like she loved every single kid in that whole entire class, but I don't know if they had as strong a bond with their mom. I don't know if they felt as close to her as she felt to them," she said.

Katie remembered meeting Steven Letourneau for the first time. Though he was just a year younger, he wasn't connected to his mother like so many others in the class were.

"He just looked at her like a mom. Like, *this is my mom*. It wasn't like a friendship thing. *This is my mom. She loves me and takes care of me, but there isn't a strong friendship.*"

Katie's mother, Judy, mulled it over.

"She felt closer to her students than her own children. God knows, she spent more time with them."

Calls or visits from her husband to Shorewood Elementary during that time frequently meant tears and a knotted stomach for Mary Letourneau. Often she'd just let Steve wait on the phone whenever the office secretary announced a call over the classroom intercom.

"It was like, I'll talk to you when I damn well please," said a friend from the school.

The kids could see the stress, and at times, members of the Round Table group were sought for comfort. From what Katie could see—and what little Mary had told her—the Letourneau marriage was failing. Katie remembered one time when Steve came to school and starting yelling at Mary in the hallway in front of the classroom. Mary just stood there. When it was over she reached out for her student.

"I just need a hug," she said. "I'm having a really hard time."

Katie hugged her tightly. "Yeah, you are," the student said.

Nothing more was said about what happened in the hallway that day. Nothing needed to be said. Whatever it was, it most likely had been Steve's fault. Students in Mrs. Letourneau's class loved *her*—Steve Letourneau was a man who lived with their teacher. It was true he was her husband, and she lived with him, but she didn't have much to do with the man. Steve was all wrong for his wife anyway.

"Steve didn't match Mary Letourneau *at all*," Katie said later. "His personality from what I could see was completely different from hers. I can understand why she wasn't happy with him. It wasn't a meant-to-be situation. I think she tried to build on it, but it ended up not working."

Steve didn't make a good impression on his wife's class.

"He always seemed rude to me," Katie said later. "He wasn't welcoming to our class. He'd bring Jackie in, 'Hi, class!' No hug for Mary. 'Just come out in the hall because I need to talk to you.' He didn't seem like he was very friendly."

Mary Kay Letourneau was coming undone. Most considered it the result of a faltering marriage made worse by stress and money matters, or it could have been that she had too many children to mother. She was on overload all the time. She looked wan. Things weren't getting better. *But how much worse could they get?* Mary Kay suffered her third miscarriage—though many didn't know until later that she and Steve had, in fact, been expecting a fifth child.

Mary Kay's reaction to losing the baby was peculiar to the Shorewood teacher who had known her for more than four years. The miscarriage had not brought tears or even much concern.

"It's for the best," Mary Kay said, seemingly detached from what she had been through a few days before. "I'm not staying with Steve anyway."

The comment struck the colleague, not because she was going to leave Steve Letourneau, but because having babies was so much a part of Mary Kay and her core values. Teaching, art, and having babies were the world to her.

Former Shorewood principal Patricia Watson was very concerned the last time she saw Mary Kay and her children. During a visit to her old school, Patricia saw the Letourneaus in the parking lot behind the school. Their windshield was cracked and the windows couldn't be raised or lowered. May Kay looked disheveled, far from the impeccably neat woman she'd always been. Her children didn't look quite right, either. They weren't scrubbed and Mary Claire wasn't wearing any shoes.

"All of them were less well kept," she said. "Unkempt even."

My goodness sakes, she thought, something has gone awry here.

TWENTY-SIX

IN THE SPRING of 1996, Mary Kay Letourneau told neighbor and teacher Ellen Douglas that she was planning on taking art courses at nearby Highline Community College in order to earn credits necessary to keep her teaching certificate current. Ellen thought it was a good idea, a *necessary* plan. Mary Kay had often delayed getting the credits and it had reached do-or-die time. If she didn't get them that summer there was a good chance her teaching certificate would be in jeopardy.

It surprised Ellen when Mary Kay said she was thinking about spending the summer with her folks back in D.C. instead. Her mother said she'd pay for her to pick up the classes *after* the summer. It seemed reckless.

"I kept thinking in my own mind there are so many classes they offer and you have to take however many to get the [right] number of credits. *Logistically, you don't have a good record for making it. You'll lose your license if you don't get them now.*"

Mary Kay gave in to reason and stayed with her schedule at the community college. She had another motive for it, anyway. She was going to mentor Vili Fualaau by taking some art classes with him. She had even arranged for a $200 grant for a "child at risk." Besides, he needed a way to get there, and she would drive.

The summer of 1996 was unsettling for the neighborhood kids. Where at one time the Letourneau household was one that invited children with a Kool-Aid mom and all the things that went with that, it was decidedly different with Vili and his older brother Perry over there all the time. Vili, in fact, the Letourneau kids said, spent the night frequently. It was a holdover from the final part of the school year when student and teacher burned the midnight oil getting the sixth-grade yearbook ready for the copy center.

Ellen Douglas's ten-year-old daughter, Jennifer, came home upset one afternoon and told her mother that she didn't like Mary Claire's baby-sitter, Perry Fualaau. Mary Kay was letting the teenager drink beer and smoke in the house. Schoolteacher Ellen gave her head a shake. She knew the Fualaau boys were hanging around, but smoking and drinking? It just didn't sound like Mary Kay at all. The next time she had the opportunity to bring it up, she asked her friend about it.

"Well," Mary Kay explained, shrugging it off, "it's so nice that he's doing me a favor that I don't want to say anything about it."

Mary Kay and the Fish twins from the Kent condominium renewed their friendship and talked on the phone more than they had in the past year. Topics always ricocheted with Mary Kay—"What did you have for dinner?" would turn into what *she* had had for dinner three weeks ago and every day since. But one subject all enjoyed discussing was the world of art. Mary Kay was especially pleased that both Amber and Angie had enrolled in the Seattle Art Institute. Amber was majoring in music and promotion and Angie was aiming for a career in video/film editing. Mary Kay recalled the fantastic job the girls had done on their high school video yearbook. She had spotted their talent back then. And, she told them, she had a new protégé of sorts.

"Yeah," she said, "I have this friend from school that I'd like to get into the Art Institute or Cornish." She went on to explain how talented her friend was and how she was even taking art classes with him at Highline Community College and at Daniel Smith, a Seattle art store, to support his dreams. The future for the student/friend was unlimited.

Amber and Angie talked about it later. They were amazed by Mary Kay's dedication.

"I knew she didn't have enough time for her family and school, and here she was taking classes with this student," Angie said. "What kind of teacher goes to classes with her student?"

Angie later remembered calling Mary Kay in July 1996 to arrange for a visit.

"We wanted to see them. It was almost an excitement when she would hear from us. 'Oh, hello! We want to see you!' It was a thrill for us because we loved the family. I would usually make Amber call; I hated calling because I didn't want to get stuck on the phone with her for an hour. She just wouldn't shut up. She'd talk about everything and anything."

The girls took Steven, eleven, Mary Claire, nine, and Nicky, almost five, to the Burien Baskin-Robbins for ice cream. They left toddler Jackie with her mother at home. It was a good time, *like the old times*. Mary Claire chattered on about anything and everything and Steven was excited about Amber's new Ford Escort.

"He was just getting into music and he really liked the new stereo," Amber recalled.

The following month, Mary Kay called and arranged

for her two youngest children to be baby-sat by Amber and Angie at Carriage Row.

As the twins entertained the children they asked what their parents had been up to.

"Daddy doesn't like the brown boy who smokes," Nicky said. "Mommy and Daddy fight about the brown boy."

Amber and Angie didn't know what to make of the remark. They asked if the "brown boy" was their regular baby-sitter.

Nicky said no.

"Why are they fighting?"

The little boy said he didn't know, and the girls just dropped it.

TWENTY-SEVEN

AND AS THE days went on during the summer of 1996, Mary Kay Letourneau and her now-thirteen-year-old protégé, Vili Fualaau, seemed inseparable. Vili's brother filled in as a baby-sitter when teacher and student took art classes, went to art supply stores, and visited galleries in Seattle. As a mother, Mary Kay had never been the type to hang out around the house and vacuum; she was always coordinating some activity. But that summer those activities always involved Vili.

When Mary Claire was invited to a slumber party with assorted cousins at Grandmother Nadine's in Puyallup, Mary Kay said she was so swamped she wasn't certain she would have time to get her there. She was running here and there, one appointment after the next. Classes to attend. Shopping to take care of. To make matters even more difficult, the day Nadine wanted Mary Claire down in Puyallup was the same day mother and daughter were planning on heading up to Anchorage to join the rest of her children and her husband who were already up there visiting. Mary Kay altered her plans, and made arrangements to go as far as Auburn to meet one of Steve's aunts in a kind of relay race. The aunt agreed to take the little girl down to Nadine's for the slumber party.

When she arrived in Auburn, she not only had Mary Claire with her, but she also had Vili Fualaau along for the ride. She said she was going to fly up to Anchorage that afternoon, on a 4 P.M. flight. The women picking up Mary Claire thought it was strange that Mary Kay had the Samoan boy with her, and mentioned it to Nadine.

"Why did she have that boy with her?" Nadine wondered.

Sharon Hume called her mother the next day. Mary Kay hadn't made the 4 P.M. flight after all, she arrived five hours later than planned. But there was more. She was troubled by something else.

"Mother, she brought this kid, Vili, with her. This kid that she's supposedly teaching art and everything to."

"What?" Nadine asked. "She had him with her when she dropped off Mary Claire, but she didn't say anything about bringing him to Alaska."

Sharon, who was audibly upset, told her mother that something else was curious. When they arrived at the Letourneaus' Anchorage restaurant, Mary Kay asked Dick Letourneau for the keys to his new truck. She said she "wanted to show Vili the stars. They were gone for hours."

What was going on? Mary Kay had left her kids, tired and cranky, at the restaurant for hours? What was she thinking? What was she doing? And all the while when they were in Alaska, Mary kept singing Vili's praises to Steve's family.

Nadine later recalled how her daughter Sharon felt about the thirteen-year-old.

"They didn't like Vili. They thought he was illiterate. Also she [Mary] kept saying, 'Isn't he wonderful? Isn't he something else?' Sharon thought, 'What is there about this kid that I'm supposed to think is so wonderful?' "

Later, Nadine couldn't shake off the idea that so much had been going on right under Steve's nose. Right under everyone's noses. In Normandy Park, and in Alaska, too.

"She sat up til four A.M. holding his hand on the dav-

enport downstairs. Steven was in the bedroom. It blows
your mind. It was like Steven was hypnotized,'' she said.

Other incidents raised an eyebrow or two among
Steve's family. One family member was puzzled by Mary
Kay's behavior at the last family gathering she attended.
It was a wedding reception. She never once spoke to any
adults. She was always hovering around the kids' table,
conversing and playing with them as though they were her
peer group. It was very peculiar and not like Mary Kay at
all. Sure, she was attentive to her children, but she liked
to be noticed and praised for her lovely outfits by the
adults, too.

That night she was a child, too.

When Mary Kay and Vili returned to Seattle they
brought with them some art photographs of a pair of puf-
fins nuzzling each other.

''They mate for life, you know,'' Mary Kay told a
friend.

If Mary Kay Letourneau lived for the telephone and its
link to the world outside her Normandy Park home, one
of her favorite people to converse with was Michelle Jarvis. That had been true when they were teenagers and had
continued into adulthood. A four-hour marathon was nothing out of the ordinary; and both women had phone bills
to prove it. One particular phone call in late September
1996, however, had been on Michelle's dime. The childhood friend and mother of three hadn't heard from Mary
Kay for a while, and assumed that her long distance service
had been discontinued for lack of payment—a common
occurrence.

They got on the phone at ten and didn't hang up until
after 2 A.M.—on a day both had to work. Mary never
needed as much sleep, but Michelle could always feel the
residual drag the next day after an all-nighter with Mary
Kay. Much of their conversation that night centered around
Vili Fualaau, whom Mary Kay considered a particularly
gifted student. She said she had realized his potential when
she taught him in second grade and the ensuing years only
verified his artistic ability. Mary Kay said she wanted to

help develop his talent. They discussed everything from showing the boy's artwork in a gallery exhibition for students to finding a mentor among the local artists who lived in the area.

This is great, Michelle thought at the time. She's got this child that she recognizes this incredible talent in. What an awesome person she is for caring so much . . .

Mary Kay had always been interested in her students. But Michelle had never heard such extreme concern for and awareness of a particular individual. From what she gathered, Vili Fualaau seemed deserving of the interest. Mary Kay described him as boy from a troubled home, being raised by a single mother in poverty with a father in prison. His prospects were bleak and she saw his future in his art. Her help could be his ticket out of poverty, she said.

"It is ironic," Michael Jarvis, Michelle's husband, said later. "It *was* his ticket out of poverty. Not how she planned it. Not what she had in mind."

In October, Mary Kay called Michelle now living in Costa Mesa to tell her that she had fallen in love. In fact, she was in love like she had never been in love before. She practically gushed into the phone, spewing out adjectives and descriptions of the most wonderful person in the world. He was the person that she had been searching for her entire life. She was not going to settle for a life without love anymore. She'd found the perfect love. There hadn't been any sex, but they were considering it.

"He's so wonderful. We talk about everything. He's my soul mate . . ."

Oddly, for a woman who showed no compunction about sharing intimate aspects of her love life when she and Michelle were teenagers, Mary Kay didn't provide many concrete details about the wonderful new guy in her life. She offered nothing about his job or his social status. Not even the subject of his ever-important appearance was broached. Nothing much beyond the fact that he was wonderful and she was in love.

"She told me he was a student and she had a class with him over the summer," Michelle recalled. "I was thinking he was a student in college that she had met through taking this class. So without coming right out and saying who he was, she led me to believe that he was a college student. In my mind I was thinking he was about twenty or so,'' she said later. ''But she never really said an age.''

But she was so happy that Michelle didn't pry.

I wonder what took her so long to find someone to love? she thought.

A few weeks later, more news came in another phone call from Mary Kay.

''I'm pregnant,'' she said, ''and it's not Steve's.''

Michelle didn't condemn. She was happy about it. Mary Kay seemed overjoyed and after all the years with Steve she certainly was entitled to some shred of joy. Mary Kay said that the father was the same person, the student, she had fallen in love with over the summer. Of course, there would be no abortion. She was going to divorce Steve and have the baby.

''Does Steve know?'' Michelle wondered.

''No,'' she said, adding that she had recently slept with Steve to buy some time while she figured out what she was going to do. There was no love lost between them and getting him into bed hadn't been easy, but the mission was accomplished. Intercourse had allowed the *possibility* that the baby was her husband's.

Michelle didn't fault her childhood friend for the deception.

''Will Steve believe that it's his baby?'' she asked.

Mary Kay doubted it. ''The baby will have black hair,'' she said.

At that point, Mary Kay said she was biding her time. Things were tense enough and adding a baby from her affair to the mix would be trouble. Steve was agitated and suspicious enough.

''Mary Kay, I'm very afraid for you,'' Michelle said. ''I'm afraid of how he will react to this.''

Her friend told her not to worry. Cake was sure she could handle it.

*   *   *

Whatever was going on at the Letourneaus' house had to be pretty bad. Scott Douglas came home very upset one afternoon and told his mother that Steven's parents were not going to have a party for his twelfth birthday. Ellen Douglas wasted no time in telling her son that they'd celebrate his friend's birthday by inviting Steven over for pizza and videos. The words ran through her mind: "Just because your family is falling apart, doesn't mean your friends don't love you."

Later Steve Letourneau talked with Ellen and the subject of the stress in his family came up. Steve said that big trouble had, in fact, been in the offing for a while. He refused to elaborate.

"I can't tell you now. But you're not going to believe it."

Ellen didn't push, though the grade-school teacher was certainly intrigued.

Don't give me a little bit of the story. . . . it's like licking the spoon without eating the cookie, she thought later.

TWENTY-EIGHT

GRANDMA NADINE KNEW that something was up with her grandson and his wife, but she had no idea how bad it would get. No marriage was perfect and the rumblings she'd heard about Steve and Mary Kay seemed like more of the same. Instead of brooding about something over which she had no control, she looked forward to filling her mobile home with children and grandchildren for the holidays. Holidays, she knew, were stressful enough without worrying about someone else's marriage.

But all of that was put on hold when she answered the phone one evening. It was her daughter Sharon, in Alaska. Her voice was ragged and her words constricted. She was upset. Nadine could tell something bad was coming. It was about Mary Kay.

"Everything I suspected is true," Sharon said, finally

diving into the reason for her call. "She's having an affair with that thirteen-year-old."

Nadine sat down on the sofa up against row after row of family pictures. Steve and Mary Kay. Mary Kay and the children. Every combination of every member in the family. All of the beautiful blond-headed kids smiling wide and sweetly. The faces stared down on her as she spoke to her daughter.

"And she's pregnant."

She could barely believe her ears.

"You've got to be kidding me," was all Nadine could come up with.

"No. Steven has all the proof in the world."

Nadine's blood boiled. "I'm glad for that," the older woman said, surprised at her daughter's disclosure, but not shocked. It was a strange feeling. Although the words were outrageous, she believed Mary Kay was capable of such an act.

"Those poor kids," she added.

Sharon swore her mother to secrecy, as Steven had requested. He was going to handle it his own way. Sharon said that Steve didn't want to make it public until he had all of the evidence. And though Sharon had known about it for a while, she needed to talk to somebody about it. She could no longer hold it inside so she called her mother.

Whether they kept their mouths shut or not, there was going to be no hiding it. The boy was a Samoan and the baby would look like him, too.

"This will come out," Nadine said.

"It will, Mother," she said, adding that she wasn't going to the authorities, at least not without Steven saying so. They had to think about the four children and what was best for them.

Sharon had known since shortly after Mary Kay's visit with Vili that summer. Steven had told her. She also told her mother that Dick Letourneau and his wife, Phyllis, knew.

Nadine didn't breathe a word of it to anyone. She watched and waited. And she wondered. *Why was Steven*

*staying with his wife? Why didn't he take the kids from
her and dump her?*

Then the answer came to her. Despite it all, she knew
that Steve still loved Mary Kay. Maybe the whole thing
would blow over.

"I think Steven hoped she'd lose the baby," Nadine
said later.

The Letourneau clan didn't keep their vow of silence
among themselves. Whenever Nadine and her daughters
got together, the subject was the first order of business.

They felt so sorry for Steve. Outside of his four children, they saw Steve as the true victim in the whole thing.
They felt he had been manipulated and brainwashed by his
wife and the forces working with her. Nadine thought the
priest was supporting Mary Kay.

"She went to the priest even and talked about it and
took Steve. Tried to get the priest to talk Steve out of
dissolving the marriage and just accepting the baby and
going on."

Nadine saw the meetings with the priest at St. Philomena as an attempt to buy time. She couldn't believe that
Steve was so naïve as to think that she'd really stay with
him and raise the schoolboy's baby as their own.

*Kind of hard to do if the baby has coal-black hair and
dark skin! she thought.*

She viewed it as more of Mary Kay's manipulation of
Steve, whom she was sure was shell-shocked by the disclosure.

"She was trying to cover her own tracks, that's all she
was doing," she said. "He was still in denial, trying to
make himself believe it [that he could raise the boy's
baby]. How evil she was!"

Nadine never believed the pregnancy was anything but
intentional and she told family members just what she
thought.

"They planned it. *She* planned it. Same as she planned
the pregnancy with Steve."

Sometimes stories would filter from Steve to Sharon to
Nadine, an information line that went from Washington to

Alaska and back to Washington and pulsed with regularity.

Some stories brought outrage.

"She left Mary Claire one night all by herself—a nine-year-old girl—and took the rest of the children, probably Vili, too, to a movie because she was mad at Mary Claire. That was punishment! Steven came home at eleven at night, nobody around. Heard this little [girl] sobbing and went into the living room, curled up on the sofa, sobbing her little heart out. 'Mary Claire, where is Mom? Where is everybody?'

"You call that a loving mom?"

TWENTY-NINE

IN THE FALL of 1996, Danelle Johnson sat at her kitchen table, sucked hard on a cigarette as she tried to figure out what was going on with her thirteen-year-old twins, Drew and Molly. The turn of events was almost beyond belief. The spring before, her youngest two couldn't wait to get out of Shorewood Elementary and into the halls of Cascade Middle School.

Couldn't wait to leave grade school behind.

The mother of two children who never excelled at school had very mixed feelings. She didn't know what to make of what was going on. Should she be happy or angry? Without provocation, the children were going to Shorewood nearly every day after class and staying until curfew time in the evening to help Mary Letourneau. It was so peculiar. The first time it happened Danelle asked Drew what was going on at the school. The boy said a bunch of former students were helping their former teacher with class projects, paper grading, bulletin boards. Among the group were Vili and a cousin.

"I thought it was strange, weird, but how nice. I'm thinking they're safe, going down there after school, helping a teacher and getting involved and interested in education. So, Mary Kay's a cool teacher. What harm could

the little thing do? Could be nothing but good for them,"
she said later.

Not long after Drew started hanging out in room 39,
his twin sister Molly and her friend Nicole joined in. It
was only when the girls started coming home late, saying
they had stopped off at McDonald's on Ambaum Boulevard, that Danelle's blood began to churn.

"But we're helping Miss Letourneau," Molly said.

Danelle shook her head.

"I don't care what you're doing down there with her.
If she's not giving you a ride home, then you're not going
down there to help her."

And as teenagers do when they can, they ignored their
mother and continued to go to Shorewood, but they made
it a point to get home on time—or at least closer to the
8:30 P.M. curfew.

Later, Mrs. Johnson remembered how it was that she
allowed her children to hang out at the school so late in
the evening. She felt as though her kids were safe with
their former teacher's unorthodox after-hours help sessions.

"I thought it was good for them. I was worried about
their schoolwork. Worried about them going from sixth
grade to the seventh. They were getting interested in
school. I swear to God, I thought it was a help. I couldn't
imagine that anything she could do would be wrong."

It was sometime after ten P.M. on a school night in October 1996 when Danelle Johnson began to wonder what
was really going on at the school. Her son and daughter
were in bed and the mother of six was watching television
when she heard a knock on the door. It was Mary Kay
Letourneau standing on the front step looking agitated and
flustered. Behind her was a young boy whom Danelle recognized a friend of her son's.

The teacher apologized for the intrusion at the late hour,
but she had no choice. Her words were rapid-fire and
aimed right at Mrs. Johnson.

"He was helping at the school. He got locked out of
his house. His dad's not home. I can't wait around for him
to come home. Is it okay if he stays here with you?"

Danelle Johnson was flabbergasted.

"What the hell is he doing down there this late at night anyway? My kids are in bed already. They went to bed at nine. I don't understand. Why would you want these kids down there that late at night?"

"Well, he was helping me with the bulletin board and then he just got locked out. I've got to get home. I don't know what to do," she said.

"Yeah, he can stay here," Danelle finally said, as she led the boy inside and shut the door as the teacher quickly turned and walked back to her van.

A few minutes later, the impromptu care provider had the kid's father on the phone.

"Are you sure he's there?" the man asked, as if he'd been that route before and wasn't exactly sure that the call was legitimate.

Why would I make that up? Danelle wondered.

"Yeah, I'm sure," she said. "And he's scared to death that he's gonna get in trouble from you, but I don't think it was his fault."

The father agreed that it would be all right for his boy to spend the night—as long as Danelle made sure he'd get to school the next day.

Years later, Danelle tried to put two and two together.

"Now that I think about it," she said later, "I'll bet she had Vili out in the van also. She was trying to get rid of the boy so she could be alone with him."

It was Mary Kay Letourneau's sweet and young-sounding voice on the line. It was mid-December 1996. It was a call out of the blue. Not for Christmas greetings or school fund-raising or anything that anyone might come up with to characterize a call just before the holidays.

"I'm concerned about Molly," the teacher said.

Danelle Johnson repeated the statement as a question.

"Why are you concerned about Molly?"

"Molly comes down to the school all the time."

"I know that. Her and Nicole, Vili, Drew—all those guys come down. What's the problem?"

"Well, Molly seems to think that I'm her best friend.

That I'm the only friend she has . . . She tells me all kinds of things and stories about school and life up at the junior high and I don't think she should be hanging around here so much. I don't even know her!''

"She was in your class! And those guys have been helping you for three or four months. What do you mean you don't know her?''

Mary Letourneau sputtered to a finish.

"Well, I don't know her. We're not best friends. I'm kind of worried about her. She should have friends her own age.''

Danelle Johnson was furious. And she was hurt for her daughter, who had mixed up a relationship with an older woman. It was a friendship about which Molly spoke often. It was Ms. Letourneau this, Ms. Letourneau that. All day. Every day.

"All right," she said softly. "I'll tell her to quit coming down there and bothering you or whatever she's doing to you. Seems to me like you've encouraged these kids to come around there and help you. I don't want to hurt her feelings.''

"I don't want to hurt her, either. I'm just worried about her. She shouldn't think she's my best friend.''

"She has a friend her own age," Danelle said. "Her friend comes down there with her to help you. They think they're doing something great there.''

"I'm just real worried about her," Mary repeated.

Danelle Johnson thanked the teacher for her concern and hung up. She was very troubled.

There's something wrong. Why would the kids think they should be going down there and helping her? And why would she call me to tell me she didn't even know Molly?

Later that day Danelle found a moment to talk to her daughter about the call.

"Ms. Letourneau doesn't want you to come around anymore," she said.

The girl asked her mother for an explanation.

"She says you act like you're her best friend and she

thinks you should have best friends your own age. She thinks you're getting way too involved. She asked you to stop—''

"Yeah, whatever, Mom."

Danelle mulled it over that night and in the days and weeks after. She rationalized it. She worried about it. She figured the kids had become too rowdy and Mary Letourneau couldn't have them around as much. Maybe another teacher complained?

Teenyboppers aren't a lot of fun twenty-four hours a day. Maybe they got on her nerves.

Drew and Vili continued to go to Shorewood, while for the most part, Molly stayed away.

Not long after the phone call from the sixth-grade teacher, Danelle spoke to her new husband about it. It disturbed her that the kids were spending so much time with their former teacher.

"There's something weird going on," she said. "Why is this woman hanging around with these kids from junior high school?"

Her husband didn't have an answer. No one did.

That Steve Letourneau had become violent and abusive toward Mary Kay to the point of hitting, kicking, and pushing her to the ground had been a shock to Michelle Jarvis. In all the years Michelle had known Mary Kay, she had never once heard of any abuse. Sure, Steve could be a jerk and punch some holes in the wall, but he didn't knock his wife around. But as Michelle learned, a few weeks after Steve found out that Mary Kay had become pregnant in the fall of 1996 things worsened in Normandy Park.

Mary Kay would reiterate some of the things that Steve had been saying and doing, and as the weeks went by, the information she shared with Michelle began to scare her. She not only worried for her friend, but she worried about the four Letourneau kids. In his embarrassment, hurt, rage, whatever, Steve never lost an opportunity to remind them what their mother had done.

"I know it for a fact, because I heard him when she was on the phone with me. She would write down all of the things he said to her. And he said things in front of the children. He would talk about where she had sexual relations with Vili. To little children!"

And always, Michelle Jarvis, more than anyone, would focus on the Letourneau children and how their parents had handled a terrible situation. It seemed that Mary Kay thought only of Vili and Steve was fixated on making Mary Kay pay for what she had done.

"The kids were an afterthought when she did what she did and they were an afterthought for him in that all he focused on was his own rage and his own need to get even or get back at her," Michelle said later.

Michelle wrestled with the idea that maybe she could take in the children, and she discussed it with her husband. It was more thinking out loud than much else. How could it be otherwise? She had no claim to the kids. They were Mary Kay's and Steve's. She told Mary Kay that once the verbal and physical abuse started, she should take the children and leave. She should call the police and have Steve arrested. But Mary Kay kept insisting that Steve would come around and things would get better. They didn't. As the name-calling worsened, the children were left to absorb it all. Michelle worried that long-term damage had been done.

"The things Steve said about their mother . . . these kids are going to be in therapy forever. I doubt very much they are going to fully recover. They've been messed up for life. Damage control could have been had."

The kids were oddly casual about the subject matter and it bothered Danelle Johnson when they told her that Mary Letourneau had been beaten by her husband, Steve—at least that's what she told Drew and Vili during one of the late-night bulletin board sessions at Shorewood Elementary.

The kids related how Mary had told them Steve had hit her and was "mean to her and all of that."

Danelle wondered about it later.

Why in the hell would a grown woman be telling this twelve-year old-kid about her family life? About her husband beating her and things like that? Where would that come from? And, she wondered, where would it lead?

THIRTY

ONE AFTERNOON A Shorewood teacher looked out of her window and saw Vili Fualaau driving Mary Letourneau's van in the courtyard. It was worth a double take. It was so outrageous and potentially disastrous. The van moved slowly toward the window and the teacher worried that the boy was going to drive it right though the glass. He wasn't even a teenager as far as she knew. He was a child. Just as she bolted from the window to avoid a disaster, Mary came running out of the annex to save the day.

The teacher was relieved. Why had Mary given a kid her keys? Why hadn't she supervised him, though it was possible Vili had taken the keys without permission?

The teacher couldn't help but notice the expression on the boy's face.

"You could see this big smile on his face. 'I'm this evil little person doing something . . .' "

Later when she thought about it, the teacher dismissed it as just "weird interaction" stuff between Mary and Vili. It was not anything unusual for Mary Letourneau.

"Mary was always weird. She did strange stuff."

Years later a teacher who worked for many years at Shorewood shook her head at the memory of an encounter she had with a student in the hallway near the school library. A girl came up to her and asked her if she knew where Mary was. The teacher thought the girl was looking for a student.

"Mary who?" she asked.

"Well, you know, *Mary.*"

"No, I'm afraid I don't. Whose class is she in?"

The girl got snotty. "Mary *Letourneau,*" she said.

The teacher was miffed by the attitude and reminded

the student that at Shorewood teachers were addressed by
their last name.

"If you are looking for Mrs. Letourneau, I'm sorry,"
she said, "but I haven't seen her."

"Whatever!" the girl said before stomping off in a huff.

The teacher held that little scene in her mind as a perfect example of the boundaries that Mary seemed to ignore.

"She allowed the kids to call her by her first name. She
gave them her phone number, address, call anytime," she
said later.

When she told another Shorewood teacher about it, she
too thought it was inappropriate—and dangerous. Foster-
ing that kind of closeness wasn't right in a professional
setting. It could only invite trouble.

"I don't give out my name and address unless it is an
absolute emergency. Parents can send a note to school,
leave me a message at the office." the other teacher said.

For some the noise coming from room 39 was more
than they could take. It seemed that no matter what time
of day, Mary Letourneau's classes seemed to buzz with a
boisterous energy that sometimes seemed to border on pan-
demonium. Friends seemed to understand that was just the
way Mary did things, but newer teachers—teachers who
didn't have an emotional investment in a relationship with
the woman—found they could tolerate it less.

"Mary had a comfort level that was probably different
than some people, but when Mary wanted to have their
attention, she had their attention," said a veteran teacher
and friend. "So if she allowed kids to behave in a way
that was comfortable for her, but uncomfortable for other
people, that was her style of teaching. But she also had
very good control when she needed it or wanted it."

One newer teacher who occupied the classroom next to
Mary Kay's bit her tongue until she could no longer take
the invasion of noise coming through the walls.

"Sometimes I couldn't hear myself think," she said
later.

After much exasperation and soul-searching, the woman
finally went over to tell Mary that the noise level was

disturbing her students. She had tried to choose words that would not offend, because she didn't want to cause problems or make Mary feel bad. Nevertheless, Mary was offended.

"The next day she made sure to come over and tell me that we were being too noisy," the teacher remembered.

THIRTY-ONE

NO ONE COULD figure out her waning sense of style. Mary Kay Letourneau always prided herself on her appearance. Always had. Her hair and makeup had been a priority since those agonizing hours Michelle Jarvis had had to endure in Mary Kay's bedroom back in Corona del Mar. But as the school year went on, people noticed that the woman who shopped at Nordstrom with a maxed-out credit card wasn't dressing that way anymore. Instead of a classic pleated wool skirt and blouse, Mary wore tennis shoes and layers of T-shirts—sometimes as many as three or four at once. She also wore tights and sometimes two skirts—at the same time. Parents noticed, too.

"She never wore anything that fit her," a mother recalled. "Yet she was so beautiful. It was strange."

When the kids asked about her layering, Mary shyly explained that her choice in attire was the result of a comment.

"One of my friends said I was bony," she said.

She wore the layers to cover up what most considered was a beautiful figure, yet somehow Mary had got it in her head that she was grotesquely thin—a nineties Twiggy. No one thought she had an eating disorder. In fact, most marveled at her ability to eat whatever she wanted without gaining an ounce. Even so, it was apparent to many that Mary Letourneau was obsessed about her weight, or lack of it. But there were other options. A number of students at Shorewood favored baggy clothes, the rapper or gangster style. Some wondered if Mary Letourneau was making a fashion statement when she wore clothes that hung on

her like a sheet on a drying line. But something else was
going on, too. One time she came to class without her
usual layers. Instead, Mary wore a woman's long-sleeved
cotton T-shirt and a wool skirt. Without mentioning names,
she later told a friend what happened: "Somebody was
obviously scanning me, giving me the eye, looking at me
at places where I wouldn't want anyone to look. He said,
'Hey, now we can see it all.' I went out to my car and put
on another shirt. It upset me. I think when I talked to him
later I even used the word 'harass' when I said I felt uncomfortable with what he was saying and where he was
looking."

Students tried to encourage her whenever possible. One
time when bolstered by her sixth-graders, Mary wore a
green dress that was stylish and the Round Table kids told
her how terrific she looked. Mary accepted the compliment
and wore the dress several more times. She never looked
better that entire year.

Though none of them knew it then, the next time they
would see that green dress was when their teacher appeared on TV. On her way to court.

Though Mary Letourneau had never seemed particularly
happy in her marriage with Steve, things worsened during
1994–1996 at Shorewood Elementary. She told a teacher
friend that she had married Steve Letourneau only because
she became pregnant. Her Catholic-to-the-hilt mother had
put her foot down. "There was no way she was *not* going
to marry Steve."

Mary told the other teacher that she had loved another
man and had been engaged to be married, but she had been
jilted. Steve Letourneau had been a rebound relationship.

It surprised the Shorewood colleague when she learned
that Mary was pregnant with her fifth baby. She knew from
previous conversations that Mary hadn't slept with her
husband for months. And, equally puzzling, Mary hadn't
been the one to tell her that she was pregnant. She learned
it from someone else.

"Whose baby is it?" the teacher asked, knowing immediately that her question was odd, but it just came out. She had assumed that Steve was not the father. She didn't know who, though.

Mary thought about it for a second and answered.

"Actually, it's *my* baby," she said. She went on to say that she knew her body and could gauge her ovulation with complete precision.

It didn't answer the question, but it did confuse the friend. *Was she saying that she was pregnant by Steve, after all? Or had she found someone else and decided to have a baby?*

Later when Mary showed her the silvery films of an ultrasound examination, the friend asked if Steve had been accompanying her to the obstetrician's office.

"No," she said firmly. "This is *my* baby."

Money was always a big worry for Mary Letourneau and most at Shorewood knew it. Of course, with teacher salaries being what they were, a husband who threw baggage for a living, and four kids with another on the way, money would be an issue for just about anyone. Mary never had any money of her own and it bothered her. Her paycheck was used to pay the mortgage on the Normandy Park house. Steve had insisted.

"Steve had control of the money," said a teacher who knew Mary well. "Her check went to the house payment because 'that was the house *she* wanted.' "

Though she said she never wanted the van in the first place, Mary was glad for it because it afforded her an opportunity to do some secret stockpiling. During the 1996–97 school year, the pregnant sixth-grade teacher told a colleague that she had begun to squirrel away extra cash.

"She had secret places in the van to hide it," the teacher said later. "She wanted to have some money herself."

The disclosure wasn't that peculiar; the teacher knew that Mary and Steve were having serious marital troubles. Mary freely talked about those problems. But when a teacher tried to talk to Mary about her own finances or any other subject from her life, she doubted Mary was paying much attention.

"It never seemed she was much interested in what I had to say back. I could be telling her something, but I knew her mind was going somewhere else."

THIRTY-TWO

MARY KAY LETOURNEAU was elated by the pregnancy; she reveled in it. She told her sixth-grade class that she was going to have her fifth baby—*before* she told any of her colleagues at Shorewood. She told them she was due in May, just before the end of the school year. The baby was so wanted and the teacher beamed whenever she brought up the subject. One afternoon seventh-graders Vili Fualaau and Katie Hogden met with their former sixth-grade teacher in the classroom when she brought out the sonogram images from among her drifting sheaves of papers and school bric-a-brac.

Mary traced the lines of the image, pointing out the baby's head and arms.

Katie had never seen her teacher so joyous. "She was glowing with happiness," she said later.

But so was Vili Fualaau.

"Vili was just so happy too that she was going to have a baby that it was kind of awkward," Katie recalled some time later when many of her memories had been tarnished by the story that had taken over the lives of her two friends.

"I knew them so well," she said, "but I didn't pay attention to the most obvious thing. I missed the *big thing*. It didn't occur to me then that Vili had anything to do with it."

Judy Hogden had a different reaction when she first heard about the impending birth. She thought it was peculiar that Mary had turned up pregnant in the first place. She knew from comments Katie had made that Mary and

Steve Letourneau were struggling through a rough patch in their marriage.

"I guess it worked this time," she said when she talked to her daughter about Mary's pregnancy. "Stranger things had happened."

Later, when it was hinted that Mary's husband was not her baby's father, Judy couldn't make sense of the man sticking around in the same house in Normandy Park.

"If he knows that's not his child, then why would he stay with her?" she asked.

Nobody in the neighborhood knew what it was, but it was clear that something was going on with the Letourneaus. Some saw changes in the children, particularly Steven and Mary Claire. Steven Letourneau ditched GI Joe action figures for an attitude and the grungy, baggy look of a gangbanger. The change seemed sudden to Ellen Douglas. Steven even adopted the shuffle-walk and the dull, apathetic gaze of a kid who didn't care or who thought the world owed him something.

Ellen talked about it with her schoolteacher husband, Daniel.

"We'd look at him and we'd look at Scott, and say, 'Wow, he's really growing up, but not in a real positive way.' "

Yet Ellen noticed how once he came over to play with her son, Scott, he'd abandon the tough, cool-thug demeanor and be a little boy once more playing with Legos and running around the house.

After a while it dawned on Ellen that the boy's affect had been a complete pretense. *Maybe something was wrong at home?*

Ellen and her husband couldn't figure it out. All they could come up with was that the kids were not happy-go-lucky anymore and they didn't know why.

"It made us sad," she said later. "Something was going on in their childhood. Life was not real happy at home."

But what was it?

*   *   *

What on earth is going on here?

The Shorewood Elementary teacher stared at the driver of Mary Letourneau's Voyager. It wasn't Steve Letourneau behind the wheel as the vehicle still adorned with the Alaska plates pulled up the service driveway. It was the end of January 1997.

The teacher recognized the driver as Vili's brother, a boy who, as far as she knew, wasn't old enough for a driver's license.

What the—? she thought. He's underage!

She watched for a few minutes until Mary Kay came bounding out of the building and jumped into the passenger side. She had obviously given the boy her keys to move the van from God-knows-where to pick her up.

The flabbergasted woman followed them as they drove from school. She stayed back a bit, not really knowing why, but only that she was so shocked at the idea of a kid driving a teacher's car. She followed the blue van to a house off Twenty-first and the boy got out and Mary Kay slid behind the wheel and drove off.

The teacher who tailed Mary Kay Letourneau was ready to tell Principal Anne Johnson what she had seen, but she stopped herself. Just like she stopped herself when she nearly hit Jacqueline Letourneau when the little one darted out in front of her in the parking lot one day. Just as she stopped herself the times when the frazzled teacher was late for school—nearly every day—arriving at 9:15 or 9:20.

"For years it was, 'Oh, that's just Mary. Mary can do this. Mary can do that.' I just thought, that's okay," she said later.

Reporting Mary in the past for anything seldom brought results, not even a reprimand that the teacher could remember. For whatever reason, the principal did not act. So why should *she* bother?

One night around seven P.M. when the linoleum hallway of the Shorewood annex was quiet, the Shorewood custodian came across Mary Letourneau coming out of the girls' bathroom just to the west of her classroom. The man

was on his way in to clean the toilets. The lights were off.
Mary Kay seemed a little nervous, and quickly indicated
that her former student Vili Fualaau was upset about something and had sequestered himself in a stall. Mary said she
tried to calm him down.

"He's having one of his attitudes. You know teenagers," she said, offering a smile and shrug.

The janitor had teenagers of his own and said he understood. He liked Mary Letourneau and knew that the boy
in the bathroom was a regular visitor to room 39. He was
a good kid.

He didn't think much of the encounter and didn't report
it. Neither did he report the time he saw Vili driving his
teacher's van in the school parking lot.

THIRTY-THREE

IT WAS NO surprise that Steve and Mary Kay Letourneau
were late. They had never made it on time for anything.
Steve's cousin Kyle Gardner and his wife, Linda, not only
expected perpetual tardiness, but often placed a bet with
each other about *how late* they'd show up. An hour? Two?
The smart money was always a little later than that. Linda
bet for money; her husband bet for sexual favors. Linda
usually won.

But in January 1997, Steve and Mary Kay didn't show
up at all to an engagement party at the Tacoma Country
Club for one of Steve's cousins. Chronically late was one
thing; not appearing at a family function was very peculiar.

Kyle Gardner's mother and Steve's father, Dick Letourneau, were siblings and their respective sons were
practically raised together, until Dick and Sharon moved
to Anchorage.

Standing in the buffet line, Linda asked another Letourneau cousin where Steve and Mary Kay were.

The young woman looked at her with a serious, but
puzzled look.

"Don't you know?" the cousin asked.

As Linda indicated she didn't know anything, an aunt nudged the cousin, her daughter, out of the way and abruptly ended the conversation.

Linda stood there with her plate wondering what was going on.

Something's funny here for her to be whisked away like that.

Linda Gardner was a fireplug of a woman. She was outspoken in a family where it seemed they preferred agreement or compliance. Linda was not a troublemaker, but a woman who knew that by age thirty-two, she was old enough to speak her mind. She and her husband, Kyle, were raising a son and a daughter and they were doing it on their own—without family handouts. Linda was planning a dream house that she was going to build herself. If she broke a nail, who in the hell cared?

She was also a lover of information-gathering and digging deep into a subject to bring out what no one had known before. This was not to say she was nosy or pushy, though some family members might have thought so. When Linda ferreted out the truth behind a family relationship, Kyle nicknamed his wife Secret Squirrel, after the crime-fighting rodent cartoon show of their childhood.

It was the encounter at the buffet line at the engagement party that put her into Secret Squirrel overdrive. Everyone had been so quiet about Steve and Mary Kay. No one would say a word, though one did let slip that the two were having marital problems. That was news to Linda.

"I thought they were the perfect little Catholic family," she said later.

Of course, Linda had no idea what was really going on. She had no idea what was going on with Mary Kay and she never would have guessed it in a million years. And she certainly didn't know that Steve was already involved with another woman, a beautiful Alaska Airlines flight attendant from Newport Beach named Kelly Whalen. The two had purportedly met in Mexico when Steve took a little holiday to get away from his troubles.

THIRTY-FOUR

IT ATE AT Secret Squirrel like splashed acid. Linda Gardner couldn't stand the secrecy and the silence surrounding Steve and Mary Kay's faltering marriage. *What was the frickin' deal?* No one even mentioned them anymore. It was like they had taken a swan dive off the face of the earth. The Gardners had sent their daughter on a trip to visit grandparents in Arizona for midwinter break. The couple decided to stop by the new house of another of Kyle's cousins near SeaTac Airport before the plane bringing their daughter rolled down the tarmac.

By then Kyle seemed just as interested in the silence as his wife had been. When the new homeowners were showing them around their yard, Kyle asked about it.

"What's going on with Steve and Mary Kay? Everyone is so quiet."

Before the cousin or his wife could answer, Linda spoke up.

"Well, I know something's wrong. I know it's Mary Kay. I think she's having an affair and it's not with a man. Either she's a lesbian or something worse."

The cousin's wife's mouth went agape.

"You guys really don't know, do you?" she said.

"No," Linda said, "we don't know. What?"

The cousin answered for his wife, saying that they couldn't tell.

"I have sworn that I won't tell anybody what I know," he said.

Secret Squirrel's mind raced as it went into high gear. *Oh, my God. She's a lesbian, she thought.*

On their way home, they drove past the house in Normandy Park, just to see. Linda slumped in the passenger seat, as if being detected would matter or as if she were on some kind of a spy mission. She had never been to the house before, and after what she had heard, she thought the place looked like a dump—not the showplace Mary

Kay had let others believe. She saw Steven walking down the street, but no other sign of the distraught family with the lesbian mother.

When they arrived at their home in Bonney Lake, Linda urged Kyle to phone his mother in Kentucky to find out what was going on. He called from the kitchen and Linda got on a bedroom extension. Kyle told his mother that they didn't like being in the dark. Everyone in the family knew something was up. Everyone but them.

"You two have to swear that you will not tell anybody or do anything," she said. "You have to swear to me."

Linda crossed her fingers. "I swear," she said, echoing Kyle's promise.

"Mary Kay was having an affair," Kyle's mother said.

"Yeah."

"She's pregnant."

"Oh, really?" That was news to Linda. She hadn't heard a word of any pregnancy. Then Kyle's mother dropped the bomb of all bombs.

"It's with a twelve-year-old," she said.

Linda didn't say a word, but a phrase bounced through her head as though she had been screaming from a mountaintop.

Oh, my God!

It shocked Linda that no one had turned Mary Kay in to the police.

The mother said the Letourneaus were hoping that the boy, who had been one of Mary Kay's students, would come forward and break the story. Steve's family had kept silent because of the children involved. Once more, Kyle's mother made them promise not to breathe a word.

"Her attitude was very firm. 'Do not tell anybody. Do not do anything about it.' She didn't say it was right," Linda said later. "She didn't say it was wrong. 'Do keep your mouths shut.' "

Putting together the pieces wasn't easy, not even for Secret Squirrel. Linda Gardner had always considered Mary Kay Letourneau a bit of a phony—at least she was so overly nice it seemed that no person could be genuinely that sweet. Linda remembered the last time she saw Mary

was at the Western Washington State Fair in Puyallup,
south of Seattle. She and her two children bumped into
Mary and her four kids quite by accident. It was mid-
September 1996.

Since the children were shirttail cousins, Linda thought
it was nice that all could be together at the same time,
even though the meeting was merely accidental. But Mary
was in a hurry; she was preoccupied. She didn't seem to
want to pal around like she might have done in the past.

"She was real fast. At that time she wasn't her bubbly
self. She wanted to get away from me pretty fast," Linda
said later.

Of course, at that time, the Letourneaus' world was beginning to unravel. Mary Kay was pregnant and no one
knew it.

That night, Linda Gardner poured herself a big glass of
wine and told her husband that they had to confirm his
mother's story. What she had said was so unbelievable, so
off-the-wall, and so ugly, that Linda didn't think it could
really be true.

"Are we imagining this?" she asked.

It was so disturbing.

*A thirty-five-year-old teacher having sex with a sixth-
grader! How dare a teacher we put in the classroom with
our children do this?*

She was also bitter at her husband's family for their
conspiracy of deceit. They knew that fall. They knew at
Thanksgiving. They knew at Christmas. At the engagement party in January.

"Kyle's mother came out for the holidays and she knew
and she didn't tell us a thing. When I look back at this it
angers me. From a parent's point of view, here she was
still teaching. She was still in the classroom," she said
later.

Linda was consumed with worry. She wondered if this
boy wasn't the only one. She feared for Mary Kay's two
sons or others in the classroom.

"You don't all of a sudden go from being an outstanding teacher and having sex with a twelve-year-old boy. You just don't,'' she told her husband.

At his wife's urging, Kyle phoned Steve's younger sister, Stacey, in Alaska to discern what she knew. Stacey recounted the same story, adding that everyone in the family had known about it for months. It started in September when Steve discovered love letters and journal entries written by Mary Kay. He confronted the boy at his house and told him to back off his wife. Dick Letourneau had wanted to turn Mary Kay in to the police, but decided not to because of the impact it would have on his four grandchildren.

"He knew what would happen," Linda said later. "They all knew."

Stacey explained that her brother had seen an attorney.

"They got a lawyer. They were trying to get him a quick divorce, but it cost too much for Steve to do it, so he backed out."

She also disclosed that the boy was Hispanic or Asian—family members had met him when Mary Kay brought him to Alaska that summer.

Linda could barely take it. She spoke up and told Stacey that Mary Kay had to be stopped.

"Stacey, I'm going to give your dad one week to do it. If he doesn't do it, I'm going to turn her in."

Stacey understood. She had been tortured over the whole thing, too. Mary Kay was a sick woman. Stacey hated what she did, but her hands were tied.

Kyle and Linda got into their hot tub and talked about what had happened. The shock of it all. What could be done? Several hours and glasses of wine passed. Linda didn't think she could wait for Dick Letourneau to do the right thing. He had known about it for months and hadn't taken care of it. Why would he do it now?

"Kyle, I have to turn her in," she said finally.

Her husband understood, but he was reticent about getting too involved. Not because he approved of what Mary Kay had done, but because his family had made it so clear that loyalty demanded silence.

"If you do it," he said finally, "just don't tell me."

Linda Gardner couldn't keep it inside. After a sleepless night she phoned her brother and told him what they had learned about Mary Kay.

"Linda," her brother said, "if you don't tell, I'm going to. She has to be turned in."

"I waited," she said later. "I stayed awake all night sick to my stomach. I knew what I had to do."

Linda Gardner kept her promise to her husband. She didn't tell Kyle Gardner the morning of February 25, 1997, that she was going to report Mary Kay to the authorities after their grade-school-aged daughter was out the door. She was scared. She felt sorry for Steve and the Letourneau children. She knew Mary Kay would lose her job and that prison was a possibility. She had separated Mary Kay the wife and mother from Mary Kay the woman who was having sex with a boy.

She's going to keep doing it, she reminded herself in an effort to bolster her resolve. She's got to be stopped.

She checked on her toddler son before working up the nerve to pick up the phone. The image of her sweet little boy was all the courage she needed. Linda Gardner never wanted anyone to harm a child. She was a mother, too. She couldn't understand how anyone could take a child's innocence, as she believed Mary Kay had.

She dialed the number for Child Protective Services, gave her name and phone number, and told her story.

"You're going to have to call the school district," the woman said. "You have to talk to them because she's a teacher."

Linda was flabbergasted and she hung up.

Hello? she thought. *I just told you that a teacher is having sex with one of her students and you want me to call the school district?*

She didn't think she could do it again, but knew she had no choice.

She called Highline School District offices in Burien. A secretary answered.

"I need to talk to somebody," Linda said. "The superintendent. I need to talk to somebody high up. This is not a minor thing.''

When the secretary pressed her for the urgency of the call, Linda told her.

"This is regarding a teacher that has been having sex with one of her students.''

"I'll take your name and phone number,'' the secretary said. "Someone will call you back.''

A little while later, Dick Cvitanich, area administrator for the district, phoned Linda and calmly listened as she nervously spat out her story. She wasn't certain of all of the facts and said so. She wasn't even sure of the kid's identity, or even the name of the school where Mary Kay taught. But the man didn't ask many questions. He was strangely brief considering the subject.

"I'll check it out,'' he said.

And that was it.

This is weird, Secret Squirrel thought.

PART THREE
RAPIST

Having fun with me was risky. One time you got hurt. Sometimes you were just yelled at or questioned. Then Steve found out and you gave up on us.
—Mary Kay Letourneau, in a note to Vili Fualaau, fall 1996

Call me as soon as it's safe. I know for sure you don't want me calling you at the wrong time. So you call. You are allowed to. He said you can. Anyway he's going back to work so he goes to sleep at 9:00.
—Mary Kay Letourneau, in another note to Vili Fualaau, fall 1996

I think what I've done is horrible and I wouldn't want anyone to think I believe it's acceptable. It's not.
—Mary Kay Letourneau, in a July 1997 interview with the Seattle Times.

The initial horror upon hearing the charges "rape of a child" is natural . . . But the continued creation of a little-boy victim and sick perpetrator has to stop!
—Mary Kay Letourneau in a press release, November 1997

PART THREE

RAPIST

THIRTY-FIVE

THE MORNING OF the day after she made the call to the school district was Linda Gardner's thirty-third birthday. She was still jittery over the day before, but the worry and struggle over doing the right thing was behind her. Ahead that night was dinner at Harbor Lights in Tacoma with her husband and her father, up from Arizona. At 8:30 A.M. the phone rang. It was Patricia Maley, a detective from King County Police explaining that CPS had forwarded a report about her call. Linda's heart smacked against her rib cage.

"You're going to have to call me back. I'm getting my daughter ready for school," she said.

The police!

Later when they spoke, Linda asked the sex crimes detective to promise to maintain her anonymity. She didn't want anyone to know that she'd been the one to blow the whistle on Mary Kay.

The detective listened as Linda recounted the conversations with her mother-in-law and Steve Letourneau's sister. The detective promised that she'd do her best to keep Linda out of it, but there was no guarantee. The allegations were very serious. Linda told her the boy's name was Billy.

Later that Wednesday morning, Dick Cvitanich, the Highline area administrator, called to see if Linda would come to the district office to discuss her story with their lawyers. Linda flatly refused.

"I've already talked to Pat Maley of the King County Police. I'm done."

The casualness of the first conversation with the district had been gnawing at Secret Squirrel. It seemed suspicious.

"Dick," Linda said before hanging up, "you guys already knew, didn't you? You already knew something before I called, didn't you?"

"As a matter of fact someone had called last week and tipped us off," he said.

As the president of the Highline Education Association, the district's teacher's association, Susan Murphy had fielded more than one call of a purported sexual relationship between teacher and student. Most were untrue and remedied by a quick investigation. But the one coming at the end of February 1997 was different. Joe McGeehan, Highline School District Superintendent, phoned Susan at her Riverton Heights office with a heads up.

"I need to let you know that we've had a call that one of our teachers is pregnant by a seventh-grade student."

It almost required repeating the words, they were so staggering.

Susan was told that the allegation was under review and had not been made public. She was alerted because, the superintendent said, "it will come out."

A teacher in the district since 1969, in the middle of a three-year term as president of the HEA, Susan Murphy had never heard of a female teacher becoming pregnant by a student. She caught her breath as the superintendent told her what little he knew. It was a family member who made the phone call to the district, and at that moment district officials were doing all they could to either verify or disprove the charges.

The allegations didn't seem like they could be genuine. Conventional wisdom had it that such sexual liaisons only happened between male teachers and their female students, usually in the high school setting. Never had she heard of the reverse. And even more unbelievable to Susan Murphy was the tremendous age difference.

A seventh-grader and a teacher?

Susan hoped that the internal investigation and any police involvement would clear the teacher without embarrassment and without long-term career damage. Teachers had been targets for such crank calls from family members or students and parents with axes to grind.

The HEA president didn't know the woman in question, only that she was described in that first call as an elementary school teacher in her thirties. None of it computed, she later said.

"What could she possibly, possibly, have in common with a student of that age? That was the initial reaction. Even before the breach of trust, the anger, the embarrassment and all of that."

It was not Billy. It was *Vili*. The night at the marina had not been forgotten by the district security director and the officers who had heard about it through the district-employee wife of a cop. When they thought of Mary Letourneau and a relationship with a student, they came up with only one name. Like a charades game, it sounded like Billy.

After calls to the school district, and the Des Moines Police, about that early morning at the marina the previous spring, Detective Maley drove to Cascade Middle School in White Center to see Vili Fualaau. It was shortly after 10 A.M. when she came face-to-face with the boy. He was slight framed, a little over five feet, with a shy, almost sweet demeanor.

Later, in her report she wrote:

"I asked him what kind of relationship it was. He was very quiet and did not say anything at that time. I asked him if it was a boyfriend-girlfriend type relationship. He said it was. I asked him if it went any further than that. Vili said they had sex."

The detective knew what she had. She arranged for an emergency joint interview with an assistant King County prosecuting attorney and drove Vili downtown. There, Vili told a story that included the exchange of rings, love letters, and, finally, sexual intercourse starting in the spring of 1996.

The prosecuting attorney wrote Vili's version of the first time:

"He said he spent the night at her house and it just happened... Mary's husband was working... the kids were asleep. He said they were in the den watching shows, he thinks Braveheart. *He said she started talking to him about psychics and stuff like that; that a psychic she supposedly talked to said she was going to have a hard life, and told Mary that she was going to meet someone with dark skin and be with him... then they just did it."*

Vili told the lawyer and the cop that Mary Kay said her husband beat her and that he shouldn't tell anyone what had happened. She could lose her job. He also acknowledged that his brother and his best friend knew about the relationship.

His brother had walked into the bedroom at the Normandy Park house one time and saw them together on the bed.

After the interview with the thirteen-year-old Samoan boy, Pat Maley took the boy back to his house and drove to the school, and minutes later Mary Kay Letourneau was called out of a Shorewood staff meeting. It was 4:30 P.M.

"I think you know what this is about," Pat Maley said.

Mary Kay stood there for a moment with her hands at her sides. Her face was white. Her red Nordstrom T-shirt and black pleated skirt hung over her belly. It was clear she was six months pregnant.

"I think I might have an idea," Mary Kay said.

One teacher who saw her leave with the police officer assumed that there had been a death in the family, maybe a terrible traffic accident involving Steve. It looked rough. She hoped Mary Kay would be all right.

It was out in the detective's car that Mary Kay Letourneau was arrested for rape of a child. She was upset, but focused on two things. She wanted to know if Vili was all right and she wanted to know what would happen to her class. Would she be returning to school? Detective Maley told her that she thought Vili was doing fine, and that Highline security would probably be contacting her about her job.

In the interrogation room at the King County Police precinct in Kent, May Kay began to unravel. She cried and stopped. And cried some more. Mary Kay told the detective that she didn't know what to say or do. She wanted to know how Vili's family felt about her and the situation. She wanted to know if it was Steve who had turned her in. The detective refused to answer. When Pat Maley asked about the letters that Linda said Steve had found, Mary Kay said Steve sent them to his family in Alaska for safe-keeping. She described the letters as a "blackmail tool."

The detective wrote: *"She said he was using these letters . . . to keep her from leaving him and obtaining a divorce."*

When the detective pressed Mary Kay for the identity of the father of the baby she was so visibly carrying, the teacher said there was a "99.9 percent chance" it was not Steve's.

"I told her at that time that I hoped it would be her husband's and not a thirteen-year-old child's baby. She said she did not want it to be her husband's."

Mary Kay cried some more. She told the detective that she was tired of being alone and she had found comfort in the relationship with Vili. She knew the relationship was wrong, but there was a reason for it. They were in love. But the detective wasn't listening to her.

She later said she thought the detective was cold and sarcastic.

"Just the way she asked the questions," Mary Kay said, mimicking a snotty, condescending voice. "It was like, 'so where's the ring?' 'So tell me about this psychic.' "

That evening, Mary Kay found her way to Shorewood music teacher Beth Adair's Seattle home. The visit cemented a bond that would grow stronger over time. In her fifties, divorced, with children ranging from a teenager to one about Mary Kay's age, Beth Adair had known Mary Kay since her student teaching days at Gregory Heights.

"We had a connection and an understanding," Mary Kay said later. "Beth is a wonderful woman and we connected on that level, woman to woman. She understood me. She considered us her kids, Vili and I."

The music teacher scooped Mary Kay up in her arms and told her she'd be all right. That night there were tears and phone calls. Mary Kay called her father and told him what had happened. John Schmitz promised he'd come see his daughter; he'd bring her a car because Steve would have the van. She'd be able to get through it. When she finally got home it was after three the next morning. Steve and the children were asleep and it felt so good to be home. In some ways, she thought, it felt like nothing had changed.

But it had.

The sun came up and the children were dressed for school. But their mother wasn't taking them that day. The balance of the hurried morning race had been altered. Mary Kay watched the clock, and as it moved closer to 9:05 she knew just how different her world was about to become. She wasn't going back to Shorewood Elementary. She thought of her class back in room 39. The children had left HHH the day before, never to see their teacher again.

"I tried to put my heart out to each one of them," she said later. "I imagined myself in front of the class, the clock, the bulletin boards, and their faces. I went around the room looking into their faces, each one, sending them an angel of peace to let them know it would be all right and I hadn't forgotten them."

The baby would be ultimate proof, of course, and Vili Fualaau's statement was on record about the sexual relationship. The case wasn't a difficult one for law enforcement. But the *why* of it all was more elusive than in most cases. It was the papers gathered under a search warrant from Steven Letourneau, Sr., that same day that provided the greatest glimpse into what was going through Mary Kay Letourneau's mind. Steve handed over a sheaf of papers, notes scrawled on scraps, comments made on envelopes. The author was his wife, Mary Kay. But was the writer the person so many admired and loved? There were six pages of lists of song titles and the recording artists, but, oddly for a schoolteacher, names were horribly misspelled. *"Maria Carie—You'll always be a part of Me;*

*Witney—I'll ALWAYS LOVE YOU; Dion Warwick—That's
what friends are for.''*

The downward spiral that had begun so many months
ago had quickened its pace as indicated by the coherency
of the writings. Her handwriting was erratic; and her
thoughts reflected a woman falling apart. Mary Letourneau
found herself falling faster and faster toward the point of
no return. She wrote of attending a late-fall family wedding in Chicago, dancing with her father, and thinking of
Vili. Steve had called the Schmitz home before Mary's
arrival and warned them that their daughter was headed
toward big trouble. He refused to elaborate, telling them it
was something she had to tell them herself.

When she returned she made some notes in her journal,
but then the neat handwriting had started to reveal the
stress of the author. Her words were ruptured, the edits
were careless, the phrasing typical of a schoolgirl:

*"So I told my mother and father everything! I told them
about he baby. I told them about you even that you are
under age (not exactly how young—I think they think
you're about 15.''*

She wrote how after she told her father that Vili was
one of her students, he said he remembered the boy. Mary
gushed how "my mom acted like she likes everything
about you . . .''

But according to the notes, Mary and John Schmitz
were also worried. They warned their daughter that she
could be in "big trouble" if someone found out. Her letter
continued:

*". . . promise on your life not to ever ever no matter
how someone questions you to ever tell about us—not even
a kiss can be told . . .''*

Other notes were revealing, too. Among them was the
briefest communication, but fifteen words, that suggested
a dynamic not considered.

He had written:

"Who said you can put your Legs Raped around ME.''

Mary's note back:

"I was just getting comfortable.''

If either cop or husband had taken a moment to really

assess what was going on between teacher and student, they might have found a clue in the smallest exchange— not in the obvious spelling mistake of "Raped" instead of "Wrapped." The note had been written when speaking was not advisable. More than likely when Steve was asleep in the bedroom and Mary and Vili were camped out on the couch watching videos. She was trying to snuggle and fantasize about a future with Vili. And yet she was apologizing for wanting to be close him; Vili was telling her to back off. Not because he didn't want to have sex with her, but maybe he just didn't want the closeness for which she had longed.

Who had been in control of the relationship? For those who bothered to consider the tiny note, a different scenario was possible. Vili Fualaau was in charge. Other missives and writings indicated that Vili called Mary when he wanted sex. He *allowed* her to see him when it was convenient and didn't interfere with hanging out with his buddies or the young girls he preferred.

Mary Kay had wanted love and attention. She could only have Vili's attention when *he* gave *his* permission.

In another note she wrote:

"I see and feel you wanting me to fill in for the sex you're not getting from your school girlfriends. That's not why I'm in your life. Don't call me ever to be a fill in."

She was functioning like a junior high girl writing lists and making plans for a fairy-tale future. They were a reincarnated love. She worried about getting his mother's permission to see him; her parents' support when she needed it. She was a girl in love with a boy from the wrong side of the tracks. A favorite song asked the question: *"How could it be wrong, if it feels so right?"*

Rumors percolated through the Shorewood neighborhood that something bad was brewing at the elementary school. Real bad. A teacher there was in big trouble. Word around the area was that soon "everyone was going to know some shocking news."

Danelle Johnson didn't need anyone to tell her who was in trouble.

"God, I know it is going to be Mary Letourneau. I just know it," she told her husband. "All those seventh-graders going down there. It's gonna be her."

As the hours ticked closer to the disclosure of "something big breaking at Shorewood" Danelle saw something in her son that suggested he knew a bit more about what might be happening.

She remembered later a time just before the news broke when her son, Drew, was out in the yard sobbing uncontrollably. It was as if his heart had been thrashed. He refused to say what it was that was hurting him so. After much prodding from his mother, Drew finally gave a lame excuse that some girl had dumped him.

Then they all learned what so many had suspected. It was Mary and Vili.

Danelle was dazed—not that it was Mary, but that it was Vili. She loved Soona Fualaau's son. He was a wonderful and talented boy. But she couldn't fathom what people were saying Mary Letourneau had done.

"I just couldn't imagine a grown woman having an affair with him. I couldn't even imagine the concept of what she could have possibly been thinking."

There's a little break area on the ramp at SeaTac International Airport where Alaska Air employees can escape the wintry chill of the tarmac and catch a cup of coffee—Starbucks, of course—and share the latest in passenger horror stories and, if there was any, a little airport gossip. If anyone had heard what was happening at the Letourneau house in Normandy Park, they kept it to themselves. It was so ugly that no one dared bring it up.

Finally, Steve Letourneau approached some employees shortly after he had been contacted by Pat Maley of the King County Police.

Usually a somewhat affable presence, Steve was apparently upset about something and wanted to talk. Joe Bendix, the flight attendant and former neighbor from Carriage Row condominiums later described him as "just heartbroken and freaking out."

The look in his eyes telegraphed that he was in great pain.

"I want to tell you something before you read about it in the paper," Steve said, choosing his words carefully. "Mary's been having an affair with one of her students."

"Oh, well, you know things happen," Joe said. While he heard the word "student" he hadn't considered the idea of age. In his mind, he thought that the affair involved a young man, maybe one she had taught who was now in high school or maybe even older. Mary had been teaching for some time and it was possible, Joe Bendix thought, that the student was nearly grown. "Student" didn't mean a child.

Steve was taken aback. Embarrassed as he seemed, it was clear that his message wasn't getting through to Joe.

"This kid is like a year older than Steven," he said, to hammer the point home. "She was arrested for having sex with one of her students."

Joe didn't know how to respond. He said he was sorry and he hoped everything would be all right. Though Steve hadn't said anything about the depth or duration of the affair, Joe concluded that it had been a fling, a one-time transgression. A fluke.

"Things will work out," he said. "Things will be okay."

Later when Joe told Fran what he had heard, the two of them could make no headway in understanding what Steve had disclosed and what they would later read in their newspaper. Fran had never really cared for Mary Kay. She thought she was snooty. So Steve's revelations naturally brought forth some disdain and, very surprisingly to Fran, a measure of unexpected sympathy.

She didn't think what Mary had done was okay by any stretch.

"Even if you are unhappy with your spouse it's not grounds for having a relationship with a child—even if you think you might be in love with him. Or are you just grasping for attention? I really think she has a problem," Fran said.

Her husband didn't disagree. And while neither of the

Letourneaus' flight-attendant former neighbors knew what was going to happen with what they had once considered "the perfect family," they hoped Steve would get custody of the four children.

The thought of the children brought a bittersweet smile.

"There's no doubt in my mind that Steve loves all of them. I think he was probably the most perfect father you could get. He doted over those kids and was proud of them," Joe said.

THIRTY-SIX

NONE COULD HAVE prepared for the emotions that the letter from the Highline School District would bring when children from Shorewood brought home word from the superintendent regarding allegations against Mary Letourneau. While many kids were teary and confused about what was going on, it was the reaction of the parents that brought the greatest wave of emotions. Lyle Mattson stood apart from many classmates. He was nonplussed about the whole thing. He merely had an apology for his mother when he handed her the envelope. He quietly announced it was about Mrs. Letourneau and Vili Fualaau.

"I should have told you sooner," he said. "It was kind of disgusting, so I didn't want to say anything."

Tandy Mattson studied the contents of the letter.

"Did she ever do anything to you?" she finally asked her son, who had transferred into room 39 after Christmas.

"No."

"Okay," she said.

The age difference between Mary Letourneau and Vili Fualaau did indeed disturb Tandy Mattson, but she had a hard time seeing what happened between teacher and student as a terrible crime. It wasn't as though such things hadn't happened before. Tandy had known of teacher-and-student flings from her own days as a teenager. It wasn't out there in the open, but it was known.

"When I was in high school I knew plenty of girls

messing with the football coach,'' she reminded her husband.

Nick Mattson had a different take. He didn't buy that kind of thirty-something justification. He also refused to see what had transpired as a love story or a "mistake," and because of their stubborn positions he and Tandy went round and round about it.

"It's child rape," Nick said as his wife reached over to hit the "mute" button on their giant television set. "The boy is a child. I don't care if it was a woman molesting a boy or an older guy molesting young girls. She's a sick woman."

Tandy didn't feel that way at all. She thought that it was within the realm of possibility, maybe even probability, that Mary and Vili loved each other.

"But," she conceded while her husband held to his hard line, "it may be puppy love, though. And I can't say it was his first time. I heard he's in a gang."

Danelle Johnson's twins were among those who just couldn't see that anything that happened between Mary Letourneau and Vili Fualaau was wrong. Vili was a gentle soul, an artist. Mary was the beautiful and wise love of his life. For Danelle, there was no getting through to her son and daughter. It was a love affair, not a crime.

"Whatever illness she's got, she's got a pretty good illness," she said later. "She actually convinced him, and them too, that she was in love with him. Then when they got in her way of using him—even though I don't think she thought she was using him—then she started turning on them, trying to get rid of them so they wouldn't be in her way."

Drew told his mother that she was wrong. He knew that Vili was in love, but Danelle dismissed the idea.

"He's too young to decide what he wants. And she's of an age where she should know that even if she did want it she should wait."

Not everyone was mortified, disgusted, or outraged when word went beyond Shorewood school grounds that Mary

Letourneau and her former sixth-grade student Vili Fualaau had been having sexual relations.

Katie Hogden nearly jumped out of her skin with joy when the first layers of secrecy began to peel away. The dark-haired teen with braces, the budding writer, the girl who never had a cross word for anyone, responded with euphoria.

Oh, my gosh! she thought. Two of my closest friends have found each other. That's so cool.

The idea that there might be dire consequences didn't hit her.

"The age thing didn't click," she said later. "When you hear that your friends are starting a relationship and they have liked each other for so long . . . they are just perfect for each other."

To Katie, it was beautiful, right, and romantic. It wasn't until she saw the news reports that cast it as a crime that she could acknowledge that it might have been wrong.

It had been a year and a half since Kate Stewart had seen Mary Kay Letourneau. The break in their face-to-face contact had been the longest since their friendship started at Arizona State in 1982, but it was not an estrangement. Both chalked up the lapse to marriages, careers, but mostly to the responsibilities of running households with small children. Mary Kay and Steve had four children, and Kate and her doctor husband were right behind them with a son and two daughters.

When a friend considered moving to Seattle, Kate suggested looking up Mary Kay for the scoop on the city's neighborhoods and schools. When the woman returned to Chicago, she told Kate that she had better call Mary Kay. There was urgency to her suggestion.

"Your friend is in trouble," she said. "She's about to break."

Kate suspected marital problems and, frankly, wasn't all that concerned if that was the cause. Mary Kay could get past that, and, Kate thought, it was certainly high time for a divorce.

"How are you?" she asked over the phone.

"We-ell." Mary Kay hesitated, drawing out the one-syllable word to two. "There's a lot going on."

"What's going on? You're getting divorced?"

"Yes."

"Yeah, so."

We've all been waiting for this, Kate thought, without saying it. Is there someone? I hope there is someone! Now maybe you can love someone.

"Yes, there is someone," Mary Kay said softly.

"That's great."

"And I'm pregnant," she said.

"Well, you said there was someone. So what!"

Kate learned nothing about the other someone, though she understood he was a wonderful person, and younger than Mary Kay. But as she had when she first told Michelle about it, Mary Kay did not let on just how much younger her beau was.

Kate, of course, would learn more in the weeks and months to come and she would consider why Mary Kay couldn't come out and tell her friends what had been going on and with whom.

"It was too much for her," she said later. "I think there was a shame factor there—religion hassles, which I don't think she's come to terms with. She's got this divider, one side, she's devout and believes in God, wants to do the right thing. The other side of her says, 'There's nothing wrong with having fun. God wants me to have fun. God wants me to live life, and damn it, I've embraced that.' "

The police had been by to make sure no other children had been molested by their favorite teacher; the school made offers of crisis counseling for those who needed it. And, of course, the media was sniffing around. As for Vili Fualaau, he was still in class at Cascade Middle School. Shorewood music teacher Beth Adair wrote a note to Mary Kay describing how Vili was: *"spaced out and subdued."*

THIRTY-SEVEN

HANGING OUT AT a friend's house in Kent on a rainy Friday evening, February 28, 1997, Amber Fish answered an urgent page from her older sister, Lisa.

"Amber, did you hear the news?"

"What news?"

"Get a hold of Angie quick!"

"What news?"

Lisa didn't want to say and instructed her sister to call their mother and she would fill her in. Amber hung up and dialed. Joy Fish answered and told her that a teacher had been arrested for molesting a student.

"On Channel Four they're saying it's Mary Kay."

Amber got into her car and drove to another friend's house where Angie was visiting. The twins and their friend watched the news report on the local late news. In shock and full of disbelief, Amber and Angie realized there was only one thing to do: they drove to Normandy Park to see Mary Kay. They knew it was late and that all hell had broken out, but Mary Kay was their friend and they wanted to support her.

Something's not right here. There has to be a mistake, Angie thought.

Amber said it out loud.

"It's just allegations. It was some kid just making this up. *Mary Kay?* I'm just sure."

Angie agreed.

"Not Mary Kay."

Just as the Fish twins, then just nineteen, turned into the driveway, the Letourneaus' '94 Plymouth Voyager pulled in ahead of them. The driver didn't get out right away and just sat there. The girls thought it was Mary Kay and got out and approached the driver's side.

Mary Kay kept facing straight ahead, until Amber got her attention, and in an instant a look of surprise and exaggerated delight washed over her face.

"Girls!" she said, getting out of the car and hugging them, first Amber, then Angie, who lingered a bit behind her sister.

"Look, you guys," Mary Kay said, gesturing to her pregnant belly. "I'm six months! Can you believe it's number five?"

Amber and Angie were breathless. Though they hadn't seen Mary since July, they had talked on the phone at Christmas and there had been no mention of a pregnancy.

Mary Kay kept rambling.

"Oh, I missed your birthday," she said. "I'm really sorry!"

The sisters said that was all right. They had come to see her because they had heard some things on the television news about "some allegations."

The smile vanished. "Great," Mary Kay said, "this will probably be in the newspapers tomorrow."

Then she started to cry and slumped back into the driver's seat and fiddled with the keys, still in the ignition. Amber and Angie moved closer and stood next to her; the rain fell hard, but it didn't matter much to them.

Mary Kay admitted that she had stayed in the van in the driveway without getting out because she thought some reporters might have followed her.

And then she talked for the next hour or two, and though the former neighbors and favorite baby-sitters knew nothing about what Mary Kay Letourneau was saying, they didn't ask any questions to fill in the gaps. In fact, neither said very much at all. They didn't know what to say. They didn't know if she was confessing to a crime or telling them the whole thing was some big mistake.

Mary talked in a stream-of-consciousness manner that was almost incoherent and then stopped to cry. Her tears seemed to fuel her and she would talk some more.

Amber and Angie started to cry, too.

Mary Kay said she had just returned from "a meeting with the boy's mom." They were trying to work things out. The boy's mother was very upset; she had just found out. It was a mess that she was trying to sort out.

"They say I can't see him until he is eighteen," she said.

"That's a long time," Amber said, offering the kind of remark used to soothe.

"Don't tell me that's a long time," she said, almost as a wish that it wouldn't be so. Tears convulsed her once more. Mary Kay was coming undone and the Fish sisters didn't know how to make her feel better.

At one point, she turned around and said, "Steven actually asked me if I loved the boy more than I loved him. Can you believe that he would say that?"

"What did you say to him?" one asked.

"I explained to him, no, I just love you in different ways."

Both sisters were sobbing at the thought of Steven and his brother and sisters dealing with the terrible allegation against their mother.

"Amber," Mary said, almost teasingly. "I've never seen this side of Angie, this is so odd."

The comment hurt. Angie had never been the "emotional" one, but she had always loved Mary Kay and her family. As much as her sister, though she didn't always show it. As the time flew by, the girls noticed that Steve Letourneau was home, peering out the window every so often. One asked if they could go inside. Mary Kay shook her head.

"Steve's really upset about this," she said. "I don't want to bring any of this inside. He found some letters that say how I feel about the boy."

"... *sometimes I feel your kisses, but you're not there. I miss the sounds we make together. I want your arms around me holding me forever ...*"

A couple of hours went by and Amber and Angie still felt as though they didn't know what had really happened. It was late, well past one A.M. They hugged Mary Kay good-bye and she asked them to keep in touch. She especially wanted to be informed on what the media was saying about her. The sisters agreed.

"I'll call you soon," she said.

On their way back to Carriage Row, the sisters decompressed. They were confused and in shock. They believed the allegations were not true. Mary Kay hadn't come out and said there had been any inappropriate contact. If there hadn't been any inappropriate contact, then the whole thing would blow over.

"I don't think she touched him," Angie said.

Amber wasn't so sure.

"No, they kissed, she said."

"No way," Angie said.

"Yeah, Mary Kay said they kissed."

Angie disagreed. "I didn't hear her say that."

"She did. She might have said it under her breath . . . 'All it was was a kiss . . .' "

Mary Kay mentioned a "meeting with the boy's mom" that had taken place before the twins met her in her driveway, but she didn't elaborate on what had transpired. In fact, it had not gone well. As most would expect, Soona Fualaau was not a happy woman. *How could she be?* Her son's teacher, only three years younger than herself, was pregnant by her son Vili. Soona was overwhelmed and angry. She had seen her son go off with Mary, she had seen a closeness develop between the pair. *But this? This was too much.* She brought the director of the Boys and Girls Club at White Center to keep her from decking Mary Letourneau when they met at the Des Moines marina in front of Anthony's Homeport restaurant. Mary gave Vili's mother a letter explaining her feelings.

Soona recalled the encounter later: "She kept saying the sex was wrong, but I do not believe that she fully understands that she had crossed the boundary that should never have been crossed . . . She never said 'I'm really sorry.' And it goes back to that I think she's crazy."

A caring woman who was smarter than her résumé, Soona Fualaau was charitable toward the teacher carrying her grandchild.

"She really needs help because I think she's living in fantasyland."

THIRTY-EIGHT

IT SIMPLY COULDN'T be true. Normandy Park neighbor Tina Bernstein had hoped that whatever was unfolding at the Letourneau place next door was the result of a disgruntled student, an enemy, maybe even an off-the-wall mistake. She also considered the possibility that Mary Kay might have been framed, maybe even by Vili Fualaau. Tina struggled with what she'd gleaned from early news reports, because she had little recent firsthand knowledge of what Mary and Steve had been up to. She hadn't seen Mary much over the course of the past few months—not much since the summer when school closure meant the neighborhood was the center of activity for all moms and kids.

As she ran through the scenarios of what had happened—what she had allowed herself to take in—Tina felt there had to be an explanation for it.

Maybe whatever happened, only happened once, she thought. Yes, I'll bet it only happened once.

Tina was at a loss for what to do and she thought of flowers. *Mary loved flowers.* She drove to the QFC grocery store that sits at the bottom of the neighborhood hill and bought a mixed bouquet from the in-store florist. She wanted Mary to know that she still cared about her and what was happening, and in the end, she'd be there for her if Mary needed her.

She parked at her house next door and walked up the Letourneaus' sidewalk to the front door and knocked.

Mary timidly poked her head from the doorway.

Tina could already feel the tears coming on.

"You need a little sunshine around here," she said, handing over the flowers and reaching out to hug her neighbor.

Tina Bernstein would never forget that day. Seldom had she seen such trouble in someone's eyes.

"She was very hesitant to say anything and I didn't

want to pry. It was very personal. We didn't have that type of relationship, but yet I felt if you've been wrongly accused here, maybe there was something she wanted to say . . . we started talking. I asked if I could come in. She looked like she needed someone to talk to. She was pretty hysterical. She had a hard time stopping crying. Steve was gone. Out for a run or something.''

Inside, when her composure came, Mary focused her anger on Steve and their marriage.

"If you haven't noticed," she said, "our marriage hasn't been that good.''

Her tears drying on her cheeks, Mary went on to tell Tina how indifferent Steve had been to her father's bout with prostate cancer. When she'd learned of the dire prognosis more than a year before, Steve had offered no comfort. The clock was ticking on a great man's life—a wonderful father, a brilliant legislator, a candidate for the presidency—and Steve Letourneau was nothing short of impassive about it. It hurt her. At a time when she needed him most, Mary said, her husband turned his back on her.

Tina knew there were two sides to every story; every broken marriage had distinct versions of why everything went down in flames. Mary blamed Steve and Tina didn't defend him.

"Steve did have an attitude," Tina Bernstein said a couple of years later. "He had possibly a chip on his shoulder. Yes, there were times when he could be really nice, very pleasant to talk to. Treated the kids well. There were times when he . . .'' Tina hesitated. "Let's say I could see what Mary was saying about certain attitudes he would have toward people. I understood what she was saying . . . I don't want to give examples, though.''

Tina didn't ask about the potential charges, other than to see if Mary had legal representation. Mary said she had talked with a lawyer in Bellevue, but wasn't sure.

"Let's talk to Dave Gehrke and see what he says. He might know someone,'' Tina offered.

A few minutes later, Steve, looking glum, came home and made his way to the back bedroom. Mary caught his eyes, and pointed to the bouquet.

"Oh, look," she said, "Tina brought us flowers." She tried to smile.

Steve said nothing and left the room.

This is pretty intense, Tina thought.

When it was time to leave, Tina hugged Mary once more. The shattered woman told her neighbor that she thought everything would work out. She thought things could be resolved within the family. The family would be moving after the school year—a school year that Mary intended to finish at Shorewood.

"I did something very wrong," she said. "I made a very bad mistake."

When Tina got home she told her Boeing worker husband, Lee, what was going on and Lee got on the phone immediately to call David Gehrke, a lawyer, neighbor, and a buddy since high school. It was a rough week all around for those with ties to the little pod of houses in that Normandy Park neighborhood. Ellen Douglas's brother—and one of David's closest friends—had died in a tragic motorcycle accident just as the investigation into Mary Kay Letourneau began.

Married to a schoolteacher, David Gehrke was by his own admission a late bloomer. At almost fifty, he was the father of two small boys, with a "busy enough" law practice in Seattle. He could be doing better, but he had no real complaints. He was a sensitive man with eyes that welled with tears when emotional subjects were broached. People who knew that side of him joked that he was the "first lawyer known to have a heart." He wore a bracelet with the initials WWJD—What Would Jesus Do. David and his family lived in a house above Pacific Highway in Des Moines that was only a stopping spot until they could build a dream home on property in the Normandy Park neighborhood where the Douglases, Bernsteins, and Letourneaus resided.

"It's Mary," Lee said on the phone that day.

David instantly knew about whom and what Lee was referring. He listened while his friend filled in some blanks, saying that Mary was freaking out, worried about the media, worried about what she was going to do.

Poor Mary, David thought. How terrible to be accused of something you didn't do.

David knew the Letourneaus only casually. He knew Mary Kay better than Steve, whom he thought was a commercial fisherman.

"He was just never around," he said later.

With people coming in for the wake for Ellen Douglas's brother on Saturday, it wasn't the most convenient time to arrange a meeting. Mary Kay and David talked briefly later that night and agreed to talk in-depth at the Gehrkes' later that weekend. When Sunday came, the pair sat for three hours at the dining room table overlooking a backyard with a swing set and littered with soccer balls and other boy stuff. Bagels from the morning sat on a plate. Mary Kay sipped tea, told her story, and wondered about her options.

Knowing Mary as he did, at first the lawyer assumed that the charges were unfounded. Mary set him straight.

"It's all true," she said. "We are in love." She went on to describe the boy in "glowing" terms. He was a great artist and a sensitive soul. He was the love of her life. Mary said she and Vili walked with the same rhythm and saw the wonders of life through the same eyes.

That complicated matters. Big-time. David told her that the law didn't recognize the possibility of love between a thirteen-year-old and a grown woman. In fact, Washington State had recently drawn a hard line and changed the statutory rape law—consensual sex between an adult and a child. It was now called "rape of a child."

The options included denying the charges and fighting it out in court. If she pleaded not guilty, David said she could suggest that the boy had been the aggressor, or maybe it was all some teenage fantasy that went too far. Maybe the sex never really happened. Mary Kay saw that scenario as ridiculous. Almost laughable. She didn't think it would work. "I'm carrying his baby," she said.

Scratch that.

Another option was pleading guilty and seeking treatment in lieu of any jail or prison time. From what he knew of her, David considered Mary a perfect candidate for treatment. She was a first-time offender. There had been no other victims. She was highly regarded by the community. *She wasn't some pervert.* The only hitch was that by seeking treatment she'd have to admit she had a problem. She'd have to register as a deviant, a sex offender. The program that David Gehrke considered her ticket out of serious prison time was the result of Washington's Special Sex Offenders Sentencing Act or SSOSA. The 1984 law allowed for supervised outpatient treatment for sex offenders with no other felony convictions. In reality, it was a brutal regimen of counseling, drugs, behavior modification, and constant supervision. Some sex offenders who'd tried it said they preferred prison—or castration. Female sex offenders were so rare that Washington didn't have a program in place at the women's prison.

The choice was not pretty.

Mary Kay wasn't in tears that afternoon, though she might have been if she fully understood the restrictions that David Gehrke said would come with a SSOSA program. She left the meeting seemingly upbeat. Somehow it would work out. She didn't even think it was a crime, and maybe if that was understood by others things would be all right.

"I didn't think two people being in love could be wrong," she said later. "I knew that as a teacher it was a big no-no falling in love with a student; a shame on the profession. And I'd have to resign. But a crime? No."

David Gehrke had the case of his career and he probably didn't know it. Not long after he talked to Mary Kay, he enlisted his friend Robert Huff, a struggling lawyer ten years younger, to help out with the case. Robert Huff was one of those men pushing forty who appeared to favor the *Miami Vice* stubble look of the early eighties. He was a pleasant-looking fellow, with chic glasses and a decent wardrobe. He also had a car about to be repossessed and a stack of complaints at the Washington Bar Association, mostly from disgruntled clients complaining that he didn't answer phone calls or letters.

Next to Bob Huff, David Gehrke, with his Jesus bracelet, soccer kids, and office in Seattle's landmark Smith Tower, seemed as rock solid as they come. David provided the heart of the case, the guy the public would come to know. As Vili and Soona Fualaau's lawyer and Mary Letourneau's "media representative," Robert Huff was the guy supposedly pulling the strings.

The two were quite a pair. Whether tipping back Lemon Drops at a bar, partying at a Jimmy Buffet concert, or plopping down on a nude beach and ogling the women like they were a couple of schoolboys, the two were best buddies. It wasn't that hard to figure out the symbiotic nature of the relationship. On the surface David provided respectability and helped Bob out when he got into trouble. And Bob? He provided the fun.

And Mary Kay Letourneau put her future in their hands.

"I didn't really 'hire' him," Mary Kay said later when people asked how she ended up with David Gehrke over a lawyer with more experience in sex cases. "He just came to me to offer help. I didn't even know for sure that I needed an attorney at that time. It just happened that I got David."

Over the course of the spring, summer, and into the fall, Mary Kay Letourneau would be in and out of court, motions filed, pleas negotiated. Everything about the case would be complicated. She was pregnant. She would be nursing. She needed evaluations. Drug therapy wasn't possible because of her unborn baby. Delay after delay after delay. There was also the turmoil of her husband and their broken marriage. Strangely, Steve didn't move out after Mary was arrested in February. He stayed put.

Throughout it all, there would be David Gehrke and Robert Huff and the case of their careers. And, despite the sometimes surreal worldwide interest that would follow that more seasoned media players might find difficult, David and Bob would later insist that they did their best.

"This Mary thing had so many extreme emotions," Bob Huff explained later. "It was like a whirlpool or a flushing toilet, depending on your visual preference. We were going crazy. I started calling it the Letourneau Triangle. The Letourneau Triangle is a place where normal laws of physics and human dealings do not apply."

*   *   *

Among those who knew her, there was no shortage of concern for Mary Kay Letourneau when the news first broke. Though contending with the sudden loss of her beloved older brother, Ellen Douglas was one of those who tried to get in touch with her neighbor, friend, and fellow teacher. She left a message on the Letourneaus' answering machine.

"Whatever happens," she said, "take care of yourself. Eat right. If you can't get out and get groceries, let us know. You can count on us."

And across Seattle almost immediately everyone weighed in with an opinion. She was Anne Bancroft's boy-eater Mrs. Robinson of *The Graduate* and Jennifer O'Neill's lonely wife in *The Summer of '42* all rolled into one. She was a schoolboy's dream; a parent's nightmare. She'd stolen a boy's youth. She'd made him a man.

THIRTY-NINE

ONE WOULD HAVE thought that an explosion had taken place in Mrs. Letourneau's Shorewood classroom the morning after she had been led away by King County Police Detective Pat Maley. But of course it hadn't. The classroom merely looked the way it always did. The only thing missing was the pretty, but frazzled, presence of the schoolteacher.

A bulletin board presentation was peeling from its mounting, the words "The American Dream" curling from the wall and falling to the floor. The irony of the statement was not lost on the teachers who pitched in during the aftermath. One said later that she'd have killed to have a picture of the pathetic scene. All the kids in the class had signed a petition on the board confirming their beliefs in the freedoms of the United States.

"*After all,*" they concluded, "*we are da bomb.*"

A handful of shell-shocked teachers toiled for hours picking up the piles and digging through the debris that seemed a metaphor for the woman who had occupied the room the day before. Papers more than a year old were heaped next to her chair. Junk was everywhere; bulky class projects formed a miniature mountain range around the perimeter of the classroom. Several paper cutters of varying sizes were unearthed from blankets of construction paper. The finding of the cutters was of particular interest. The guillotinelike devices were not allowed in any classrooms since a boy had clipped off the tip of a finger.

"Guess whose class it happened in?" asked a teacher later with more than a touch of sarcasm.

In nearly every child's desk, it seemed to one who had been there, was an X-Acto knife. Again, a direct violation of school policy.

Said one later: "When I see the pictures they show of Miss Perfect's little room, I think . . ." Her words trailed off into a sigh.

The father of one of the students filled in for a few days until a more permanent substitute could be hired. Visitors to the classroom during those subsequent days felt sorry for the man and the others who had helped out during that tumultuous time. Not only was the place a mess and the kids crying, but there was no indication of what had gone on as far as actual curriculum was concerned.

At first, word came down not to change the room one bit. Mary Letourneau was only *accused* of something. She was on administrative leave with pay while the legal system made a determination about her fate. Who was to say that she wouldn't be exonerated and allowed to return?

After a while, the personnel director instructed a teacher to "change everything. She didn't want a shred left of Mary Letourneau."

Though many tried to comply with the substitute's call for order, a few students made it exceedingly difficult. And for good reason. They were used to having control of the classroom to such a degree that Mrs. Letourneau was more a peer than a leader. Word got back to other teachers about the difficult time the sub was experiencing. The students were up in arms.

"We only do that once a week! We're not going to do that!"

The woman on the front lines scurried from teacher to teacher seeking input about the sixth-grade curriculum that had been ignored much of the year. She had to get the students of room 39 focused on their schoolwork and get them to the end of the year.

Mary Letourneau was not coming back. The sub wasn't the enemy and they weren't holding down the fort until the return of their favorite teacher.

Recess dance parties were over and kids were told to get outside and play like the rest of the sixth-graders. It might have been what they "were used to" but it was not going to fly any longer. Homework was doled out and report cards were actually drawn up on time, a first for the year according to a teacher at Shorewood. Other kids looked into the classroom with smiles as big as a goalpost because they knew the party was over. Mrs. Letourneau's kids had to work as hard as they did.

It was about time.

And though it wasn't easy, the children began to accept the substitute. One boy told her that he knew that Mary and Vili had been "dating." Other kids in the class knew, too.

Some students needed reassurance and consideration and so did their parents. It was a thankless task, juggling emotions, the law, and the loyalty the students felt for Mary Letourneau, but other teachers could see the woman who stepped into room 39 was capable of handling the heavy challenge.

Teachers shook their heads and even laughed when the substitute told them that her students wanted her to dress more like Mary.

"You'd look really cute in a short skirt and a big sweatshirt, tennis shoes, and maybe some bright pink lipstick!" they'd said.

"Thanks for the tip," she said.

In time, devotion to the disgraced and absent teacher eroded.

"The boys were the first to start calling her names," one teacher remembered.

*   *   *

The staff lounge at Shorewood Elementary was not only a retreat from the somber faces that roamed the hallways; it was also a place where they could talk about what they had heard about Mary. All didn't talk openly. Some were closer to Mary and felt their allegiance to her eroding. They wanted so much for her to get help for her sickness, be cured, hospitalized. Whatever it took to get her better, preferably far from Shorewood. Those who were less invested in a relationship knew when to back off and keep quiet. As public as it all was, for many at the school it was a personal, emotionally charged issue.

Pieces of the puzzle came rapidly together and with each new bit of information came the understanding that whatever had been going on between Mary Letourneau and Vili Fualaau had gone on under everyone's noses.

When the teachers learned of the marina incident, the date reminded one of the group of the last day of school in June 1996. That night the Shorewood graduating sixth-graders convened with friends, parents, and other students to celebrate the end of the school year. As had been the case for several years, the event was held at a local swim club. One teacher who was also a Shorewood parent remembered something about Mary.

"One of the parents brought a karaoke machine and Vili was there, he was the star, singing. This one girl in particular was hanging all over him . . . and probably ten minutes before the party is set to end, in runs Mary bouncing around and looking and looking. And I remember her looking and she saw Vili and this girl singing—and she was just so giddy."

Here I am!

"That was the night of the marina incident," the teacher recalled.

Another teacher recalled a sixth-grade field trip in which the bus had been kept waiting because Mary and Vili and another boy had lagged behind before showing up, skipping merrily along, arm in arm. A teacher told her that it was "not appropriate behavior."

And a teacher remarked about the time Mary Kay was

seen "slow-dancing with Vili" during recess. The teacher told Mary Kay to knock it off.

"It didn't look right," the teacher said.

The investigation by the police and a worried school district continued in the days after Mary Kay Letourneau's arrest in the school parking lot. Information came slowly. Vili's buddies had known about the sexual relationship since the summer before seventh grade. One boy told police investigators how Mary Kay had picked Vili up one night in her van to have sex near some apartments in White Center. Another time, the kid said, Mary Kay got Vili from the Boys and Girls Club for sex.

"They came back in around ten minutes," the kid said.

FORTY

AFTER MARY LETOURNEAU was gone, Shorewood teachers who knew her were left with snapshots of memory they couldn't reconcile with all the recollections percolating in the staff room. One young teacher who knew Mary only casually would never forget her impression of the teacher just the day before the Highline school superintendent came to break the news. She hadn't seen Mary much in the previous weeks—Mary hadn't been in the staff room.

"I remember looking at her and thinking how beautiful she looked. She looked so happy. She was pregnant; she was radiant. I just remember thinking, Wow, that's great."

The day after the news came was intensely disconcerting for the young teacher. The allegations were preposterous.

"She couldn't have done anything," she said to another. "How could someone who knew she was in so much trouble be so serene?"

"Well, you never know," the other offered.

Wrong, she thought.

Almost two years later, tears would come to her eyes as she recalled the memory.

"To find out that she had all this in her head and pretended to be so fine. That's struck me ever since."

What was she thinking? How was she able to cover such a devastating reality?

Another teacher who shared lunch duty with Mary Kay the day of her arrest was also struck by the deception, the denial—whatever it was. While they were helping out with the students, Mary Kay told the teacher how excited she and Steve were about welcoming their fifth child to their family in the spring.

"She said they had both come from large families and had wanted a fifth child. Other people told them they should stop at four."

It bothered teachers at Shorewood when the media proclaimed knowledge of a foot-long waiting list for parents who wanted to get their children into Mrs. Letourneau's class, but could not be accommodated. There was no waiting list.

"That isn't how it is done at Shorewood," a teacher said later.

In fact, another said, "There were parents who made sure their students did *not* end up in her class. They wanted more structure."

A few parents told a colleague of Mary Kay's that they noticed that sons, more so than daughters, "were not pleased with her as a teacher. The boys did not necessarily consider her their favorite teacher. But the ones who had girls had that little friendship connection. . . ."

Some parents said they never felt welcome in room 39, and again, more often than not, those who got a cold shoulder were the parents of boys. Those who had girls with whom Mary had some kind of friendship connection said they helped out because they felt "needed."

As time passed, some teachers speculated about their colleague and her alleged crime.

Could she have abused any others?

One Shorewood teacher couldn't rule it out, though she thought it was unlikely.

"I had a parent tell me that her older son felt uncomfortable in class," she said a couple of years later. "But I still think if Vili hadn't been in her room she wouldn't have picked anybody else."

Who was this woman they all thought they knew? It was a question that for the longest time went unspoken within the walls of Shorewood Elementary's staff room. For a while the charges and whether they could be true was all they thought about, all they talked about. One teacher later described herself as feeling like a snowman in one of those little plastic domes trying her best to be still and numb. But now and then someone would give her plastic dome a shake and particles would fall once more.

Who was Mary Kay Letourneau? Even the way the media called her Mary *Kay* was unsettling to many who knew her at Shorewood. It almost made her seem unreal, like some character they didn't know. Mary Kay? She always went by Mary at school. The only one they knew who called her Mary Kay was her husband, Steve, and that was to differentiate her from Mary Claire, their daughter.

But who was she really?

The answers prompted only more confusion and even some dissension. It seemed that no one could really agree on her true character; everyone believed Mary Letourneau was a different woman for different people.

One saw her as a master manipulator who got whatever she wanted. Arriving late, skipping meetings, doing whatever she pleased.

Another saw her as a charismatic, if unhappy, woman who wanted nothing more than to be a good teacher. Devoting hours and hours for the good of her students.

She was competitive, a teacher thought. She wanted to be seen as the best, the most popular teacher in the school.

"I see Mary as a cheerleader who wanted to be very popular and wanted everybody to like her," said one.

Still another saw her as a rule-breaker, a person for whom the guidelines of the school had no meaning.

"You can't chew gum in the classroom, but Mary let

her kids do it. We might not all agree with the same rules
... but we try to uphold them.''

A teacher who was relatively new to Shorewood
thought that Mary appeared to act like a junior high school
student. In fact, the teacher said, she even looked the part.

''Shorts, skirts, big baggy sweatshirts. She looked very
cute. She looked to me like a teenager,'' she said later.

Mary would discuss nothing but her pregnancies, and
child-rearing concerns, with another teacher sharing a similar personal load.

Another was given insight into her marital problems.

In time, even one of her most devoted friends on the
staff would begin to wonder if all had been duped by the
pretty blond woman in room 39. Had they ever really
known her at all?

''A sex offender's forte is deception and knowing one's
audience and you play to them what you want them to see.
And if you have to play different parts for different people
you can do that. And they lay a blanket on whatever's
behind; whatever they don't want you to see,'' the teacher
said later.

John Schmitz arrived in Seattle less than a week after his
daughter called him from Beth Adair's after the arrest. He
brought her a car, an Audi Fox, and the promise that he'd
stand by her. Mary Kay and Steve showed him the ''peaceful coexistence'' contract that had been drafted by the Jesuit priest that she and Steve had consulted when they first
discovered she was pregnant by Vili.

''It was a contract based on respect for each other and
the understanding that what must be done is done in the
best interests of the children. There would be no reconcil-
iation and the priest said he wouldn't even pray for a miracle to have us reconcile. We would transition the children
to their new life, divorce, and they'd remain with me. I
was their mother, their primary parent. After my father left,
Steve ripped up the contract. He accused the priest of being
in conspiracy with my family.''

''You won't get your way this time,'' he said.

It was at this Des Moines, Wash., marina where police discovered Mary Kay Letourneau and Vili Fualaau in the teacher's van in the early morning hours of June 19, 1997. Highline School District officials learned of the disturbing incident, but since no one was charged with a crime, did nothing. *(Author)*

Mary Kay Letourneau, pregnant with her student's baby and her world falling apart, was all smiles when she posed for this class picture in the fall of 1997. Her baggage handler husband Steve Letourneau had already discovered proof of the sexual relationship between his wife and her student. *(Jose Avila)*

Twelve-year-old Vili Fualaau was a popular kid in Mrs. Letourneau's sixth-grade class. Teacher and student shared their first kiss not long after this photo was taken in Shorewood's classroom 39. *(Katie Hogden)*

Mary Kay's was the only bedroom with an ocean view in the Schmitz home on exclusive Spyglass Hill in Corona del Mar, Calif. Family friends wondered what role the tragedy of little Philip, who drowned in the pool, might have played in Mary Kay's life. *(Author)*

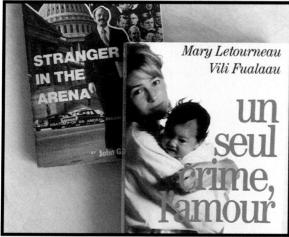

Like father, like daughter – John Schmitz and favorite daughter "Cake" shared many similarities. Both had two children by students. Both published memoirs. *(Author)*

John Schmitz's ultra-conservative politics brought demonstrators to the Congressman's house. No one would dispute that Mary Kay was her father's staunchest defender. *(Irv Rubin)*

Mary Schmitz, lawyer Gloria Allred and Hank Springer as they appeared on KNBC's "Free For All" public affairs television show in the late '70s and early '80s. *(Pat DeAndrea)*

Not long after it was learned that he had fathered two children with Carla Stuckle, John Schmitz, disgraced and no longer a viable political candidate, lived in this trailer park in Tustin – a mile from his mistress's home. *(Author)*

Steve and Mary Kay Letourneau and their children lived in this modest home in Normandy Park, Wash. Ultimately, marital infidelities on both sides and financial pressures would cause them to lose their dream house. *(Author)*

Sixth-grader Katie Hogden considered her favorite teacher a friend and spent hours on the phone chatting with her. After Mary Kay's arrest for rape, the teacher asked the girl to relay an important message to Vili. She refused. *(Judy Hogden)*

Some teachers at Shorewood Elementary School in Burien, Wash. were embittered by what they considered a lack of support from the district administration during the scandal. *(Author)*

Defense lawyer David Gehrke represented Mary Kay through her second arrest. He infuriated Mary Kay's friends by calling them "groupies." The friends, in turn, begged Mary Kay to dump the lawyer. *(Noel A. Soriano)*

KIRO-TV reporter Karen O'Leary was sued by Vili's family after she interviewed the teenager in a park near his home. The reporter considered the lawsuit an attempt to silence the media about the true relationship between the teacher and student. *(Courtesy KIRO)*

Nick Latham, Public Information Officer, Highline School District, was on the frontlines of the media storm. *(Courtesy KIRO)*

Dr. Julia Moore diagnosed Mary Kay with bipolar or manic-depressive disorder. Dr. Moore's testimony at the sentencing hearing in November 1997 was critical to securing sex-offender treatment over prison time. *(Donald Moore)*

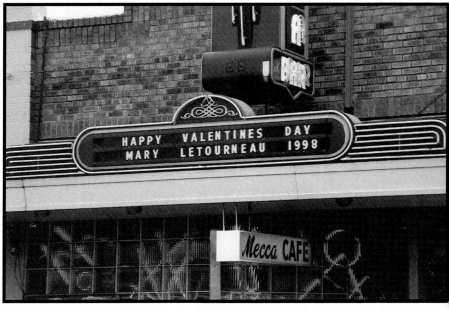

The Mecca Cafe in Seattle got caught up in the media fever. *(Jim Fielder)*

The story turned tabloid when lawyer Bob Huff brokered the Fualaaus' "exclusive" story to the *Globe*, "Inside Edition" and *American Journal*. Their French tell-all, *Un Seul Crime, L'Amour, netted* them more than $200,000. *(Author)*

Mary Kay Letourneau after her release from jail in January 1998. Though she looked it, the fallen teacher was not at her low point. Some encouraged her and enabled her to see the teenage father, and the results would be disastrous. *(Seattle Police)*

Michelle Jarvis (here, with her husband Michael) flew to Seattle to bring Mary Kay home from the hospital after Audrey was born. Michelle worried about possible violence against her childhood friend by Steve Letourneau.

Twins Amber and Angie Fish babysat Mary Kay's new baby, Audrey, until Mary Kay was sent to jail in August 1997. The twins worried about their friend's mental stability. *(Breea Bridges)*

No longer a teacher but an inmate at the Washington Corrections Center for Women near Gig Harbor, Mary Kay Letourneau spends her days writing and answering fan mail. Since her incarceration, she has not seen the two babies she had with the Samoan teenager Vili or the four she had with Steve Letourneau. *(Jim Fielder)*

After her second arrest, an avalanche of media interest enveloped Mary Kay. The former teacher made the cover of *People*; articles in *Time, Paris Match, Mirabella, Spin* and *George* were among the many that appeared in the spring of 1998. *(Author)*

FORTY-ONE

HAD THERE REALLY ever been a graceful way out of the mess that Mary Kay and Steve Letourneau had made of their lives? It was a question that, once Mary Kay was arrested, Kate Stewart could never really answer with certainty. For a time—through Christmas, New Year's, Mary Kay's birthday, even the Valentine's Day a couple of weeks before the arrest—it seemed that there was, in fact, a little room for the concept that things could be worked out quietly and discreetly. But Kate felt that in the long run, it didn't seem possible that "Plan A" (as her former roommate described it) would ever really work: Steve and Mary Kay would divorce, she would quit her job, and Vili would move in with her and the kids. *And they'd be one big happy family.*

Plan B hadn't been any better. It was even more preposterous. Steve and Mary Kay would move away to raise Vili's baby in a new town, far from the prying eyes of those who knew them. It wasn't that Steve didn't love Mary Kay enough to do that; Kate and others knew that he *worshiped* her. But it wasn't up to him alone. His family would never stand for it and his ego wouldn't allow for accepting his wife's student's baby as his own. Once that little black-haired baby was born, it would be all over at the Letourneaus'.

Sometimes, Kate understood, people just can't look the other way. Even if it is in the best interest of everyone involved.

Kate could only hope that the divorce between Mary Kay and Steve would be swift and involve as little finger-pointing as possible. Finger-pointing would lead to defensiveness; defensiveness would lead to nothing but trouble. In reality, this was a divorce for which there was plenty of blame to go around.

But if Steve Letourneau was in turmoil, much of it his own doing. And certainly, there had to be a measure of

guilt thrown into the mix. Steve hadn't been exactly faithful. If he was smart, he'd be the last one to throw any
stones.

"The marriage had broken down to the point where she
didn't even know where he was," Kate said later. "They
could probably have swapped sex stories if they had to or
were in the mood to at home. It was out in the open between them. At one point he was going to be gone and
told her that he was going to see a girlfriend."

"Now that's all right? You're okay with this?" Steve
asked.

"Fine," she answered.

But it wasn't fine. Mary Kay had reached out to a sixth-
grader. Yes, Kate knew, over the years there had been
transgressions on both sides. There had always been the
understanding, however, that when the night was done,
both Steve and Mary Kay would return home. If Steve
hadn't strayed, maybe Mary Kay wouldn't have been so
inclined to do the same.

During the weeks and months before she and Vili
crossed the line to the point of no return, Mary Kay Letourneau was falling apart and her husband was seemingly
oblivious.

When Kate and Mary Kay started talking after the two-
year hiatus of their friendship, the subject of sex with Steve
came up. Mary Kay said that it had never been that great
with her husband. The revelation surprised Kate. She had
always assumed that sex was the glue that bonded their
marriage. But it was more than just mundane sex that troubled her. Steve wasn't the man of Mary Kay's dreams. He
had no conviction. No passion.

Steve Letourneau, as his wife presented it to Kate, went
whichever way the wind blew. When he was with Mary
Kay, "they'd be sleeping in the same bed crying together"
and trying to find a way to save their marriage. When he
talked with his family he whined about the nightmare his
wife had caused.

"He has no backbone," Kate said. "He is not strong.
That's the whole reason she could never love him. He
doesn't know his own mind."

Steve Letourneau loved Mary Kay—which was the strangest part of the whole tragedy surrounding their broken marriage. Though he strayed, though he pushed her around when she was pregnant, it had more to do with his badly bruised ego than hatred for Mary Kay. Mary Kay told her friend that her father had put it in very simple terms.

"How do you expect him to handle it? He's been upstaged by a thirteen-year-old!"

Kate understood where Steve was coming from. "He never wanted a divorce. He loved her. If she called up and said, 'Oh, my God, I made such a horrible mess. I need you so much. We just have to get the kids and move to Canada,' he'd be right there."

Kate Stewart was another who just couldn't accept Steve and Mary Kay living together once things went from civil to ugly. She was worried for Mary Kay when the violence started to escalate between the two. Mary Kay was pregnant, in a state of confusion, and her husband was hurt, bitter, and humiliated. Not a good combination for resolution or even a truce. Mary Kay told Kate that alcohol had been thrown in the mix and she was even more worried. Steve made frequent trips down the hill to the shopping center for big cans of Foster's. When their car was out of commission, he'd walk the long walk down the hill to the shopping center.

One time Kate overheard a shouting match between father and son when she was on the phone talking to Mary Kay.

"Get out of there! Leave her alone, you big drunk!" Steven's eleven-year-old voice called out in the background.

Some nights Mary Kay couldn't take the yelling and the shoving. She grabbed a blanket and a pillow went to sleep in the van.

Kate could only wonder if the nightmare Mary Kay was living through would really be worth it. Somehow, as incomprehensible as it seemed, Kate understood that her former college roommate loved teenagers. She also recognized that Mary Kay's feelings for the boy were stronger than they had ever been for Steve Letourneau. Yet Kate couldn't help but play the devil's advocate during their phone conversations from Seattle to Chicago. She pressed the notion that although Mary Kay and Vili were "in love," they were from two very different worlds.

"If you are at a black-tie cocktail party and Vili's next to you and there's a lot of politicians and all these people in the room—*people in high-powered places*. You're in an arena that you are very comfortable in, how will you feel?" Kate asked.

There was no hesitation from Mary Kay. She said she'd be fine.

Her friend pushed harder. "You won't worry about Vili?"

"I've spent my whole life worrying about what my husband was going to say when he opened his mouth; I can't tell you how comfortable I'd be with Vili. He can hold a candle to anyone in the room. I would never worry about what comes out his mouth," she said.

Several weeks had transformed the tail end of another gray Western Washington winter into a wonderful, wet, and warm springtime. Gregory Heights teacher Mary Newby found herself at an executive board meeting at the Highline Education Association offices near the airport. An HEA director told her that Mary Letourneau was there taking care of her pension and other matters related to her employment as a teacher for the district.

"If you want to talk to her, this might be a good opportunity," the director said.

The veteran teacher was torn. She wanted to see her former student teacher, but felt she'd get teary-eyed and start to cry. No matter what had been said about Mary Kay Letourneau, it could never shake the sympathy that so many shared. How could it? Mary Newby was like so many others; what she had seen firsthand was a gifted teacher and devoted mother, a far cry from a predatory monster.

Finally, Mary Newby gathered her strength and went

out to the parking lot and marched right over to the younger woman. She put her arms around her. It was a moment Mary Newby will never forget.

"I asked her how she was doing, at that point I felt she was on very, very thin ice, emotionally."

Mary Letourneau, still pregnant, didn't seem upset.

"I'm fine," she said. "Everything's going to be okay."

It was almost as if she had found it within herself to comfort the comforter.

"You wrote to me, didn't you?" Mary Letourneau asked.

"Yes."

Mary Kay smiled. "I thought that you did. I received several hundred notes and just couldn't answer all of them."

Years later, Mary Newby struggled to get a fix on the attitude of the pregnant teacher in the parking lot that evening. The word that came was "bravado."

"There was almost a sense of bravado, that everything would work out."

Mary Newby continued to worry about her former student teacher and the impact of her relationship with the artistic Samoan boy.

"When she finally comes face-to-face with the fact that they aren't going to be together by his choice, what's going to happen with her?"

FORTY-TWO

OTHER INQUIRIES WITH lawyers had gone nowhere for both Mary Kay and Steve. After her arrest Mary Kay hired David Gehrke, and Steve hired a lawyer of his own, a young Tacoman named Greg Grahn. Steve met Grahn through a referral from his wife, Susan, also an Alaska Airlines employee. At the time, Steve was looking for advice, not necessarily a quick divorce. There were too many issues to be resolved. Mary Kay's criminal arrest, her pregnancy, and the foreclosure of the house in Normandy Park all loomed to cast a pall of uncertainty on people who needed resolution.

More than anything in those early days of the criminal case, Steve Letourneau was embarrassed about the attention his wife and marriage were getting because of her involvement with her student. He met with Greg Grahn in March, shortly after the arrest of his wife.

The thirty-two-year-old lawyer had practiced both civil and criminal law, and had even worked on a couple of child molestation cases. He saw Mary Kay as a pedophile. He wondered how Mary Kay could have hoodwinked Steve. But after conferring with his new client, it became clear that Steve hadn't been tricked by anyone. He simply didn't see the truth because it was so incomprehensible.

"Initially, Steve looked at it as Mary Kay was just taking this pupil under her wing. He thought, 'Hey, it was inappropriate. Teachers shouldn't be having students at the home. That was kind of uncommon, a bit odd. He never really thought it was sexual.''

Why would it ever be?

Steve told Greg Grahn that he believed his wife was starving for attention and Vili was providing what she needed to feel good about herself.

"He thought with Mary Kay maybe it was more of an ego-patting thing for her, that she was just intoxicated that somebody else was finding her to be such a wonderful person.''

Steve said he had tried to be a better husband, a more supportive person. By then it didn't matter. Mary Kay was getting everything she needed from Vili.

Those who knew Mary Kay Letourneau knew she loved the telephone more than face-to-face conversations. She thought nothing of calling to chat about one subject and ending up talking about a million others. During the time she was pregnant, Ellen Douglas was on her calling list. And throughout the conversations that the two shared, schoolteacher Ellen would take notes so that she could share what had been said with her husband, Daniel.

One of the reasons she made notes was simply because Mary Kay seemed so out of it, was so far gone at times, that it was difficult to remember every tangent that she drifted to.

Though facing treatment or prison and pregnant with a former sixth-grade student's baby, Mary Kay didn't seem to grasp that her world—*her old world*—had come to a complete halt.

She talked about staying in the house after Steve was gone.

"Well, we'll have to see what happens," Ellen said.

Mary, come on and wake up. You don't have the money. You're being foreclosed on.

She talked about continuing her teaching career.

"Uh-huh," Ellen said.

You're in denial. Life will not go on as it did. You won't have your children.

Ellen just couldn't tell Mary Kay the silent responses that went through her mind. It would be cruel. It was unnecessary. It wouldn't have helped her fragile state one iota.

"She was pregnant and life was tumbling on without her and things were happening and it was too late. No matter what I said to her it wouldn't have made a difference," she said later.

Whenever Ellen Douglas would hang up, by the look on her face and the duration of the call, Daniel Douglas knew his schoolteacher wife had been talking to their troubled neighbor. Ellen referred to her notes and shared what the two had discussed, but not all of it. Though she and Daniel were very close, some of it just seemed too personal to disclose. She shared nothing that was said with anyone at the school where she taught.

Of everything they discussed, one issue seemed paramount to Mary Kay. She frequently referred to Steve's callous treatment of her.

"She needed people to know that he wasn't a goody-goody," Ellen said later.

FORTY-THREE

IF ANYONE OWNED the Mary Kay Letourneau story—
outside of the principals involved, of course—it was television reporter Karen O'Leary. In many ways it was a
good fit. Not only because Karen was an excellent reporter
with a surprising reserve of sympathy for the teacher, but
also because the two shared some common ground.

Karen O'Leary came from money. Her family lived in
exclusive Pacific Palisades in Southern California. They
owned a villa in Puerto Vallarta, an apartment in New
York, a home in Lake Tahoe—Karen grew up blond and
beautiful in the California sun. A tennis star as a teen and
at Stanford University, she was fit and driven—the coed
with the golden future in television news.

So driven, friends thought, there seemed to be no time
for the right man. But those friends were delighted when
she married not long before the Letourneau case broke.
But by the time the case was over, so was the marriage to
a lawyer with political aspirations.

For more than fifteen years at KIRO, Karen O'Leary
was in the kind of job that ensured she'd never win a
popularity contest covering the unseemly of Seattle. Karen
reported on the Green River Killer investigation and the
infamous South Hill Rapist from Spokane, Kevin Coe. She
sat with Jim Lobsenz, a lawyer who would later represent
Mary Kay Letourneau, and witnessed the execution of
Lobsenz's client, a triple murderer, at the state prison in
Walla Walla. And throughout all her stories, Karen
O'Leary was always tough, dogged, and when necessary,
pushy.

"It's hard to like Karen sometimes," a former co-
worker said. "She's a tough broad."

She didn't know it at the time, but more than ever, she'd
need to be tough when it came to the Letourneau case. In
time, Karen O'Leary would be fighting for her name, her

career, and her dignity when the media circus came to town.

On March 12, 1997, Karen stood with the other pack of reporters in a King County Superior Courtroom to get a look at the thirty-five-year-old teacher in the olive-green gingham dress when she entered not-guilty pleas to two counts of rape of a child. As a sex offender, *a child molester,* she could have no contact with the victim or his mother; nor could she be left alone with her own children. Since she was a candidate for treatment, there would be weeks of tests, counseling sessions, and legal wrangling to see if she could be placed in program under the guidelines of the Special Sex Offenders Sentencing Act, or SSOSA. Otherwise, Washington's determinate sentencing left no room for wiggling. She'd serve seven years in prison. Certainly the thumbnail premise of the schoolteacher's criminal case was remarkable, but not nearly so as how the perpetrator appeared that day in court. It could not be denied that Mary Kay Letourneau was not just any sex offender. Even the reporter who had seen it all was shocked.

"This person was so pretty and sweet-looking and frail *and* pregnant," Karen O'Leary said later.

And it was the pregnancy that immediately raised an eyebrow.

Could it be the kid's? Karen thought.

FORTY-FOUR

MARY LETOURNEAU'S REQUEST made Katie Hogden feel uncomfortable. It also made the teenager feel more torn than ever. What was she to do? There was a time when she would have done anything for Mary or Vili or any of a number of people about whom she cared. She never felt used. She hung up the phone and sought out her mother.

Judy Hogden could see the confusion in her daughter's eyes. She knew it had to be about Mary.

"Mary wanted to know if I could pass a message between her and Vili."

Judy shook her head. She didn't think it was a good idea.

Deep down, Katie felt the same, though she explained Mary's motives. She knew Vili was hurting and there was no direct way to contact him.

But everyone was hurting.

"She said it was a three-word phrase that would let Vili know that everything would be all right. She said, no, I can't ask you to do that. But if you could tell him 'three words,' he'll know what it means."

"I'll have to talk to my mom about it," Katie had said.

Judy got on the phone later. She chose her words carefully, but she didn't allow Mary to cut into the conversation. Judy had some things to get off her chest.

"Before I say anything else, I want you to know we'll always be here for you, we'll always be your friends. If you need anything, a place to stay, to get away from reporters, come here. We won't tell anybody you're here. I don't approve of what you did, but that doesn't change how we feel about you."

Mary Kay seemed to take it in and seemed to appreciate the support. She thanked Judy Hogden for the offer, but it wasn't likely she'd take her up on it. She was going to be fine right where she was—at home.

"And as far as Katie getting involved," Judy said, tackling the most difficult part of the call, the reason for her conversation with Mary. "I think you are in some really big trouble and I don't think it's best to involve Katie, even passing along a three-word phrase."

Mary agreed and apologized for even asking.

"I'm in such a panic for him to know that everything is going to be okay," she said. "There are three words that if he heard he'd know that everything's going to be okay."

Judy felt sorry for Mary, but Katie would not be her little dove sending messages from her to Vili.

"I can't allow it," she said.

Katie phoned Vili after her mother got off the phone.

She didn't know what the three words were but if she did she would have told him. *Why hadn't she asked?*

"Is she okay?" Vili asked.

"Yeah," she answered.

"Is she crying?"

"Yeah, she is."

"Did you calm her down? Did you tell her everything was going to be okay?"

Alone in her upstairs room, thinking it over for the gazillionth time, Katie Hogden held on to one great hope that Mary Letourneau was in love with the right guy.

"He was just as concerned for her as she was for him," she said later.

She wondered what the three words were. Was it so basic as "I love you"? Or was it more creative? Deeper? More personal? She also wondered why she hadn't asked what the words were. Just in case.

When Mary knew that she was not going to be with Vili for a long time because the courts had restricted their contact and some jail time was all but a certainty, she timidly asked Katie Hogden the same question she had posed to so many others. It was a question that none of her friends liked to answer.

"Do you think Vili will wait for me?"

This was difficult. Katie knew that Vili loved Mary at some level, but if it was a lasting love she couldn't be certain. Wise as she was, Katie was only thirteen years old.

She tried to be kind, to keep Mary's sagging spirits lifted. But she wasn't a liar.

"He may not be there when you get back," she said. "But he'll remember and he'll probably want to come back."

Mary understood.

"I'm sure you'll always be friends," Katie said.

It broke their hearts to see the Letourneau family crash and burn. The four kids were about to be scattered to the winds and the parents were living in the same house, but not speaking to each other. Steve slept in the bedroom and

Mary Kay stayed camped out on the hide-a-bed. Amber
and Angie Fish saw it as the end of the perfect family.
They never, ever could have imagined that anything could
break up Mary Kay and Steve.

They could never have conceived of Mary Kay falling
in love with a student, either.

Almost as much as they wanted to support Mary Kay,
they wanted to let Steve know how they felt about him.
How worried they were and how much they loved him,
too. But he would never look into their eyes.

Only one time did he even make a halfhearted attempt
to speak to them.

"He was very short, abrupt," Amber recalled later. "I
kept trying to make eye contact with Steve. I just wanted
to talk to him. I never got the chance . . ."

Steve didn't appear to want anyone's help.

When people called, he hung up. When a neighbor
knocked on the door to let Steve know that he was supported by lots of people, he barely listened.

"Yeah, thanks," he said before shutting the door.

The twins talked about Steve's behavior with their
mother.

"Steve's hardly around," Angie said, "and he's got a
baby coming."

"He's not around because it's not *his* baby," their
mother said.

The girls thought their mother was way off base.

"There's no way," Amber said. "Of course it is."

Joy Fish didn't think so.

"It probably isn't," she said.

It was too much. The fact that the teacher had been having
a sexual relationship with a student was bad enough.
Shorewood parent Danelle Johnson thought it couldn't get
any worse, but of course it did. Danelle had a better pipe-
line for information than the Fish girls or their mother. She
learned from her children that Mary Letourneau was carrying Vili's baby.

"The kids thought it was just another awesome sign

that it was a meant-to-be romance. I thought it was god-awful," she said later.

Parents, for the most part, didn't see it the same way. In fact, few thought the pregnancy was positive proof about anything, other than it *proved* the woman hadn't been teaching birth control. Some fathers joked about wishing they could have had a tutor like Mary Kay Letourneau.

Many played the gender-reversal "what if" game. Danelle had a unique take on that kind of supposition. As mother of boy/girl twins it was easy for her to flip the roles.

"Molly tells me she's in love with a thirty-five-year-old man and they got pregnant to prove their love, and I'm gonna kill the motherfucker. End of story. Same with my son. I'm gonna kill *her*. Mary can be as sick as she wants to be, as demented as she wants, and I *would*," she said later.

With her honeydew-round belly, Mary Kay Letourneau thumbed her nose at the court order prohibiting unsupervised contact with her children, and the five of them boarded an Alaska Airlines flight to Southern California. They stayed with Michelle and Michael Jarvis and their three children in their home in Costa Mesa. Mary Kay knew her time with her children would be limited for a while and she wanted to spend every minute with Steven, Mary Claire, Nicky, and Jackie. Disneyland was their prime destination, and was wonderful as always. Mary Kay reminded her brood that their grandfather had once worked at the theme park as a Cobblestone Cop. Later, they played in the surf at Newport Beach. Mary Kay even took her kids up to Spyglass Hill to drive by the old house and to remember what once had been and imagine the future.

"I felt like it was *us* again and that everything was going to be all right," she said later.

Michelle was heartsick during the visit, but she didn't show it. Mary Kay was so upbeat and energetic that it didn't mesh with the reality of her situation in Seattle. She was in the trouble of her life. Moreover, she wasn't telling

Michelle every detail, either. There was one detail in particular that she hadn't shared with her best friend. It was the identity of the baby's father.

"I knew she was pregnant by someone other than Steve when she got pregnant, but I didn't know *who*. She didn't tell me. I knew who Vili was, she talked about him, but I didn't know he was the father. But going from here to there was like crossing two galaxies to me. Taking it from this kid, to being a father, was a leap that I couldn't even fathom."

FORTY-FIVE

THE SPRING OF 1997 had not been easy on Soona Fualaau. Her beloved father, just fifty-nine, died, leaving her with a broken heart and a grieving mother. Her hands were also full—*overflowing, really*—with her youngest son's imminent fatherhood and the criminal case facing the mother of his baby. And if she ever doubted things could get worse, they did. The last thing the soon-to-be grandmother needed was any more trouble with the police. But that is exactly what she got that spring, when Vili and his brother shook down a kid for his Fila jacket and a basketball jersey at Cascade Middle School. According to a police report filed after the second-degree robbery incident, one victim was clobbered with a broom handle, the jersey and jacket "ripped from them." The other was left with the threat that if he called the police "he would be killed." The boy wanted his jacket returned badly enough to risk it. The police were called, and the Fualaau boys were identified by pictures in the school yearbook.

Later that same day Vili and his brother were read their rights, booked, and fingerprinted at a local police precinct.

One of Vili's lawyers later dismissed the seriousness of the charges and considered it nothing more than "stupid kid stuff."

*   *   *

The stress and violence also intensified inside the Letourneau home. Each day closer to Mary Kay's baby's delivery date turned the flame up another notch. By May it was a blowtorch. Normandy Park police officers responded to a 911 call from Mary Kay on May 9. They found the pregnant woman with a red mark two inches wide and four inches long across her stretched stomach. She said her husband had hit her.

"We want to see the law bury you and it can't happen too soon," Steve had said, according to Mary.

They had argued over the spiral notebook she kept of his threatening remarks and he grabbed at her and struck her.

"The battle has begun," he said before leaving.

Mary Kay refused to press charges and the officers departed.

But later that day Steve returned. Mary Kay later said she met him outside in the driveway. While Steve stayed in the driver's seat, Mary Kay told him that the police had been to the house earlier and had taken a statement. She didn't think it was a good idea for him to be there. He could be arrested.

A police report chronicled what happened next:

". . . Steve suddenly pulled away and she felt the vehicle bump her and knock her down . . . She said she struggled to crawl toward the house and at some point [a neighbor] came and took her to the hospital."

Mary Kay Letourneau was admitted to a Seattle hospital for observation overnight. Her pelvic bone had separated, her left shoulder was bruised, and her left leg and elbows had been scraped by the fall. A day or so later she talked with Steve.

"He said he wished he had killed her and the baby."

Weighing in at nine pounds, ten ounces, Audrey Lokelani Fualaau was born on May 29, 1997, at Swedish Hospital in Seattle. Named for a beloved aunt of Mary Kay's and given a Samoan middle name meaning "rose of heaven," the baby's hair was as black as her teenage father's. And just as John Schmitz had done some sixteen years before when Carla Stuckle gave birth to their son, Vili Fualaau emerged from the waiting room and held his baby in secret.

But Vili wasn't alone, and neither was Mary Kay. Her music teacher friend from Shorewood, Beth Adair, was there to support and encourage Mary and Vili on their happy day. Also in attendance were scads of Vili's relatives—brothers, cousins, aunts, and uncles.

"Every Samoan in Seattle was there," Mary joked later.

Strangely, presiding over the scene was not the new mother, but the mother of the boy who had just become a father. "She's the Samoan Queen," Mary told a friend. "She's the matriarch of the family in any way that you can imagine. No question. She is in charge of every move that family makes."

Before *her* baby was born, Mary Kay wrote a message that she hoped would someday help the child understand her love for Vili and how difficult it had all been. *"People are putting me down. Accusing me of being mentally unfit because I allowed him to love me and I returned that love . . ."*

FORTY-SIX

THE PAST COUPLE of years had been rough on the news team at KIRO-TV. The station changed hands repeatedly. First a CBS affiliate, then an independent, it eventually went back to network status. Shakeups in the newsroom are inevitable during such turmoil. Friends who were no longer on the inside knew that Karen O'Leary was vulnerable. She wasn't over the hill by any means, but she wasn't a fresh-faced kid anymore, either.

Mary Kay Letourneau came along at a time when it benefited the veteran reporter, too. The story gave Karen— rather, she *took* it—a high-profile case at the right time. And though she had a résumé of important Seattle stories a mile long, the teacher-and-student saga was like nothing she'd broadcast before. It had sex, a pretty perpetrator, a boy who said he wasn't a victim, and inquiring minds wanted to know.

It gave Karen the vehicle she needed to prove herself to new management. And she worked it to death.

"That story has made her career," said a close friend several months after it all happened. "It saved her at KIRO."

Later, Karen O'Leary would downplay the importance of the Letourneau story. It was only one of many that she covered during that time. The pastor of the state's largest church had been caught in a purported homosexual encounter in a public restroom was another, so was the prominent plastic surgeon who had been charged with assaulting a patient. But even Karen had to concede that none caught the public's attention more than the teacher from Shorewood Elementary.

"Yes, my news director wanted stories about Mary Letourneau," she said later. "Yes, ratings go up whenever she's on. But that's not why I did the stories. I pay no attention to ratings and never have. If two people watch or two hundred thousand watch, I don't care. But I have bosses who care."

FORTY-SEVEN

SOME OF THE teachers at Shorewood Elementary felt they were in an emotional battle zone without a general, much less a sergeant, in command. It seemed that after the big to-do of the arrest—a four-member crisis team of counselors, the promise of supporting teachers through the difficult time, and the ensuing media firestorm—for the most part district support vanished. The superintendent never came back.

Said one teacher embittered by the abandonment: "They brought the whole group in that first day to tell us and the children and we did not see them once after that. We never heard from Nick Latham. We never heard from

Susan Murphy. We never heard from a single person.''

District PR guy Latham later took issue with the notion that he hadn't offered ongoing support.

''We gave the teachers every opportunity to share their feelings with us,'' he said. ''I called the school and talked to [Principal] Anne Johnson many times about offers to help. I went through proper channels—through the principal and administration. It is possible, however, that the information didn't get to the teachers.''

The beleaguered teachers had been left to their own devices, while Highline administrators and others seemed to bask in the eye of the television camera. Nick Latham fielded inquiries from media outlets all over the world. Highline Education Association President Susan Murphy taped a segment of Dan Rather's *48 Hours* on CBS. Even Highline superintendent Joe McGeehan got in on the act: he appeared on NBC's *Leeza*.

One person was missing in action on the PR front. Shorewood Principal Dr. Anne Johnson didn't pose for pictures or appear on television. In fact, the principal kept a very low profile—even among her staff. Yes, the somewhat aloof, petite woman with the cropped hair appeared shaken, but as the days passed some contemplated if she was just upset for being caught with a mess in her own backyard. And even more troubling, as additional information was revealed to colleagues, some were left to wonder just how much their principal knew in the first place. Had Anne Johnson been made aware that Highline security had been alerted about the marina incident in June 1996? Had there been parent complaints?

No one knew. Anne Johnson wasn't talking. Her only public remarks appeared in the district newsletter.

''If anybody had known anything, why hadn't they come to me about it?'' Dr. Johnson wrote when the wound was still fresh.

But teachers *had*. Even though none ever had the slightest inkling that Mary Letourneau was engaging in any kind of sexual activities with a district student—and most assuredly would have turned her in to the police in an instant if they had—they had noticed and complained about other behaviors in the past.

Dr. Johnson also defended the district against some teachers' charges that they had been left to fend for themselves on the front lines. She said the administration was very aware of what was going on at Shorewood.

"She wasn't giving the teachers any information unless they asked about it. Food and cards came from different schools so we knew people were concerned but we never had support or concern from the district, not once," said a teacher from Shorewood.

And they needed support in the most desperate way. They had children crying in class because of the stress of losing the beloved teacher in such a stunning and public way. Others acted out because they were mad at the replacement the district had hired. For a time, even the parents picked at the wound.

"One father said of the substitute that she was fine, but she was no Mary Kay Letourneau," recalled a teacher. "Thank God she was no Mary Kay Letourneau."

The goal of the Shorewood teacher group was to just get through the day and do their best to make sure that the children received the best education possible. No matter what had been disclosed that day—and every day seemed to bring another tawdry revelation—the teachers numbly went about their duties. When 9:05 arrived and the kids would come in, they'd put on a different face and pretend that nothing about Mary Kay Letourneau mattered at all.

"Trying," one said, "to protect the kids from being hassled."

The media intrusion was a hindrance to the educational process in ways that no school should have to endure. The media that was camped out on the street had been ordered to stay away from students.

"They could step on the sidewalk, but not one foot on the lawn," recalled a teacher.

But they tried. They followed kids. They shadowed teachers as they walked into the building. Their satellite trucks sprang like oversize toadstools all along the street in front of Shorewood. One second-grader came up to her teacher and pointed out the window to the television vans lined up.

"So we had this impromptu lesson. What's a good time to be on TV and what's not a good time to be on TV? What do people say when they don't want to talk? No comment. That's what you need to say."

It upset the Shorewood teachers when Mary Letourneau's class photo and another taken by a teacher at camp found their way into the pages of magazines and newspapers. They were outraged when they learned that the district had given permission for their use. *Weren't students supposed to be protected?*

Further irony came later when a national magazine published the class photo and only Vili Fualaau's image had been blurred to protect *his* privacy.

None of the other students had their identity obscured in any way.

"I'm surprised no parent sued the district. I would have," said one Shorewood teacher.

Instead of making matters better, the counselor at the school inadvertently fanned the flames, according to a teacher who witnessed her "approach" to the crisis.

"Our own counselor was more of a problem," said the teacher.

The counselor went before the students of room 39 and asked questions that led to nothing but pain for the woman who was trying to salvage the school year for the group abandoned by their beloved teacher's arrest.

"What did you love about Mrs. Letourneau?" the young woman asked.

The kids piped up with a litany of praise. She was fun. Pretty. Let them do what they wanted. Lots of art. Music. Fun.

"What do you hate about Mrs. [new teacher]?"

The kids didn't volunteer anything, so the counselor prodded them.

"Is there anything you are doing in class that you don't like? Is there anything that Mrs. [new teacher] is doing that you don't like?"

Finally the words came.

"I don't see why we have to . . ."

Other voices joined in, as the kids complained about

the new order under Mary's replacement. The lessons. The extra work. All of it.

Later, when the kids in the class had left for the day, a dumbfounded teacher who had witnessed the exercise berated the counselor for turning the students against the substitute teacher. *How was that going to help the students move on?* Other techniques at healing the wounds of the scandal only served to anger the remaining teachers even more. It particularly miffed some teachers when the counselor allowed Mary Letourneau's students to keep a notebook of the articles written about the "love affair" between teacher and student. The kids were told they could look at the contents of the binder any time they wanted— even when class was in session.

FORTY-EIGHT

SHE NEVER SAID it out loud because it would have hurt her friend so much. But the idea spun circles in Michelle Jarvis's head when she made her first trip to Seattle a day after Audrey was born. Where was someone, *anyone*, from Mary Kay's family? It was Michelle who had the duty of bringing Mary Kay home with her newborn daughter.

Where's her support system? she asked herself. I can't believe that I'm it. I'm the only one.

If ever someone needed the love of a family, it was Mary Kay. She had been arrested, lost her job, run out of money, and was alone. Her four other children were dispatched to live in Alaska, Washington, D.C., and Tempe, Arizona, with relatives. Her hostile husband, living with his cousins in Bonney Lake, was around enough to make things as uncomfortable as possible. And all Mary Kay had was Michelle Jarvis and Beth Adair. Mary Kay spent the first night out of the hospital with Beth, the music teacher from Shorewood. She hadn't wanted to spend the first night at home alone. Michelle came up and drove her to Normandy Park the next day.

The house was a mess. The kitchen floor was so dirty,

it could have been plowed. Boxes were everywhere. Michelle cleaned up, filled the refrigerator, and made casseroles for the freezer. She tried to put some order back in Mary Kay's life. Things had slipped so far in the months since she became involved with the mystery student. Or had they? Michelle reminded herself that the only glimpses she'd had of Mary Kay's life with Steve in Seattle had been school pictures, and the orchestrated photographs of the family dressed in matching sweaters in front of a perfect Christmas tree nestled in a drift of gorgeously wrapped packages.

This place was not only in utter disarray, it was dangerous, too. Carpet tack strips had been left along the walls and in the doorways from the day the Letourneaus decided they wanted to refinish the hardwood floors. When Michelle stepped on the tacks for the second time, she asked Mary Kay how she could live like that.

Mary Kay shrugged it off. It wasn't a problem.

"What about your kids? You let them run around the house like this?"

"Oh, they learn to avoid stepping on it."

Michelle was astonished. A mother of three, she wouldn't have dreamed of leaving such a hazard and having such a cavalier attitude about it. It would have taken only a couple of hours to pry off the most dangerous tacks. But Steve and Mary Kay hadn't bothered.

"There were other things that were much more important." she said later. "Which is kind of the Schmitz mentality. You keep up appearances at all cost."

One other thing surprised and worried Michelle during her stay at the house in Normandy Park. Steve Letourneau was still around. Mary Kay had led her childhood friend to believe that Steve had already left the residence. But during the week that Michelle was there, Steve returned several times and each time tension filled the air. Mary Kay repeated her concern that she feared additional rage when "he saw . . . the black hair, and the olive skin . . ." And at one point, Steve's anger at the situation and his apparent hatred for his wife frightened Michelle enough to pick up the phone and threaten to call the police.

In many ways Mary Kay was her own worst enemy. Maybe it had always been that way. But her defiance of the court order stipulating no contact with Vili troubled Michelle. Yes, Michelle could concede, the two had feelings for each other, but "feelings" wasn't enough. Whenever Mary Kay got off the phone with Vili, Michelle met her with an icy stare and a word of warning.

"You are playing with fire and you better knock it off."

Mary Kay didn't care. She was going to do what she wanted to do. She deserved it. It was her chance at happiness.

"She ignored me, like she always does," Michelle told a friend later.

After a week of cooking, cleaning, and worrying, Michelle took Mary Kay and Audrey to a restaurant for a last meal together. After they ate, they watched the sun set and sipped Grand Marnier. Audrey slept soundly and Michelle told her friend she thought she had been blessed with such a good baby. Both cried as they said their good-byes. Mary Kay trusted that she'd never go to jail, and in time, the whole problem would be sorted out.

"I'll be all right," she said.

There was a hole in the neighborhood when the Letourneau kids were gone—and never coming back. Ellen Douglas was left with the difficult task of supporting her son and daughter through a crisis that had reached out and abruptly snatched their best friends. She knew how tough Mary Kay's arrest had been on her son and daughter, but she knew that whatever their pain and confusion it had to be a billionfold for Steven, Mary Claire, Nicholas, and Jackie. With Audrey's birth and their parent's divorce inevitable things had to feel very unsettling.

Ellen would never forget how excited ten-year-old Mary Claire had been on the phone because she and her siblings were going to Washington, D.C., to go to school— and they were leaving right away. They'd be living with their Aunt Liz. After school was let out, they'd be visiting other relatives, including their father's in Alaska.

I'm sure this is cool, Ellen thought as she listened to

Mary Claire burble on about the new school without a clue about what was to come, but there's something going on that you haven't allowed to sink in. Life as you know it is falling apart . . .

Ellen's daughter, Jennifer, didn't get it completely, either. When Audrey was born the little girl asked her mother if they could go see the baby. Ellen knew it was important for Jennifer to see Audrey because the infant was her daughter's best friend's new baby sister. The difficulty for Ellen was the fact that she was a schoolteacher in the Highline District and she saw the pain that had resulted there—because of Mary Kay's relationship with her former student.

Concern for her daughter won out. Ellen picked out a lovely little outfit as a baby gift and the pair went down the street.

Cradling her newborn, Mary Kay welcomed mother and daughter inside. The house was eerie in its emptiness. Boxes and cartons bordered walls smudged by children who no longer lived there. A child's easel and plastic pool had been left behind in the carport. Talk centered on the baby's delivery with no mention of the disintegrating family or the acts that caused it.

"We knew someone was there," Ellen said later, "because she was not allowed to be alone. That was what the law said. She told us that it was her friend from California. We never saw the person. We were there twice. She said her friend was sleeping. The other time the shower was running the whole time we were there."

Ellen later wondered if Mary Kay really had someone there, or if perhaps someone who wasn't supposed to be there was hiding out waiting for the visitor to leave.

Not long after Audrey was born, Mary Kay called Amber and Angie Fish to see if they could watch her newborn. She was required by the court to participate in some evaluations and treatment—and she wasn't happy about it. The twins were elated about the prospect of seeing the baby, partly because they loved Mary Kay, but also because their

mother was so convinced that Audrey wasn't Steve Letourneau's.

Mary Kay was running late when she breezed into the
condo. Her baby was in an infant carrier hidden by a blanket.

"Audrey's asleep," she said, dropping the diaper bag.
"Here's her formula. She should sleep for a while."

Then she left, leaving the baby covered up.

Amber would never forget that visit and how she and
her sister were dying to take a look under the blanket. "We
were all peeking under the blanket, but no one wanted to
touch it. The minute she walked out the door, 'Oh my
God!' "

There was Audrey, an adorable baby with a cap of black
hair. Audrey didn't look anything like Steve, or even Mary
Kay, for that matter. The girls wondered if the baby's father had been black.

With the coast clear and the moment too good to resist,
Amber got out the video camera.

"To show my mom," she said later.

The girls called a few friends to tell them about the
baby's coloring.

"Can I come over to see Mary Kay's baby?"

When Mary returned later, the girls hedged about what
they really wanted to ask, and commented on Audrey's
black hair.

"Doesn't she just have the greatest, darkest hair?" she
said.

"Yes," Amber said. "What is she?"

Mary didn't bat an eye. "Samoan," she said. "Her
middle name is Lokelani."

The girls were still in shock, and later were unable to
recall what Lokelani meant, though Mary explained the
name's meaning and how it was perfect for her daughter.

Neither did Mary say who the father was. She said nothing about the boy, whom she still did not name for the
girls.

For as long as the Fish twins had known Mary Kay and
Steve Letourneau, they had been on a quest for the perfect

couch. The one they had in Carriage Row was typical of
many young couples—before a house full of children—it
had once been white, but after time it turned an unseemly,
dull gray. Of course at the Normandy Park address, such
a battered sofa would never do. Mary Kay told the twins
that she had finally found her dream piece of furniture and
special-ordered a custom fabric. It was a floral tapestry
with some pinks and blues and even some yellows. It
wasn't cheap. Before it was shipped, Mary Kay said the
furniture maker had told her that so many people commented on the unprecedented use of that fabric and how
it came together with the style of the couch so magnifi-
cently. "They couldn't believe it," she said.

"She was in love with the thing," Angie Fish said later.

Good thing. For the summer of 1997, the sofa-sleeper
was Mary Kay's home base. She arranged it at an angle
in the den, a small carpeted room that had three exits and
clear sight lines to outside of the house, the front door,
and the hallway. The room was dominated by sliding glass
doors to the patio. She never closed the sofa—the hide-a-
bed was never hidden.

"Everything was around her bed," Amber recalled.
"Diapers, dirty diapers sitting there and she didn't get up
to throw them away. She just kind of tossed them to the
side."

A constantly ringing phone in one hand, caller ID box
at the ready, the remote control for the television in the
other hand, Mary Kay sat at her command post. She was
in a foxhole at the center of a storm of her own creation,
and she seemingly loved every minute of it. She told the
girls she used the caller ID to screen her calls, because a
few "weirdos" were phoning and offering their support.
They told her that they understood her because they had
once loved what the law had forbidden, too.

"I'm not sick like that," she said. "They think I'm on
their level. I'm not one of them."

Drifts of mail blanketed every surface of the room. A
little hate mail, but mostly supportive missives. One time
Mary Kay pulled out a letter she said had been written by

the students of her sixth-grade class. She became teary-eyed as she read each loving word.

During each of her visits, Amber Fish couldn't help but notice notes and lists written by Mary Kay and scattered throughout the house. Most were directed toward David Gehrke and concerned areas that needed addressing for her defense. But she also posed questions better suited for a fortune-teller than a lawyer.

"When will Vili and I be back together? What will happen to Vili? Why can't Vili and I be together?"

The little notes were familiar to the Fish sisters. When they baby-sat for Mary Kay at the condo, the girls frequently saw little lists and notes that Mary Kay had used to organize herself and her thoughts.

"She was always a list maker," Angie said later.

Though she faced a more formidable adversary in the form of the King County prosecutor's office, Mary Kay focused much of her bitterness on her estranged husband. She was angered by the way friends and neighbors and then the public had taken his side by showing sympathy for the man now raising the kids on his own in Alaska. Mary Kay thought "the image" was a whole lot of baloney. At first, she refused to say much against him other than express her disdain for his smugness and holier-than-thou demeanor. Every once in a while, however, she would lift the curtain slightly to expose what had been a very unhappy marriage and a philandering husband.

"Well, there's a lot more here than you know," she told Amber Fish one day at the house. "Steve isn't all perfect, you know."

Amber knew that. No one was. But as far as she could tell from where she was standing without a father, Steve Letourneau was one terrific dad. He had worked hard to support his family, he played with his children, and he pretty much did whatever Mary Kay told him to do. She, not he, was always the force in charge of their household at Carriage Row. Amber assumed things were the same at Normandy Park.

But like a dripping faucet that no wrench could remedy,

Mary Kay kept dropping hints until hints turned into
shocking disclosure. She told the twins how he had beaten
her when she was pregnant. Neither Angie nor Amber
could really believe it.

"Steve was never violent," Amber said sometime later.
"We lived in that condo for years and you could hear the
disposal running and we never could hear them fighting.
You didn't even hear raised voices. Those walls were paper thin."

Mary Kay told the Fish twins that Steve had cheated
on her. In fact, she claimed he fathered a baby with a
girlfriend before Audrey was born.

"It's a boy," she claimed. "The mother is telling her
husband that the baby is his, but it's not. I guess they look
enough alike."

The teenagers couldn't believe their ears.

Not Steve. Not Steve of all people, they thought.

Though she talked mostly of Audrey, Mary Kay also
spoke of her oldest children. It was Steven, Mary Claire,
Nicky, and Jackie who were suffering the most, having
been yanked like rag dolls from their mother. Mary Kay
felt Steve was doing his best to make sure that her oldest
children were excised from her life. Forever. She was convinced that he was tossing her letters into the trash. Screen-
ing her calls so the kids wouldn't have the opportunity to
talk with their mom.

Sobbing uncontrollably, Mary Kay told Amber about a
phone call she had managed to place to the children when
Steve wasn't around to intercept it.

"The minute Jackie got on the phone she started
screaming. It was like a scream that she was being mur-
dered, like a scream I never heard . . . she wouldn't stop
screaming because I wasn't there . . ."

Amber started to cry, too.

*No baby should be taken from her mother. It wasn't
right.*

There were times when Mary would talk about her
plans to regain visiting rights. She told the girls that her
lawyers were going to fix it so that Steve couldn't live out

of state. They'd have to live close enough to their mother so that she'd be able to take care of them.

If she thought that she could do all of that, she sometimes let doubt creep in. Mary Kay was smart enough to know a losing battle. And she knew she had caused it.

"I made a big mistake that hurt my family," she often said, "but I never would change it. I ruined my family. I'm hurting those I love."

Amber and Angie both knew that Mary Kay meant every word she uttered. There was no fix for the mess— not when she felt so strongly that her love with the boy was worth it all. The love with the boy was forever.

Audrey Lokelani was more than the daughter of Mary Kay Letourneau and Vili Fualaau. The baby with the dark eyes and black hair was also a sibling to Mary's four children by Steve. The adults on both the Schmitz and Letourneau sides did whatever they could to ensure that whatever impact this new baby would have on its mother, it would not ruin the lives of the four already born.

All were in apparent agreement with the strategy, which included not talking about it and, heaven forbid, not promoting the fact that there was a new sibling back at their olive-green house in Normandy Park.

"Mary Kay's sister Liz was very upset when they found a picture of Audrey that Mary Kay had sent back East for Mary Claire's birthday. Her sister was very unhappy. 'I should have screened it. I should have made sure that something like that never got through.' "

But Audrey *was* Mary Claire's sister and she knew it. True sisterhood would take time, and who knew what words were said to make the kids feel differently, but a closeness would happen. Yet on the day of her great-granddaughter's birthday even Nadine had to admit later: "Mary Claire was happy because she had a baby sister."

And back in the house in Normandy Park, in the bathroom where the family of six all used to converge in morning and evening chaos, Mary Kay, Vili, and Audrey posed in front of the mirror and took a photograph. The flash burned a bright hole in the center of the image, leaving only the tops of their heads to their eyes.

"We didn't know it then," Mary Kay later said, "but it was the only family portrait we'd ever take."

FORTY-NINE

ONE DAY INTO the summer when Angie and Amber were over helping Mary Kay take care of Audrey at the Normandy Park house, she stopped referring to the baby's father as "the boy."

"I guess I can tell you his name. Promise not to say anything to anyone?"

They agreed.

"Vili," she said.

"Billy?" one of the girls asked.

"No. Vili with a V."

She retrieved some pictures from another room and showed them to the sisters. They had done this with Mary Kay before; in fact, the girls considered it something that Mary Kay loved to do. She was forever looking at her children's pictures and remarking on their physical features and whose side of the family was represented in their noses, mouths, hands, eyes.

She pulled out a picture of Vili standing next to Steven and Mary Claire by the swing.

"This is really bad," she said, as if apologizing. "He's a lot older-looking now."

Angie studied the photo. The boy was taller than Steven was, but not by much. When she heard he was Samoan, both she and her sister thought he was going to be some monster of a guy—six-feet-four and 240 pounds. But he wasn't a linebacker type at all. At five feet two inches, he was lanky and gawky—and four inches shorter than Mary Kay.

He was just a boy. The way she had described him, he was really big for his age.

Mary Kay went on to tell the sisters about how she had

wanted to get him into Cornish, a Seattle school for the arts. He interviewed and showed his portfolio there the summer she became pregnant. He was so talented and mature for his age.

From the photograph, they couldn't see any of it.

It was also the first time Mary Kay came out and acknowledged the obvious. The baby was Vili's. Although from that first look Amber and Angie knew it wasn't Steve Letourneau's child, they never asked and she never said anything.

She also pulled out some pictures of Soona.

"I can't tell who Audrey looks more like. Do you think she looks like...?" She studied the photograph and looked at her baby. "She could have gotten this dark hair from my mother," she said.

And then she suggested something that the girls would never forget. It was so strange. Mary Kay wondered out loud if Audrey could have picked up her dark hair from Steve's mother, Sharon.

The girls thought that Mary Kay was "totally out there."

Steve's mother? What would she have to do with this baby?

Mary Kay could be glib and laugh at the silliness of the media being camped outside her door, while she cradled a fourteen-year-old boy's first daughter. But inwardly, the stress of the situation was taking its toll. Shortly after Audrey was born Mary Kay developed a rash on her face and consulted a dermatologist. Though the rash was barely visible, she was obsessed about it.

"Is it getting better? Is it getting better?" she asked over and over.

She also had fits of tears about her father's cancer. Her reaction was somewhat perplexing to the Fish twins. They too had known John Schmitz was battling cancer—and had been for some time. When Mary Kay first told them back at the condo, she was calm about it. Almost indifferent. All of a sudden the reaction was emotional.

"I don't want all these family stories coming out," she said, refusing to elaborate.

Only one of Mary Kay's children saw baby Audrey that summer and by then, of course, there was no hope that any of her children could be raised with her love child. Even before the baby was born it was inevitable that she would be a symbol of what had gone wrong with their parents' marriage. But she was also a sister.

Only Steven Letourneau, that summer between sixth and seventh grade, would see his baby sister.

Mary told Amber and Angie Fish about how she had picked up her oldest son at SeaTac Airport. Audrey was asleep in a car seat.

"You know Steven," she said, "he was awkward and hardly talked to me. I know he's very upset with me. I know he's very mad at me, but when I put his luggage in my trunk, I sneaked a peek at him as he lifted up the blanket and saw Audrey."

Mary Kay cried as she told the story.

When she got behind the wheel, Steven turned to her and said, "That's a cool little girl you have, Mommy."

The story made the twins cry. They felt so sorry for Steven and his siblings. Sorrier than they felt for Mary Kay and her mixed-up future. Steven, they felt, had an especially heavy cross to bear. Steven had been around Mary and Vili during the previous summer and fall.

"Steven knew. He knew from the beginning. He knew everything," Amber said later.

Ellen Douglas once called herself a "Que Sera Sera" type person. Stuff happens. It just does. The idea that a teacher and a student could fall in love was not so impossible for Ellen to understand. She could see how it might happen with one huge reservation. The age difference was too bizarre to accept. She just couldn't see it. Maybe in a high school setting, but not an elementary teacher and her young student.

Whenever she tried to rationalize what had happened between Mary Kay and Vili Fualaau, she always came back to the impact on the children involved.

She never considered Vili part of that group.

"That child was never a child like Mary Kay's son and my son," she told a friend. "That was not a little boy playing Legos and G.I. Joe [action figures] and wearing little Ninja costumes and running around the neighborhood like our two little boys were."

Vili Fualaau, as Ellen saw him, was not in the same league as other kids that shared his chronological age—at least none that she knew. It seemed that the seventh grader did what he wanted, whenever he wanted to. Obviously, with a father in prison, his family life was outside the norm of suburban Normandy Park kids. Since he was too young to drive, someone must have brought him over to the Letourneaus and left him there—at all hours and overnight. Ellen was convinced that members of the boy's family were aware that something was going on between Vili and Mary Kay.

"His family knew," she contended.

It also became apparent to Ellen and others that a true double standard was evident in the Mary Kay Letourneau saga. The fact that it was a woman perpetrator and a young male victim, though novel and shocking, probably had less lasting impact than if the roles had been reversed.

"A thirteen-year-old girl getting pregnant is a heck of a lot different physically than a thirteen-year-old boy getting someone else pregnant. The physical difference of what happens to that child's body is different. It is a double standard. We are not equal."

Introspection comes easily to a teenage girl's heart, but so does the willingness to believe in someone or something when the most obvious evidence points in another direction.

Katie Hogden had felt so very close to Mary and Vili and had seen the signs of their closeness—the looks, the fleeting touch of their hands—that she was not surprised later when she learned the two had been intimate or had "hooked up." It was always in the back of the sensitive girl's mind like a closed door, she later imagined when she tried to explain it. A door that she had chosen to leave locked and boarded up. Always there, but always hidden. For Katie, keeping that door closed probably meant never getting hurt.

Later, Katie considered that all that she believed had been going on was a teacher trying to save a boy from his family, his past, and a future that was dark and without room for all that he could be.

"She wanted to help him because he needed the help and she needed the help. He could help her and she could help him. And their souls just like matched. He was her best friend and she was his best friend. *Look at them talking . . . it was just perfect. Once-in-a-lifetime thing.*"

Steve Letourneau wanted the whole thing to end. His wife had flung their dirty laundry all over the country and the sooner it was put to rest, the better. He told his lawyer that while he wanted closure, he didn't want Mary Kay to go to jail. Greg Grahn told Steve that he doubted such an outcome from the very beginning. He was sure as a first-time offender she'd get a treatment program. Even so, he had doubts as the summer progressed that Mary Kay Letourneau was really a good candidate for any kind of special program. He told Steve that he doubted she was a threat to their children and that she was unlikely to be involved with any boy other than Vili.

Greg felt his client's wife had some kind of emotional problem that prevented her from remaining in control.

"It wasn't a love-at-first-sight type of thing. It was a drawn-out process where Mary Kay could have just drawn the line: 'You're a thirteen-year-old child and it's not going to happen.' "

Greg Grahn was also alarmed by Mary Kay's insistence that she was still in love with Vili. She appeared to be using love as a defense.

"Honesty is a defense of slander so love should be a defense of child molestation. 'You can't put me in jail, because I really do love him.' That's just not the way the law works."

FIFTY

SHE DREADED THE day that she'd pick up the phone and it would be Steve Letourneau calling. Even though Secret Squirrel Linda Gardner had done what she felt was right, she knew that her actions led to the breakup of her husband's cousin's home, happy or not. Such as it was. Kyle Gardner had been in contact with Steve not long after the arrest and he had kept his wife up-to-date.

But it wasn't until April that the phone rang at ten P.M. and Steve's voice was on the line. Fear overwhelmed her and her heart sank. Before she could say anything—and she didn't know what it would be anyway—Steve took up the slack on his end of the line.

"Linda," he said, "I just want to let you know that you got me out of this nightmare and I want to thank you for it."

Linda didn't know what to say.

"Yeah. You want to talk to Kyle?" she asked, before setting down the receiver and looking for her husband.

Over the next few days the two would talk more. Linda listening at first, then offering advice. She thought it was ridiculous that Steve was still living there with his pregnant-by-a-sixth-grader wife. And why was he staying? The place was being foreclosed. It wasn't as though he was going to be living there after the law did whatever it was going to do with his wife.

She understood from talking with Steve and Kyle that things were getting violent in Normandy Park.

"You've got to get out of the house," she said during one of their conversations that spring. "Come here and stay with us. If you don't you're going to get thrown in jail."

Steve finally admitted that Secret Squirrel was right. It would be better than hanging around while Mary Kay had her baby.

And while her own mother-in-law would not forgive

her, it seemed that once everything was out in the open among members of Steve Letourneau's family, Linda was not completely alone. Steve's mother and grandmother both made calls of support to thank her for taking care of the Mary Kay problem.

She knew Mary Kay and Steve hadn't kept the cleanest house. Linda Gardner recalled the time one of their children was missing at Carriage Row and it was discovered that the toddler had fallen asleep in a pile of debris on the sofa. Linda remembered tiptoeing through the clutter, but she didn't think that was as bad as what her husband Kyle described when he helped Steve Letourneau move from Normandy Park to their home in Bonney Lake just before Mary Kay had her baby. It wasn't just a case of packing boxes and moving them to storage. According to her husband, more than a half-dozen trips to the dump were necessary.

"They even threw away a couch," Linda said later. "Steve had absolutely nothing when he left that house. It was all trash. Kyle couldn't believe how bad it was."

And yet Steve and Mary Kay had always seemed so neat. Linda couldn't figure it out.

Something's not right. Not right with her. Not right with Steve. How can you be so filthy at home, but when you are around everybody you don't have a scrap of dirt on you . . . you're perfect?

She asked Steve about it not long after he moved in with the Gardners that spring.

"He told me that he would come home from work and he just gave up, because she would do nothing. She would not do any housework. They had a rat in the house. It was filthy. They lived in filth," she said later.

Linda didn't want to rub salt into the wound so she kept her mouth shut, but still she wondered, "How was Mary Kay going to bring this baby home to that house? How could these kids live like that?"

When things became more relaxed and she felt she could pry a little, Linda asked her houseguest why he didn't just boot his wife out the door when he confirmed the involvement with the boy.

Steve said he just couldn't. Too many people were involved and he was afraid. He didn't know what to do, how to handle it. He knew she'd go to prison.

"She's the mother of my children," he repeated.

That didn't wash with Linda.

"When she started having sex with someone the same age as her son, she gave up the right to be the mother of your children," she retorted.

Later, when Linda would try to describe Steve's state of mind at the time, he was so wishy-washy, so noncommittal, that it was impossible.

"I think that he thought that possibly this would go away and they would be living their lives," she said.

Over the course of the next few days and weeks, the story would unfold and Linda would become increasingly satisfied that she had done the right thing. Steve said Mary Kay had admonished their children to keep quiet about Vili's overnight visits.

"If you tell anybody, Mommy will go to prison."

He showed copies of the love letters he had found.

"So here we are. We had a dream—it was a once upon a time—fairy tale story about two people that were meant to become one—and did."

In one missive, Mary Kay lamented how she couldn't show her love for Vili in public, couldn't call him, couldn't show off their devotion to each other . . .

"But each day something new happens to me and I always want to tell you . . ."

Linda later described some of the letters as depicting Mary Kay and Vili as lovers from another plane, another dimension, and another time. God, they believed, had a plan for them and that plan included a baby. Linda thought the notes were "twisted" and "sick."

"I also told them that this wasn't just sex and an accidental baby."

Later, Linda fumed about the letters: "She knew that this baby would keep them together forever. They set out to make this love child. He was talking about how he loved her, how they were destined to be together and her letters were the same.''

Steve talked about phoning Mary and John Schmitz to tell them what was going on with their daughter long before she was arrested.

"They wanted to get Mary Kay out of Washington and moved to Washington, D.C., but she wouldn't do it,'' Linda recalled Steve telling her. "Her mother wouldn't talk to her—totally wrote her off. The dad came out and brought her a car. Then he went back and the parents were not supportive of her at all.''

In time, Linda would piece together what she thought was the real reason why Steve passively sat by as his wife got involved with a student. He was busy with his own affairs. He even fathered a child with one of his flings. And Linda in her best Secret Squirrel mind-set figured that Mary Kay hung that over his head and threatened him.

"If you tell, if you leave, I will let everybody know about all this stuff.''

And there was Kelly Whalen, too. Kelly, the flight attendant from Alaska Airlines, was the woman with whom Steve was planning his post–Mary Kay future. He talked about Kelly and how wonderful she was and how he couldn't have made it through the ordeal without her. He told Linda they had met on a trip to Puerto Vallarta. He didn't tell her what was going on with his wife, but he wanted out of his loveless marriage.

"I don't agree with him having an affair,'' Linda said later. "If my husband ever had one, I'd pull a Lorena Bobbitt on him.''

A girlfriend of Mary Kay Letourneau's who went to the Shorewood open house in the fall of 1996 witnessed a slightly hostile exchange between a man—possibly another teacher—and Mary Kay. She told Linda about it later. According to the friend, she was in the classroom when the man walked up to Mary Kay and said, "You are getting way too close to Vili.''

Then he walked off.

*   *   *

Whenever they met at his Tacoma office or talked on the phone, divorce lawyer Greg Grahn always found Steve Letourneau to be true to form in one critical regard. Steve remained entrenched in his position that he wouldn't get caught up in the blame game that had been a part of the Mary Kay Letourneau saga from day one. Yes, he was pissed off at his wife for dumping him for a kid. Without a doubt, he was humiliated and bitter, but deep down there was some guilt. Pointing the finger at his dewy-eyed wife was not a good strategy. It only made Steve Letourneau look like a bully kicking her when she was down.

"He couldn't exempt himself from it one hundred percent, anyway," Greg Grahn said later. "So rather than trying to figure out what percentage is his and what percentage is Mary Kay's, he doesn't want to blame Mary Kay in public."

He had played a part in what happened, and despite what his critics would say, Steve Letourneau knew it.

"You know," he admitted to his lawyer, "I could have done things that could have stopped this."

But Steve wasn't paying attention or he was burying his head in the sand during the months his wife carried on with Vili Fualaau. Maybe he was too wrapped up in what he was doing with his girlfriend to step in and save his wife and family from the inevitable ruin? Hindsight was a killer, and Steve knew it. According to his lawyer, Steve had seen "hundreds of things" that indicated what had really been going on with Mary Kay and Vili.

"He just refused to believe it back then," Greg Grahn said. "He feels bad about it. He blames himself a little bit for that."

FIFTY-ONE

FOR SUSAN MURPHY, the president of the Highline Education Association, the day Mary Letourneau moved out of her classroom brought a combination of sadness and disbelief. It was a Saturday, not long after Audrey's birth,

that brought Mary, her newborn, and her friend Beth
Adair, along with Susan and a school district security official, to Mary's old classroom at Shorewood Elementary.

As for Mary, she had come full circle, returned to the
scene of what some considered a crime, the place where
she said she fell in love with a boy. For the others there
to oversee and help the stroller-toting former teacher, it
was the end of what had been considered a promising career.

Mary had been instructed after her baby arrived that she
would need to remove all of her belongings from her old
classroom. Other than a few books, very little of her personal effects had been sent to her after she was arrested.
Susan Murphy was on hand to represent Mary, who was
still on the district payroll—though most doubted it would
last much longer.

Susan had been told that Mary had "a couple of boxes"
to pick up. Mary arrived with her baby in the Audi Fox
that her father had brought to her before Audrey's birth.

It was apparent that her vehicle would not hold all she
had left behind in room 39.

"It wasn't a couple of boxes," Susan Murphy recalled
later. "It was closets full of stuff. Tons of projects, props
from plays. Several closets within the classroom were
overflowing with belongings that the district did not wish
to store any longer." The HEA president figured if she
were the teacher leaving that classroom, say to go to another school, she would have marched three fourths of
what they were hauling out over to the jaws of an awaiting
Dumpster. Mary wanted everything. Every scrap, every
project.

It bewildered Susan and she had to bite her tongue to
avoid what she wanted to say.

*What are you thinking? Where are you going to put all
this stuff?*

Mary, upbeat and excited, wanted it all.

"She was kind of childlike," Susan later said of Mary's
behavior in the classroom. "I didn't get a sense that she
understood the severity of the situation. She'd wander from

one thing to the next, she was sort of disorganized, kind of wandering around in circles . . .''

While the group sifted through Mary's belongings and pressed on with the business at hand, Susan came across a pink detention slip with the name Vili Fualaau. She put it in one of the boxes without saying a word. Susan also got a clue about how the children in the classroom were feeling toward Mary and her successor. Inside a drawer she found notes disparaging Mary's replacement: *"So and So Sucks! I hate So and So!"*

Mary went from one item to the next, exclaiming interest and recalling memories that came to mind as she boxed up student projects. She had a kind word for everyone and everything associated with the remnants of all that had once mattered.

When the mountain grew larger, Susan called her husband to bring his car to provide more packing room. Half a day had passed before it was time to caravan over to Normandy Park, unload, and put that sorry episode behind them.

Late spring in the Puget Sound region brings a burst of growth and incessant rain, and in a week's time lawns can be overgrown—with no dry days in sight to mow. But that was not the case at 21824 Fourth Place S. The Letourneau home stood out from the others in the tidy neighborhood. Its lawn was overgrown and dandelions were rampant. Susan Murphy felt another pang of sorrow for Mary and her family. Though she could never dismiss the professional breach of trust and responsibility that Mary had blatantly and seemingly cavalierly forsaken, somehow Susan held some hope that Mary and Vili's story was truly one of a deep and undying love. Even though it was as wrong as could be—and there was no way to make it right in her mind—she allowed herself to hold out some hope for a somewhat happy ending. Susan didn't really buy into it, but even so she hoped for it anyway. Otherwise, she knew, all of this was for nothing.

Mary skittered about the half-empty house and announced that she'd spend some of her free time going through each and every item. She thanked everyone for their concern and help.

Susan Murphy will never forget the sadness she felt for Mary Kay Letourneau, her new baby, her husband, her children, and, because she had devoted her life to it, too, the teaching career that she had squandered.

Years later, that Saturday at Shorewood still brought a sigh from Susan Murphy.

"She was never going to teach again. Her certificate had been revoked. Unless she went somewhere where they didn't care about having one. Or for some strange reason they had never heard of her . . . that would be pretty incredible. Antarctica, maybe?"

When teachers at the school heard Mary's things were finally gone, they were both relieved and a little angry. They saw her tardiness in retrieving her things as more than just putting something off because it was painful. It was about power.

"She didn't come back until *after* the baby was born, which personally I felt was a little game with her that the kids would know her stuff was still there and she was in charge," said one Shorewood teacher.

Mary Kay wouldn't have given a single thought to the Shorewood teachers after she left the school with her belongings. She had a bigger problem. She told friends that she thought that King County Police Detective Maley had it in for her. It was personal, Mary told a friend later.

"They were all saying that it was some kind of a Hitlerian mentality going on. That I had sought out a genius in order to give me a better baby than Steve could. Pat Maley was behind that. *What was with her?* I couldn't figure it out for the longest time until David [Gehrke] told me to consider that something was going on between us, woman to woman.

"I've encountered this before in my life, I won't say 'jealousy', but something like that. Resentment. Here I was with the love of my life, and I'm living on the water in Normandy Park, and she's this pockmarked detective living in SeaTac somewhere by the airport. And she will never, ever get to Normandy Park and I have. Never."

And for that, no matter what her motives, Pat Maley would probably be eternally grateful.

FIFTY-TWO

A TURNING POINT for Amber and Angie Fish came a few weeks after Audrey was born. From that rainy night in late February when they first tried to comfort Mary Kay to their baby-sitting excursions to Normandy Park after Audrey was brought home from the hospital, Mary Kay didn't let on about her true feelings for her former student.

But then she started to refer to Vili Fualaau more frequently. She started to tell the girls that she was in love with him and he was in love with her. They had wanted to make a family. And, against all odds, she was going to do everything in her power to prove it to those against the idea.

"I remember her talking about it," Amber said later. " 'Yeah, it's like *Romeo and Juliet*' and I asked her what she meant and she said, 'You know we're forbidden to be together, and I hope it doesn't end up like that.' "

Amber knew how *Romeo and Juliet* ended. *Was Mary Kay suggesting a suicide pact?*

When Mary Kay started speaking of the relationship with her student as a love story, it was such a departure from what the twins understood that they found it hard to process. They had seen the media accounts on television and read some of the legal papers scattered around the house. They knew there was a difference between a love affair and a crime. They also didn't believe Mary Kay was the criminal type. All of it was confusing.

"We really didn't know what to think," Angie said later.

Although the girls thought of Mary Kay more as a peer than an adult figure, they didn't try to dissuade her from her impossible plans. There was no point in going against her.

"I never thought it would come to the point where she'd go to jail. We just kind of blew it off. We never agreed with her, but the way she was saying, 'I'm never going to jail.' The way she talked about everything, rolling her eyes about everything. It made it seem that it was not that big a deal. It was coming from her . . . so we didn't think it was a big deal," Amber said later.

Amber Fish had a good memory and when she learned that Mary Kay had been involved with a boy that she had taught in second and sixth grades, she flashed on an incident that took place four or five years earlier at Carriage Row.

"I can remember one day standing in her kitchen and she was telling us—she came home really late and I don't know if she was with him—but she was telling us the story about this little kid, an incredible artist. He was amazing, smart."

Amber wondered if this was the same child. Mary Kay had been so animated, so excited that night. Though it was true that Mary Kay was the type of woman who frequently showed enthusiasm for the world around her, this was different. The second-grade boy she was talking about had touched her deeply.

Though Mary Kay thought the world of this child, she never spoke of him again.

Later, when she thought about it, Amber Fish would bet money that boy she had talked about years before was the same one she had been accused of raping.

Amber and Angie knew that Mary Kay was not supposed to have any contact with Vili, but they were certain she broke that rule—though she never came out and confided that she had. There were occasions when she would whisper into the phone.

"The twins are here . . . I'll have to call you back."

A couple of times, the girls would later say, Mary Kay held the phone up to Audrey's little round face.

"Yeah, do you want to hear her?"

Those calls were more important than the others were, though they were often quite brief. Mary Kay didn't want to leave the house, partly because of the media mob, but also because she didn't want to miss any phone calls.

"She had her phone in her hand at all times. All of the diapers were around her, the remote control and caller ID in her hands the whole time."

How much had her great-grandchildren really seen of their mother's relationship with her sixth-grade student? It was a question Nadine had asked herself time and time again. She worried and wondered. She knew that Stevie, Jr., was certainly old enough to figure out what had been going on. In fact, she knew from conversations with Steve and Sharon that the boy had been out with his mother and Vili in the van at night.

"For a cover," she surmised later of Mary's insistence that her oldest accompany her and Vili on their nighttime excursions. "If Steven had questioned it, 'I had Stevie, Jr., with me, what could be going on?'"

A telephone conversation between Sharon and Nadine confirmed Stevie, Jr., was not the only one who knew what was going on.

As Sharon told it, Mary Claire burst into tears one day as she sat at her grandmother's kitchen bar.

"What's the matter? Did Grandma say something to hurt your feelings?"

The girl continued to cry. "I love my mom," she said. "But I don't want to love her because I know that she did bad things and I don't like what she did. But I'm supposed to love her because she's my mom. I saw her and Vili in bed together."

Sharon Hume was devastated by the disclosure.

"What was I going to tell the child?" Sharon said to her mother, Nadine. "We know your mom did wrong, but your mom is sick. We just have to wait to see how things turn out."

Later, Steve Letourneau's grandmother learned through his girlfriend Kelly Whalen that Stevie, Jr., saw his mother and Vili in the shower, but kept his mouth shut.

"She probably threatened him," the grandmother said later.

Later Nadine recalled a photograph that had been taken of the Letourneau children not long after they were separated from their mother. The great-grandmother didn't recognize Stevie and asked a family member who the boy was.

"Oh, my God, he looks like a zombie. He looks so withdrawn and pathetic. Couldn't believe it. It was Steven."

And as the weeks passed, cracks the size of the Grand Canyon emerged when it became apparent that things had been very ugly in Steve and Mary Kay's household. As if the sex stuff wasn't bad enough, Nadine learned there had also been physical violence. And while no woman deserved to be hit, if there was one who did, as Nadine viewed it, Mary Kay was a good candidate. Steve's grandmother wouldn't put up with any man backhanding her, but she felt Steve had done the right thing because he told her that he had no choice.

His story was that he was defending Mary Claire.

"He said the only time he ever laid a hand on her was when she was seven months pregnant and he shoved her because she was going to hit Mary Claire. 'You aren't laying a hand on her,' he said. She said, 'That's my child and I will if I want.' 'No, you won't.' He grabbed her by the arm and he shoved her back on to the davenport."

Steve, of course, didn't tell his grandmother about the purported altercation with the van in the driveway, the holes he allegedly punched in the walls.

FIFTY-THREE

NOTHING STEAMED MARY Kay more in the summer of 1997 than the visits with the psychologists who were trying to figure her out. Picking apart her brain, reexamining her childhood, dissecting her marriage. The whole concept of the treatment was absurd. She thought one woman used "brainwashing" and "concentration camp" techniques as she "tried to break me down to nothing."

"These people aren't helping me any," she told Amber and Angie Fish one afternoon when they were at Normandy Park helping her with Audrey. "I know what's good for me."

The treatment provider in Federal Way was particularly cruel. She reminded Mary Kay of Steve's mother with brown hair.

"She's the biggest bitch I've met in my life," Mary Kay said.

Amber felt sorry for Mary Kay. The way she had described some of the psychologists made them seem harsh and indifferent. Mary Kay needed understanding, not judgment.

"She said they were really cold and impersonal and she didn't like talking to them at all. So I felt bad that she had to go through that," she said later.

Angie later remembered how Mary Kay railed against the whole process.

"They were trying to feed her the right things to say and she didn't want to say the relationship was wrong. She hated it. She really believed she was right and the evaluators were telling her that she was wrong and it made her mad. She was really stubborn and wouldn't agree with them," the teenager recalled.

Mary Kay also hated the idea that Audrey couldn't come with her. Because of the nature of the child rape charges, she was ordered never to be alone with *any* of her children. No one expected her to molest her baby, but a rule was a rule. Mary Kay didn't care.

"I'll show them," she said in what had become typical defiance. "I'm going to bring her anyway."

One time she called the Fish twins from Federal Way and asked them to come to the evaluator's office. She had Audrey with her and the psychologist insisted that she be in someone else's care during their session. When the girls arrived and got Audrey, Mary Kay rolled her brown eyes.

"I'm trying to prove a point," she said. "I should be able to bring my baby with me."

The Fish twins understood Mary Kay's loyalty to her romance with Vili, but neither could understand why she wouldn't go along with the program in order to avoid incarceration.

Neither did the twins know how far her defiance of the program had gone.

"This little boy you've accused me of raping? Well, he's out in the car waiting for me and we're going to go off somewhere and do whatever we want to do," Mary Kay had wanted to blurt out during one treatment session, as she later told a friend.

The treatment providers pissed off Mary Kay. She thought they were mean-spirited and didn't care about anything but categorizing her as a pervert. They had stripped her down to the core. They had probed in every area of her sexual background so deeply that Mary Kay told a friend she thought she had detailed every sexual experience she'd ever had. They wrote it all down, shook their heads, and told her she was a sick woman. According to what Mary Kay told friends, the whole process was built on humiliation.

"You're going to admit what a sick woman you are!"

"You are going to tell your children that you're a pedophile!"

"If you see—even a picture—of a child, you'll report it!"

One time a woman carrying her baby arrived in the waiting room while Mary Kay sat until she was called in for her appointment.

"They told the lady she had to leave the room because Mary Kay was a sex offender and might hurt her child. To a woman who was carrying her infant, for God's sake," a friend recalled.

Mary Kay knew she was in trouble. The SSOSA program of treatment might keep her out of prison, but it was not a cakewalk by any means. *Some alternative.* She was trying to do what they wanted her to do, but her feelings for Vili hadn't changed. They weren't going to.

"Everything that she did just incriminated herself further and further and it gave the prosecution more ammunition against her. They were just telling her to do things that were doing nothing but burying her deeper," said Michelle Jarvis a year later.

But Mary Kay told them repeatedly that she would rather go to jail than sit through the evaluations.

That's really stupid, Angie thought.

FIFTY-FOUR

ANGIE AND AMBER thought healer Leslee Browning was a bit of a busybody, but she cut such a peculiar figure—all bells, spangles, and moonbeams—they couldn't hate her. All they could muster was a bit of eye-rolling and annoyance. Leslee, with her spiky, reddish "do," reed-thin legs, oversize eyeglasses, and deep, smoky voice, was well-known by folks at Carriage Row.

"She's the daughter of that 'natural products' gal, Natalie. You know, the one with the pots of plants stormtrooping out her front door."

Leslee Browning was in her mid-forties when she reconnected to Mary Kay Letourneau. The gossip line at Carriage Row had been rife with recollections and innuendo since it first became news that a former resident, a pretty, young mother of four, had lost her job as a schoolteacher by having an affair with one of her students.

Lines were drawn in a hurry. The Bendixes worked with Steve at Alaska Airlines and held down the side for the northern-exiled baggage handler; most of the women in the complex—including Leslee—were firmly in Mary's corner.

For Leslee Browning, however, Mary Kay was a woman of contradictions.

She was guarded and cold and effusive and outgoing.

"But I don't mean that in a derogatory way," Leslee said many years later, while fabric and plastic moons and

stars hung over her healing room—the back bedroom of
her mother's condo at Carriage Row. "I mean it in an
abused way."

Mary was unhappy with the Catholic church, yet she
made every effort to get her husband and kids there every
Sunday. She told Leslee that when she became a certified
teacher she'd never work for a parochial school, though
she had standing offers to do so. She'd *never* put her kids
in Catholic school, either. But after she left Carriage Row
that is exactly what she did.

"I was just floored when she sent those kids to Catholic
school. She had been so against it," Leslee said.

Even when Steven was just an infant, Mary Kay had a
difficult time adjusting to new people, maybe even to the
role of motherhood. People who saw the pretty blond
mother getting the mail would see a different person in the
confines of her own kitchen. They saw the shy smile, the
reserved presence of a mask.

"She did tell me at that time that she was unhappily
married and would do just fine without Steve."

As the years passed, it surprised Leslee that Mary Kay
and Steve Letourneau were able to hold it together as long
as they had. Unhappy marriages were a dime a dozen at
Carriage Row. Natalie Bates had failed in hers, as had her
daughter, Leslee. Fran Bedix, Teri Simmons's mother, was
making a go of her second time around. But there was
something about the Letourneaus.

The house was chaotic all the time with laundry strung
from the kitchen to the living room like a Maytag ticker-
tape parade, but when Mary Kay emerged from the front
door she was perfect. From her shoes to her hair, Mary
Kay was perfect. So were her children. Leslee Browning
never saw any of Mary Kay's children dressed in anything
less than catalog-perfect attire.

All the kids in the complex loved Mary Kay. The Fish
twins were often joined by Brooke, Leslee's daughter, as
the pretty young mother spread a craft project out on the
kitchen table or led the kids on a backyard nature walk.
After Steve went off to work, Mary would come outside

to play. When Steve was around his wife was more rigid, more self-controlled, soft-spoken.

When she was teaching, she shared a laugh about her housekeeping with Leslee.

"You know if I had a student like Steven and could see how they would live, I'd really have to have a talk with their parents—they're being dysfunctional."

Chaotic on the inside and perfect on the outside. That was Mary Kay.

"I think she's highly intelligent, but emotionally crippled. I think she had problems early on and she cracked."

Leslee Browning was a healer and psychic and had a business card to prove it. It was in that capacity that she first thought she'd reach out to former neighbor Mary Kay Letourneau to see how she was doing. She didn't care what the media had reported—though it was only the second week in March, there had been plenty of reports.

Maybe Mary could benefit from having someone care for her?

The voice on the other end of the line was Mary. Not a shattered, devastated Mary, but the upbeat woman who would spend all day and night on a papier-mâché project and look like a million bucks when she finished it.

Leslee asked how she was and Mary said she was doing all right, getting along in a tough time. Mary thanked her, and when Leslee offered to come to Normandy Park to give her a "healing," she agreed to the offer.

The house was a shambles, just as it had been at Carriage Row. Leslee offered to clean up the place, but Mary declined. When Leslee noticed a hole the size of a fist pushed through the wall, Mary sighed and said Steve had punched through the drywall.

The idea of Steve being violent was surprising. Leslee had never known him to show any kind of temper. Never. But she knew these were difficult times in the Letourneau household.

Mary settled onto her pride and joy, the new couch. She caught Leslee's eyes looking at the volumes of psychology books spread in small piles around the sofa. Mary pointed to them and said she had been doing some reading.

"I think I might fit the manic-depression diagnosis," Mary said, "so I'm going to look for somebody to diagnose me."

"Well, you know, Mary, I think what you need is to get through a counseling program."

Mary stiffened slightly, surprised at the remark.

"No," she said firmly. "I'll go to prison before I go through counseling."

"Everyone can benefit from some counseling."

Mary shrugged off the remark.

Leslee was convinced Mary's reluctance to get help had more to do with shame associated with events from long ago than the affair with the schoolboy.

She'd rather do anything then dredge up the past, Leslee thought.

She was also very protective of the baby's father, telling Leslee that she would "not have his name get into the news."

You're so smart, but you haven't a whit of common sense, Leslee thought. This is the nineties, we're talking talk television, the Internet city. They're gonna dig it up.

There were no tears. She was defiant. She had no clue where this was headed.

Leslee was mystified about Mary's father, not only his advice, but also the very fact that he had been alive to offer it. She thought he would have died years ago. Mary had told her that he had terminal cancer back when she was finishing up her degree at Seattle University. She remembered when her mother, Natalie, and Mary discussed natural products that might help buy John Schmitz more time, or even stop the cancer.

They visited a bit longer, Mary telling Leslee that she and Steve had talked with their priest, who agreed that a quiet divorce would be the best solution. Mary said that the plan called for shared custody of Steven, Mary Claire, Nicholas, and Jacqueline—though they would live with Steve for the school year.

"We wanted to keep this to ourselves," she said. "If it became public, it would ruin the lives of our children."

It was clear that she still hoped that the plan that had been put together by the priest would still work out. Leslee didn't have the heart to tell her that she thought it was too late.

Mary didn't reveal Vili's name; again choosing to preserve his privacy, she called him "the boy." She said she was close to the boy's parents. The relationship with the boy was real, deep and lasting.

"Why can't Steve just accept it?" she asked, still supine on the couch.

Leslee didn't have an answer, and Mary didn't allow for one. She went on to tell her about some writings that Steve had found.

"I made a mistake in leaving out my journal," she said, before correcting herself and adding, "But that really wasn't a mistake, I guess."

Mary was worried about her children. She told Leslee her sons and daughters were back East with her family. The children were all that kept her from running.

"If it weren't for them, I'd get on a plane and never come back," she said.

Years later, Leslee pointed out the irony of Mary's statement.

"She said she could not bear being in a place where she could not see her kids. Unfortunately, look what happened."

The healing took less than an hour. Mary closed her eyes as Leslee moved her hands slowly over her body while imparting her energy and soothing a broken soul. Mary fell asleep, as most of Leslee's clients do. It surprised Leslee. Mary was in dire straits—"the head of the school of hard knocks"—so that such complete relaxation would have been more difficult.

Leslee Browning and her mother, Natalie Bates, talked over coffee and tea in their cluttered kitchen at Carriage Row after the healing. Leslee was convinced that there had been a pattern of sexual abuse in Mary's life. Leslee could see it from her own personal experience, having survived sexual and physical abuse from a family member.

"Mary is the classic sexual-abuse child. Everything

she's doing. Maybe within the family, maybe within the church. I don't know why. She was so adamant about hating it . . . there was something that happened in the church or school.''

A couple of years later, Leslee remained troubled by those books and the bipolar diagnosis.

''There's a part of me in the gut that believes that the manic-depression part was researched on her part and she found someone to diagnose her. I'm not saying she's not manic, but it is weird. Maybe she was researching to see if she really was manic, but I don't know,'' she said.

FIFTY-FIVE

NONE OF HER friends were in her position—and none ever could be—but all were in agreement with the idea to dump her lawyers. Mary Kay waffled on the subject over the course of the summer of 1997. She was scared and isolated, sitting on her hide-a-bed in the house in Normandy Park. She didn't think David really knew what he was doing. She told friends that the only sex case that he'd ever handled concerned a father who raped and molested his daughter for six years. And he was basing her case on *that,* she said. Even so, she felt David's heart was in the right place.

It wasn't his heart that worried Kate Stewart. She was a bit more practical than her college friend was. She didn't want to see Mary Kay go down for the count and spend the rest of her life branded as some kind of sex pervert.

''What am I going to do?'' Mary Kay asked, phone pressed against her ear.

Kate was direct as always: ''You need a new lawyer.''

Like Michelle, though not to as great an extent, Kate had also gone to work to find a new solution for Mary Kay's legal troubles. She talked to other lawyers. Friends. Anyone with a germ of an idea about what could be done for Mary Kay.

"I don't think he's been telling you the whole truth about pleading guilty," she told Mary Kay during a phone call that summer. "Don't go there. Once you go there, you are eliminating so many other things that are possibilities that could help you later on."

Mary Kay wasn't sure. Her head was spinning and she told Kate that she was on overload. She wanted to trust David Gehrke to do the right thing and he didn't think there were any other options to discuss.

"Excuse me," Kate shot back, "but you're paying him. It is his duty to lay all of the options on the table for you to choose."

Kate named some options that would be lost if she took the SSOSA treatment. She'd lose the chance to be with all of her children, lose the chance to nurse Audrey, lose any kind of house-arrest program. She'd be giving herself over to people who thought she was some kind of boy molester, a freak. As David Gehrke outlined it to his client and to her friends it was either SSOSA treatment or prison. If she didn't plead guilty there'd be no SSOSA.

Far away as she was from Seattle, Kate felt she could see things very clearly, and she was worried. She was convinced there had to be a better way.

Mary Kay had needed a psychologist who would help her out of the mess she had made of her life without ruining her future. Friends helping her were outraged that David Gehrke seemed to let the prosecution roll over him when it came to selecting evaluators. It just didn't make sense to Kate or Michelle that the prosecution had to approve evaluators that were supposed to help the defense.

"Most unheard-of thing I've ever heard," Kate said some months later. "All kinds of things went on like that, and David would advise her and tell her, 'That's just the way it works.' That's bullshit!"

It frustrated her even more when word came back that the prosecution was dismissive of a finding of a bipolar disorder.

"Then the prosecution accuses her of personality-profile shopping. That she was just trying to get the right one. Aren't *they* doing that to nail her?" Kate asked.

Mary Kay Letourneau had increasing doubts about David Gehrke, but she hated the idea of ditching him in the eleventh hour. He kept telling everyone she was ill and she hated being portrayed that way in the media. An article in the *Orange County Register* ticked her off, and when he said he was quoted out of context, Mary Kay said context or not, words like "obsessed" and "mentally ill" carry weight alone. Later, she conceded that she had even told him what her friends were saying.

"Don't prove them right, David," she said. "Will you start showing them you are what I believe you are?"

She summed it up later: "He did his best, but it wasn't good enough."

FIFTY-SIX

MARY KAY FIDDLED for what seemed like hours, with her hair, her clothes. While Amber Fish watched Audrey, the subject of growing media interest ironed and reironed outfit after outfit for herself and her baby. For Amber, it was oddly like old times back at Carriage Row. Mary Kay was running around the Normandy Park house trying to find the right outfit to wear, ironing and rejecting and making nervous jokes about it. But, of course, this wasn't old times. Steve was gone. All the Letourneau children were gone.

A short time later, a photographer from the *Seattle Times* arrived to take pictures for the article Ron Fitten was writing. Mary Kay settled on the simplest outfit and the veteran photographer agreed. She wore an oversize white T-shirt and blue sweat pants; her infant, a white T-shirt and diaper.

The shoot went well. The *Times* photographer suggested that the new mother sit on the hardwood floor in front of some boxes—all packed up with no place to go.

Even before the shutter closed, the poignancy of the scene was heartbreaking. Mary Kay was swallowed by her T-shirt, swallowed by the boxes around her . . . alone with the baby—the only thing left in her life.

Before the photographer packed up to leave, Mary Kay asked if she would do her the favor of taking some personal pictures of Audrey in a little red Samoan dress that Soona had given her. Mary Kay rolled her eyes at the ruffled and lace-trimmed garment. She told Amber that she thought it was "the most ugly thing, but we'll do it to make her happy."

The photographer reluctantly agreed. Amber thought the photographer seemed "scared" about doing the favor.

"You can't tell anyone," she said.

"She took the film out right away and gave it to Mary Kay and said, 'I can get in so much trouble for this.' "

Mary Kay laughed a little. There wasn't much else she could do.

"It isn't like I can go out to JC Penney's to get them taken," she said.

Even though Katie Hogden would later say there were times when she would break down and cry for no reason, deep down she always knew there was a reason. The reason would emerge after the sobs that shook her body, after she had buried her face into a sodden pillowcase. The reason was painfully plain. It was always about her teacher, her tears seeded by the scandal that had taken a life of its own.

How can I explain this? To myself? To anyone?

For a long time she struggled with a poem about her feelings of love and friendship for Mary Letourneau. Each time she tried to complete the verse, she'd find herself scribbling over the text and crumpling the paper into a wad. Over and over.

I'll never get this right. I'll never be able to explain, she thought.

At thirteen, Katie was trying to do what adults could not. She was trying to analyze matters of the heart and to find a way to make sense of what had happened. Most importantly she wanted to keep her closeness with Mary undying and forever.

When people told her to "get over it. It wasn't a real friendship . . . the lady was old enough to be your mother," Katie did her best to dismiss them. It was so easy for adults to miss the point. Katie used the same words Vili would use to defend his love for his teacher.

"Don't judge. You don't know me. You don't know how I feel," she said.

Mary Kay Letourneau was uncertain about the effectiveness of lawyer David Gehrke, and she told the twins so on several occasions. She explained how she found him through some neighbors and that he had never handled a case like hers previously. His specialty was drug cases or DUIs.

As time went on, instead of growing more confident, Mary confessed more concern that her defense lawyer might be out of his element.

"She wondered a lot if he was doing the right thing," Amber Fish said later.

Amber and her sister Angie asked Mary Kay more than once what was going to happen in court.

She told them not to worry. Mary Kay didn't think she'd have to serve a day in jail.

"My lawyers tell me that it won't go that far," she said.

Even so, she took every opportunity to read up on her case and she made countless notes of issues to discuss with David Gehrke. In fact, for much of the summer it was all she talked about. For a while, she barely mentioned the relationship with the boy that had brought her to the place of ruin in the first place.

One time she called Amber to let her know that her lawyer was going to be calling her. There was some question about whether Mary Kay had been alone with Audrey—which was a violation of her bond.

"I don't want you to lie or anything," she said, "and it really wouldn't be a lie because you have watched Audrey . . . but if he asked you if you've been watching Audrey and been with Audrey then tell . . .''

Amber knew what Mary wanted. She was asking for an alibi.

"If he asks if you are living in the house, I'd say no," Mary Kay told her.

Amber didn't have to worry about stretching the truth at all. David Gehrke never phoned. She even called his office, but she never heard back from anyone.

It was the strangest thing.

Mary Kay Letourneau was not a rude woman. Karen O'Leary had had her share of people slam doors in her face. While a KIRO cameraman waited in the car, the reporter and the woman about to go to jail for the rape of her student stood on the front steps of the Normandy Park home for more than a half hour, talking about the case, Mary Kay's future, and her love for her children. At one point, Karen asked to use the bathroom, and Mary Kay let her inside. The house was in total disarray and Mary Kay made no apologies for it. *Why would she? She was about to go to jail.* Before leaving, Mary Kay showed her pictures of her four oldest children.

"I felt sorry for her," the television reporter said later. "She didn't know what was going to happen. She was actually, at that point, she said, glad to be going to jail to get away from the chaos outside."

Mary Kay later recalled the day Karen asked to use her bathroom.

"I couldn't believe the nerve. She was lucky I had a *guest* bathroom. When she asked to use it, I thought, is this really an emergency or does she just want to get a little glimpse of the inside of my home?"

What Karen didn't know that day was that Mary Kay wasn't alone. Vili Fualaau was hiding in a back room listening to a Dionne Warwick CD.

"We laughed hysterically about it after she left," Mary Kay said later. "She didn't know how close she came."

The reporter and the teacher talked by telephone a few times later.

"I found her very warm, sweet and vulnerable. And a little delusional," Karen said, looking back.

With the exception of Karen and the *Seattle Times*'s Ron Fitten, most reporters had dropped the ball between the time Mary Kay Letourneau's name first appeared on charging papers until she made her most critical appearances in court.

"Karen was very smart. She spent time with Mary by going to her house. She saw potential for the story to really go big," friend and school district policeman Nick Latham recalled. "She camped out at district headquarters. She claimed the story and kept at it."

Karen O'Leary was well-known in the Normandy Park neighborhood and though she tried with all her considerable persuasive charm, the TV reporter was unable to get any of Mary Kay Letourneau's neighbors in front of a camera. She worked on the Bernsteins the most, talking with Lee quite a few times, but getting nowhere. The calls to Lee irritated Tina.

"He didn't feel quite as sympathetic of that whole thing. I think he gave negative tones to Karen."

Months later she paged Karen, but the TV reporter told her it wasn't a good time to talk. Later, one evening when Tina had company visiting, Karen returned the call. This time it wasn't a good time for *her* to talk.

Karen kept pushing and Tina hung up on her.

"She kind of irked me," she said later.

At least to the defendant's way of thinking—if there had been a hero in the media circus that pitched its sleazy tent in front of Mary Kay's home in Normandy Park, it was Ron Fitten. The reporter for the *Seattle Times* article in the newspaper's July 25, 1997, edition was headlined:

BURIEN TEACHER'S SEX WITH A YOUNG STUDENT
SHATTERS THE BOY'S FAMILY, AND HERS

It was a sympathetic portrayal by a reporter who had spent time with both perpetrator and victim. She said she was sorry. She loved the boy. It was clear there was enough tragedy to go around, and along with the photographs of Mary Kay and her baby, it begged the question: What purpose would be served by sending her to prison? It was the kind of article that won awards, changed public opinion, and caught the attention of Hollywood bottom feeders. It wasn't skin deep.

And oddly, though there was a time when he would announce that he was writing a book about the Letourneau story, Ron Fitten's byline became missing in action.

Kate Stewart would later shake her head at the reason she felt Ron Fitten had been dumped off the story of a lifetime. He appeared too close to the subject, and because of his "on the inside" perspective, very sympathetic. He had become a confidant of Mary Kay's and nearly a surrogate father to Vili.

During a marathon conversation with Kate that lasted several hours, the reporter told her that what had happened between Mary Kay and Vili Fualaau could not have happened between any other two people. That kind of message didn't go over well at the paper.

"This thing is so big politically. He's not ready to leave his job . . . you had a sympathetic writer on the case . . . and off."

The first wave of television movie producers came the summer that Angie and Amber Fish helped Mary Kay Letourneau take care of her infant daughter, Audrey. The wave was small—and nothing like it would become in the months that would follow—as Hollywood beat a path to Normandy Park, Washington. It was an interesting time. The twins felt Mary Kay courted the attention as much as she denied her interest in it. She put up blankets over the sliding glass doors to shield them, yet there were times when the media caught her peering through her temporary partition.

When the girls asked why she wanted to get involved in a television movie, Mary Kay shrugged.

"It will be done anyway," she said, "I might as well have some input into it." She even teased Amber about casting Shannen Doherty as Angie.

"Because she's such a bitch," she said teasingly.

Amber countered that with an idea about who should play the lead role.

"Meg Ryan is you, Mary Kay."

They both laughed.

"I just can't wait until the movie comes out!" Mary Kay said with a laugh, as if none of it really mattered to her. Meg Ryan or not.

Yet she continued to talk about the television deal's viability and how the whole world would want to watch it. It was a modern *Romeo and Juliet,* a cross-generation saga, a cross-cultural tale. She worried if any movie could capture the essence of her love story. She was also quite hopeful that the film would be a big moneymaker.

"If anything comes out of this," she said one day, perched on her hide-a-bed command post, remote control in hand, "I want each one of my children to have a trust fund for college. Maybe this will even put the boy through school."

Angie didn't see the point of worrying about the boy and how he might profit.

What? Who cares about him? What about the others? she thought.

The delays were over. Everyone in the little Normandy Park neighborhood knew that, as part of a plea agreement, Mary Letourneau was going to jail that first week in August, though no one knew for how long. Some neighbors had avoided her for the mere fact that she had been dubbed a criminal; still others, like Tina Bernstein, had kept their distance because of the awkwardness of the situation. Here was a woman they had known, cared about, and somewhere along the way she had become someone else. A predator. A child rapist. A criminal. For those who knew her at all, none of those labels were appropriate—or even plausible.

The night before she was going to plead guilty and more than likely go to jail, Mary Letourneau walked over to the Bernsteins'. A certified letter for Tina had been put into the Letourneaus' mailbox and Mary brought it over.

Tina could see how the events of the summer had been quite tough on Mary. She was tired and thin. Coming next door had been hard for her.

The meeting was awkward. There had been so much silence since it all started, Mary hadn't talked to Lee in months. Tina Bernstein had wanted to come over to tell Mary that she still cared about her and her children.

Tina's voice started to break. "I'm so sorry, but I didn't know what to say or do," she said. "Every time something new comes out, I'm speechless."

Mary started to cry, too.

"I know," she said. "I've been putting a lot of people through some pain and confusion. I'm sorry."

The women stood there as Mary apologized and tried to explain what had happened between her and Vili.

"She wanted me to know where she stopped seeing him as a boy and where she started seeing him as a man. She was very confused, too," Tina Bernstein recalled later.

It was last-minute, as always, but Mary Kay called the Fish girls to see if their brother-in-law could do her hair on August 5. She had two big reasons: there was an interview the next day with *Dateline NBC* at the Gehrkes' house, and the day after that she was going to jail. The hairdresser called all over the Southcenter shopping area to find a salon that would stay open until he could get there to pick up the right supplies Mary Kay Letourneau needed to get her hair done—cut *and* foiled.

"It might be the last time I get my hair done for a while," she said.

Late that night, Mary left Audrey with Soona and returned to Carriage Row, parking in front of her old condo, and went to the Fish home. She tried to appear upbeat, joking and telling Amber and Angie and their sister, Lisa, that everything was going to work out. One of the girls had the new issue of *Cosmopolitan* and read aloud a "love test." From her makeshift hair salon chair in the kitchen, Mary Kay joined in.

"I haven't been able to goof around in a long time," she said, thanking them for the diversion.

As they did the test, Mary Kay talked about Vili and how the two shared a special relationship that defied all reason. She said she was sorry for the pain their romance had caused so many people, and though she was going to plead guilty in court, it was a legal tactic, not real.

"The only crime I'm guilty of is betraying Steve," she said.

When her hair was done, the girls walked her outside. There was an awkward moment of silence. No one knew what to say.

"I'll see you in seven," she said and laughed before getting into her Fox.

Amber and Angie talked after their friend and former neighbor drove away. Neither one thought Mary Kay was going away to prison; it would be just a little jail time. *But not seven years.* There was no way.

Early in the morning of the day of her interview with *Dateline,* Mary Kay Letourneau had been on the phones trying to locate her children. She knew they were en route with their father on a Northwest Airlines flight from Washington, D.C., to Anchorage, where Steve had taken permanent residence after staying with the Gardners that spring. She worked the phone like a desperate mother or a telemarketer because Steve would not tell her the flight time or number and her sister Liz wasn't even answering her phone. She paged her son over airport P.A. systems across the country. Minneapolis. Detroit. Chicago.

Finally one airline employee ("An angel, one of my angels," Mary Kay said later) broke the rules and gave her the flight number. Steve Letourneau and the four children were listed on a flight arriving in SeaTac at 11:02 that morning. With a Nordstom bag in one hand and a sack of presents in another, Mary Kay frantically found her way to the gate. For a moment, after she had gone to the wrong gate, she thought she had missed them and started to cry.

"Jacqueline saw me . . ." Mary Kay said later, tears coming to her eyes. "She put her arms up and called for her mommy. She melted into my arms. They all did. Steve looked at me and said, 'She knew you'd be here. She was calling your name before we got off the plane.' My eyes said, F. U., but I said, 'And what if I wasn't? What if I hadn't been here?' ''

Those two hours at the airport would be the last time Mary Kay would see her children.

The next day, August 7, 1997, a haltingly repentant Mary Kay Letourneau joined the inmate population of the King County Jail. Among the prisoners there, she was by far the most educated, best mannered, and most beautiful. Just as she appeared to Karen O'Leary and other news reporters back in March when she first walked into a courtroom with her hair held up in a barrette and wearing a gray maternity dress, she didn't look like she was the type of person who belonged in jail. But there she was. David Gehrke had told the court earlier in the day that she was sorry.

"She's a very good person who did a horrible thing," he said.

And there she would stay, pumping her breasts for milk for baby Audrey, awaiting sentencing that would drag on for months as doctors, lawyers, and people she didn't know argued over her fate: treatment as a deviant or more than seven years in prison as a criminal.

FIFTY-SEVEN

AUGUST 21, 1997, was Vili Fualaau's coming-out party. Sort of. On that morning the boy and his mother, Soona, appeared on NBC's *Today* show and gave the world the first glimpse, albeit obscured, of the boy behind the woman. Karen O'Leary missed the segment that morning, but the KIRO-TV reporter caught excerpts of the interview on the NBC affiliate's noon news show. News director Bill Lord told Karen to get down to White Center to dig up an interview. The boy? His mother? Mary Kay? Gehrke?

"Anybody," he said.

Karen O'Leary and cameraman Tom Matsuzawa made

their way to south Seattle, but once there, Karen realized she had left the Samoan family's name and address back at the station. She went to see Nick Latham at the Highline School District.

"She showed up at Highline, with her cell phone, and told me, 'Bill Lord told me I've got to get an interview with Vili, help me find him,' " recalled the public relations officer. It made for an awkward moment and the beginning of a strain on their friendship. Nick couldn't tell Karen anything; the district and the Fualaaus had made it clear that legal action was a possibility if they disclosed information about Vili. Moreover, he wondered why she needed it from him anyway. All the information she wanted was on the charging papers filed by King County anyway. Name, address, probably phone number, too.

"I can't help you find him," he said finally.

It was time for a Coke and plan B. Karen went to a nearby Burger King.

"Do you know that boy who was involved with Mary Letourneau?" she asked a group of teens hanging around the fast food restaurant.

The kids didn't flinch or hesitate.

"Oh, yeah, Vili . . . Buddha," said one.

"I know his telephone number," added another. "Here it is."

It was that easy at Burger King and it probably would have been just as easy at Taco Time. The teens admitted that it was common knowledge that Vili was the mystery boy involved with Mary Kay Letourneau. Everyone, it seemed, knew.

Some secret, Karen thought. Kids aren't dumb. They are observant. Everyone knew this boy.

The house at White Center was modest and rundown. Karen O'Leary left the cameraman in the car and knocked on the door. Vili answered. He looked like a boy of thirteen, maybe fourteen. To the veteran reporter, Mary Kay Letourneau's boyfriend/victim did not look like a mature young man, as the lawyers had tried to portray him. He was small, gangly, and self-conscious like a kid. Karen introduced herself, though she needn't have. Vili immediately knew who she was and said so. She said she'd seen the *Today* show interview and the two talked about the story.

"Now that you've done national TV, we'd like to interview you for a local story."

"Okay," he said.

They talked a bit longer and Vili excused himself and went back inside. Karen could hear him converse with a couple of others. Later Vili would tell her that his sister, Leni, and his aunt were home.

"We said we'd disguise his face using pixalization. He knew what that was," Karen said later. "We talked for five or ten minutes."

Then Karen asked to use the restroom.

"I needed to use the restroom, is all," she explained later. "It wasn't any kind of a ruse. I'm a television reporter. I didn't have a camera with me. What difference would it have made that I was inside? He was already talking to me."

A few minutes later, he brought out baby Audrey to show to the reporter and the cameraman. The baby was very cute and they asked if they could take her picture.

Vili said yes at first, but later changed his mind.

"I don't think my mom would like that," he said.

They took video of some of his artwork, the bassinet, and a car seat. When it came time for the interview, Vili considered the most appropriate venue. First the inside of the house was all right, then he thought the porch would be better. Finally, he said it would be best to tape it at nearby Hicks Lake Park.

Before they left, Vili washed off a stylized *m* with a heart that he had drawn on his hand like a mock tattoo. He was embarrassed and didn't want any kids to see it when he was on television. He was embarrassed, not because the *m* stood for Mary, which it did, but because he thought friends would tease him for writing it on himself.

Sitting at a picnic table not far from the tennis courts in the park, Vili Fualaau gave his second major interview. And though she'd hate to admit it later, it was the most

important of Karen O'Leary's career. Not for what her
subject said, but for how it would affect her life for nearly
a year.

Vili talked about an uncle who had started getting involved with an older girl when he was twelve. The uncle
married the girl—and they were still married. The story
was interesting because it told Karen that Vili had been
exposed to—and accepted—early sexual experiences
within his family.

As they talked and the camera recorded the soft-spoken
boy's words, Karen O'Leary observed something that surprised her. The rape victim still cared for the perpetrator.
She wouldn't have thought that a boy would have such
strong feelings for a woman over such a long period of
time. He still cared for Mary Kay. He said that his brother
had tried to fix him up with other girls, but he refused. He
was waiting for Mary Kay Letourneau.

As they talked, he barely made eye contact with the
reporter. He seemed shy and vulnerable. Nevertheless, he
did drop a couple of bombshells. He said he and Mary
Kay had planned the pregnancy and that they were still
planning to be married. He wore a silver engagement ring,
engraved on the inside. Mary Kay, he said, wore a similar
ring.

The disclosures that afternoon were shocking because
they revealed a relationship that was ongoing and a relationship that had been very deliberate. It was not about a
teacher who had made a mistake. It was all planned and it
wasn't over.

As the interview came to a close Vili said that he felt
he was older than Mary Kay. His family, he said, considered him an "old soul." He thought Mary Kay was child-
ish or immature in some ways. He was more grown-up
than she was.

On the way back to the station to rush the story for the
5 P.M. news, Karen O'Leary was thunderstruck by the boy,
the victim, and his attitude about what had happened.

"He was a very romantic young person in the way that
kids who read books about princesses and dragons . . . live
this romantic fantasy life," she said later. The Vili Fualaau

interview aired at 5, 6:30, and 11. Then, at least for Karen O'Leary, the trouble began. There was very little reaction. Only one phone call that Karen O'Leary heard about. But it was a doozy. It was from Mary Kay Letourneau and Vili Fualaau's lawyer.

"The only call was from Bob Huff. It went to my boss. I'd heard that he'd called and insisted that we withdraw the story. And I knew we didn't do it. Just because somebody called up and was unhappy with a legitimate news story—that's gotten legitimately—were not going to not run it," she said.

For Katie Hogden, the almost-eighth-grader with the weight of the world on her shoulders, the Karen O'Leary interview with Vili Fualaau solved a mystery that had hung in the back of her mind over the summer. She watched the KIRO report as Vili fiddled with the filigree-decorated silver ring that had been a gift from Mary. The inscriptions "I'll Be There" and "Oh Happy Day" triggered the memory of her teacher's request to relay three words to Vili.

Words that will let him know that everything would be all right.

It was the ill-fated lover's song "I'll Be There." Those were the words that Mary had believed would comfort Vili.

"I knew that was what she had wanted to say. I finally figured it out," she said later. "It was like a puzzle."

Friday morning, August 22, 1997, started out promisingly enough for the reporter who had interviewed Vili Fualaau as they sat at a picnic table at a White Center park. She had brought to light new information and it was the talk of Seattle and beyond. A talk radio show praised Karen O'Leary for revealing the other side of the story; that the boy wasn't a victim, but was a thoughtful and caring boy. A boy who loved Mary Kay. Still. And she still loved him. They had planned their baby and plotted a future together.

If the good feeling of a good story can be savored only until the next telecast, it was over even faster for the KIRO reporter.

The bubble burst when Bob Huff showed up in front of KIRO's offices in downtown Seattle with lawsuit papers in hand. He had called other media for a surprise press conference to announce that the rape victim and his mother were suing KIRO, owner Cox Broadcasting, and Karen O'Leary for a dirty-laundry list of infractions including unlawful imprisonment, invasion of privacy, trespass, negligent and intentional infliction of emotional distress, negligent hiring and supervision, and fraud.

Outrage and indignation bolstered each word. Karen stayed out of it; in fact, the station sent only a cameraman down to film what was being said. There would be no confrontation in front of the competition.

Bob Huff stuck his claim to the boy's story that morning and drew the line in the sand with a backhoe. He made sure that the message was loud and clear: *Keep away from the kid.*

"It rings almost hauntingly of what they are accusing Mary Kay Letourneau of doing—coming in, gaining confidence, and abusing trust to gain something from the boy," the lawyer told a reporter after the announcement.

Karen O'Leary certainly had plenty to consider, but one thing troubled her more and more, something that hadn't been apparent until Bob Huff showed up waving papers in front of KIRO. She knew Bob Huff as Mary Kay Letourneau's attorney along with David Gehrke. Every time she had seen David Gehrke in court, Bob Huff had been there, too. But she was unaware he had anything to do with Vili Fualaau.

So strange.

"It seems like an amazing conflict of interest that you would represent both the rapist and the rape victim," she told a friend. "But Bob Huff's doing that. It seems shocking to me."

Bob Huff didn't completely disagree. He thought the situation was curious, too. The lines were blurred in the Letourneau Triangle. The rapist's chief supporter appeared to be the victim's mother. In addition, he later suggested that the prosecutor's office just wanted the whole thing to go away, and by doing battle over Mary Kay and Vili's shared representation, it would only focus more attention on their story—fallout that would only serve the strange alliance's goal—more ballyhoo.

"I was keenly aware that you can't be a representative of people with a conflict of interest," Bob Huff said later. "But that unusual thing here is that even though they were rapist and victim, they had the same commercial interests. Vili wanted to make money and Mary wanted to get her story out."

As she faced the first lawsuit in her career, Karen O'Leary found herself in an odd position. She was a reporter covering a case in which an offshoot of it was a lawsuit against her. Over the next few months, she would see what it felt like to be called a liar, manipulator, and a fraud. A dentist from Mukilteo, Washington, sent a note: *"Did you get a thrill questioning this young man about his sexual adventure?"*

The TV reporter would also see how a boy and his story was twisted and turned for what his lawyers appeared to want more than they wanted justice.

Karen O'Leary deduced two reasons for the lawsuit. One had to do with the upcoming sentencing hearing, the other had to do with money. With sentencing coming up, David Gehrke and Bob Huff were promoting the position that Mary Kay Letourneau was a victim of her own mental imbalance. She was an upstanding teacher who made a terrible mistake. She needed mercy, not condemnation. Treatment, not prison.

The KIRO interview showed a side of the defendant that didn't mesh with that strategy. Vili said the pregnancy had been planned. Mary Kay Letourneau was going to marry him. It was a deliberate and calculated relationship. The lawsuit was a muzzle on the media.

"They didn't want that out," Karen said later. "They didn't want anyone else to get to Vili. They knew Vili would talk."

At least to Karen, the second effect of the lawsuit proved to be the most enduring. Bob Huff and David Gehrke were sitting on a story that could mean money. Movies, books, television interviews. Bob Huff, who had that curious role as an associate of David's in the beginning of the case, now had a real job.

"He wanted to make sure no other reporter tried to approach Vili. He threatened everybody else. Nobody else better go to that boy! Nobody else should interview him!" Karen told a friend of Bob Huff's purported tactics.

Karen saw the *Today* appearance as a promotional effort for the marketing of the "forbidden love" story and her "free" interview in the park had thrown a wrench into the plan.

"They allowed just a little bit of Vili's story out there as a teaser, letting publications like the *Globe, Inside Edition,* people who pay, know, 'Hey, he'll talk.' Then the negotiations were supposed to start," Karen said later.

The KIRO interview undermined everything. Vili Fualaau was giving the information away for nothing. That wouldn't do. Not for him. For Audrey. Or for the lawyers. Most importantly, some observers felt, for the lawyers.

Bob Huff flatly denied that the family wanted to sell out. He made the point perfectly clear during an interview with the *Seattle Post-Intelligencer.* "This is their lives, and they're not going to cheapen it."

The KIRO lawsuit wasn't the only pending legal matter. No one knew it at the time, but Bob Huff had contacted the Highline School District the week before Vili went on TV. A notice of claim alleging the district had been negligent in the hiring, supervision, and retention of Mary Kay Letourneau had been sent to district offices in Burien. The notice of claim merely rings a warning bell. The statute of limitations for any negligence runs for three years after the minor's eighteenth birthday. The district responded a day after they received Bob Huff's letter. Their investigation showed that the district did not have any knowledge of Mary Letourneau's improper relationship with her student, and therefore had not failed to act in the best interests of the boy.

Mary Kay was livid when she learned of Bob Huff's letter.

"He did it on his own," she told a friend. "He just did

it to see if they could scare them into doing something, paying something.''

Feeling sorry for Mary Kay Letourneau was best left to those who saw her as a Joan of Arc for a forbidden love. She had recklessly and spectacularly ruined her life. But it was something she had done to herself. Although TV reporter Karen O'Leary had compassion for the teacher, it paled next to the sorrow she felt for the four Letourneau children. She could not fully imagine the devastation it had brought to their lives now, and ever after.

"[Imagine the pain of being] rejected by their mother because she's choosing a twelve-year-old over their father, but also over them ultimately," she said later.

Lawsuit or not, she felt it added up to a mental illness. It had to be. Karen was convinced that Mary Letourneau was in fantasyland and needed treatment, not prison. The Letourneau children deserved a mother who was made well, not jailed. She believed it so much that in the middle of a San Francisco vacation the Monday after the lawsuit was filed, she agreed to appear on CNN's *Burden of Proof* to argue her position. It turned ugly and Karen learned firsthand how rotten the other side of the camera can be.

"They were just vultures," the Seattle reporter recalled of the hosts and other panelists who wanted Mary Kay locked up forever. "They were terrible and I was defending Mary. They chewed me up. They all sided against me."

Whenever some teacher-turned-rapist tidbit hit the papers or television or even the White Center grapevine, it ignited dissent and discussion. The Mattson house with its big-screen TV was always a center of such activity. Rumors began to circulate that Vili would not be waiting for his teacher-girlfriend and he was already playing the field. To be fair, most considered the boy somewhat shy, artistic, a tranquil presence in a sea of middle-school turmoil. At least that's what he could have been if the relationship with his teacher had remained private. But it didn't. And those who knew him knew that the girls were after what Mrs. Letourneau had.

Shorewood parent Nick Mattson had heard stories of the Samoan boy's conquests and refused to give him any slack, even when his wife, Tandy, reminded him that Vili was no longer in elementary school, he was growing up.

"So what? Is he going after college professors now?"

Tandy Mattson shook her head. "What I'm saying is that kids his age can understand."

"Understand? He's their hero. He bagged a teacher."

"You're just jealous that you weren't one of those kids back then."

"Granted, what happened was wrong, but it takes two people to do this."

"Aw, gee. Don't get started with me."

"When Savannah is in sixth grade—"

"Oh, please," Tandy said, stretching the word "please" into two syllables.

Nick ignored her. "—and her teacher's over there molesting her, you're gonna say, 'It's okay, it takes two to tango?' "

"Oh, mister, she ain't moving out of here till she's thirty!"

Nick shook his head. His wife didn't get it.

"It was rape," he repeated.

Tandy wouldn't hear of it.

"There's a big difference between a male and a female."

"No there isn't."

"Yes there is . . ."

And so it went, from household to household, from city to city. Everyone had an opinion.

FIFTY-EIGHT

AS FAR AS many of the teachers in the staff room at Shorewood knew, there had been no personal relationship between Mary Letourneau and Beth Adair, the music teacher, until *after* Mary's arrest. And none of them knew how deeply Beth had become involved with Mary and how often she helped out with Audrey during the summer.

On the surface, it appeared an odd fit. Beth was older, not glamorous and certainly not the live wire that Mary had been. She was a mother and a recent divorcée. But Beth seemed to share at least one characteristic with her new best friend: Beth relished talking about herself and her painful divorce. One teacher who was going through a divorce about the same time handled her pain and legal matters privately. Not Beth.

"She would just be on the phone and very dramatic. Her divorce went on and on. 'Be nice to Beth. People kept saying Beth's crying.' "

From September 1997, the music teacher appeared obsessed with the Letourneau saga, making visits to the jail, running errands, talking to Soona and Vili on the phone from the staff lounge.

"She got way too into it," said a veteran teacher who was at Shorewood at the time.

"Beth would be there crying or laughing the whole year long. She was so distraught sometimes she couldn't teach class, so she'd show movies."

Her devotion to Mary Letourneau, the woman who had ripped a hole in the heart of Shorewood Elementary, was an insult to those left to pick up the pieces. While they understood that Beth needed to be needed at that particular time in her life, the staff room was not the appropriate command post. She said her involvement was "the Christian thing" to do.

"Mary needs a friend to help her out," she said. "Mary realizes it was wrong now."

The other teachers agreed—the former teacher needed the right kind of help—but they doubted that Beth's running around town on Mary Letourneau's behalf doing favors for her was the right approach. For months, the teacher group iced out the music teacher.

"She was totally isolated that year. You'd go into the staff lounge and nobody wanted to talk to her. It wouldn't be that we wouldn't have wanted to talk to her if she wanted to talk about the weather, but all she wanted to talk about was Mary."

For teachers outside of Shorewood Elementary it was equally rough. Word—"reminders," they were called— came down from the district: *Remember, Don't touch! Don't be alone! Don't let it happen to you!*

Ellen Douglas and others were miffed by the warnings.

"That was a choice *one* teacher made. I was insulted that they were implying that this could happen to just anyone."

Months had passed before everything that everyone knew was spoken. One teacher from Shorewood was so upset by the thoughts that had passed through her mind, she never told anyone about them. She recalled an incident in January 1997. It was an "early release day," and a handful of teachers had gathered in the faculty lounge to work on a school musical production scheduled for the spring. The musical was always the Big Event of the year, a traditional celebration for all students, and the big send-off for the sixth graders who were leaving Shorewood for Cascade Middle School. Beth Adair had been in charge of the program in previous years, and though the music teacher had not abdicated her leadership role in 1997, personal problems had obviously distracted her. The other teachers knew that in order to produce the show, they'd have to step up their involvement.

Mary Kay Letourneau breezed into the planning session, only to announce that she had to leave right away.

"I can't stay," she said firmly. "I have to meet with Vili."

A couple of teachers exchanged puzzled looks, but said nothing.

What could be so important? one wondered.

"Couldn't you do that later?" another asked.

"No," Mary said. "I need to take care of a student's needs. My responsibility with my students doesn't end because they have left Shorewood."

Mary left the faculty lounge for her van and was gone for about an hour. It was uncertain if the van even left school grounds, though one teacher later thought that it hadn't.

"She was so freaking self-righteous about her 'student's needs.' It was loopy. She was so arrogant. It was as if she was saying there was something wrong with us—with anyone—who didn't think the way she did. As if we didn't care about our students after they left our classrooms. Of course, we did. But we also had work to do."

When Mary returned to the lounge, her face was flushed. She seated herself at the big blond table, brimming with ideas and acting as if she'd never been gone. But it was not her rosy skin tones that stirred fleeting concern.

"She smelled like sex," a teacher said later, still shocked by the scent and the thoughts that ran through her mind that January afternoon. "I thought about it for an instant, but I banished the idea as being an impossibility. *It just couldn't be.* She was in the van with Vili Fualaau in the parking lot. *It couldn't be that she just had sex with the boy.*"

Later, Mary Kay's words haunted the teacher who noticed the heavy, musky smell that lingers after intercourse.

"She said he has these *needs*. What was she talking about? Sexual needs?"

In time, reality would set in and events that seemed odd, but not sinister, were cast in a new light. Another teacher at that planning session agreed with her colleague that the Highline administration had dropped the ball.

"We didn't know about what happened at the Des

Moines pier," said the teacher. "If someone had bothered to tell us, maybe we could have done something. We didn't have the history that we needed to make the connection between what was happening with Mary and Vili."

PART FOUR
COMMODITY

This is their lives, and they're not going to cheapen it.
—Bob Huff in an August 1997 interview with
the Seattle Post-Intelligencer

I was 12 years old and I never f——ed anyone . . . I wanted
to see what it was like . . .
—Vili Fualaau, in Time Daily, *October 18, 1998*

How do you say "fuck you" in Hollywood? "Trust me."
—David Gehrke in a summer 1998 interview

I know how to bring out the best in people. To make them
understand. I wish it was me out there fighting for me.
—Mary Kay Letourneau to a friend in 1999

FIFTY-NINE

MARY KAY LETOURNEAU paced in her jail cell in Kent. She seemed a frail-looking woman, though of course she wasn't. Her lawyer, her friends, and even her jailers knew that she had a reserve of fortitude unmatched by many. No matter that she was in jail, confined, she still knew when things weren't done properly. She ranted in her young-sounding voice.

"I can't wear this," she said. "The fabric is all wrong—it's itchy and I don't like the color."

A guard used to the tirade looked on and rolled her eyes while Mary Kay shifted her tiny frame in the yardage of fabric that made up her county-issued garb. It didn't come in any other color but orange, for goodness' sake. The guard had heard the rants before. *Everyone had.* The Mary Kay the world would come to know was nothing like the inmate guards knew as she awaited sentencing in November of 1997.

"The real Mary Kay," said one who saw her during that period, "isn't all that pretty. Funny thing, people like that are never told anything but words of comfort. She seems so weak, but inside she's anything but. Selfish and self-absorbed, that's what she is."

Local Seattle boy Ted Bundy had had them. So had Los Angeleno Richard Ramirez, the so-called Night Stalker. Although Mary Kay Letourneau's crime was nothing compared to theirs, she did inspire a bizarre and devoted following. The groupies started coming to see her in the fall

of 1997 and they didn't let up. Defense lawyer David
Gehrke and others close to the Letourneau case had never
seen anything quite like it. Whether it was her sun-streaked
California good looks, her sweet demeanor, or if it had to
do with the titillating nature of the crime, no one could
say for sure. But the former schoolteacher, without a
doubt, touched a strange chord among a cross-section of
people. Men and women from across the country and indeed the world found something in Mary Kay. It was true
that from the moment she was arrested in late February
letters and phone calls from "weirdos" had bombarded
her. But there were other callers, too. Mary Kay heard
from people who on the surface seemed as normal as the
neighbor next door. Scores of men and women who for
some reason or another saw a place for themselves in her
life. Some wanted to marry her. Some wanted to mother
her. All wanted a connection to the woman they saw in
the papers and on the television screen. One guy wanted
to set up a defense fund; another announced a Web site,
marykayletourneau.com, devoted to the woman behind
bars for love. Some were convinced through some form of
erotomania—the erotic obsession with a famous person—
that Mary Kay was as desirous of them as they were of
her.

Certainly Michelle Jarvis and Kate Stewart were not
included in the collection of groupies, but they were un-
questionably the most influential members of the "Mary
Club," as David Gehrke liked to call the widening circle
of friends and hangers-on. Among the members of the
group were Abby Campbell, a Mormon mother of five and
wife of a South King County, Washington, lawyer; Max
McNab, a writer who had written some unproduced screen-
plays and the back of a restaurant menu; Beth Adair, the
Shorewood music teacher; and Tony Hollick, a fifty-five-
year-old "retired physicist" from London.

Mary Kay, of course, didn't think of them as groupies,
but as "true, true courageous people." She later included
Ron Fitten, the *Seattle Times* reporter, as one among her
inner circle. Susan Gehrke also was a common fixture at
the King County Regional Justice Center in Kent, but Da-

vid Gehrke never considered his wife a groupie. She was only doing the right thing by befriending someone who needed it. Skeptical about Mary Kay at first, Susan became so devoted that months later she—like a dozen others—would contemplate writing a book about the extraordinary Mary Letourneau. She even signed an entertainment contract for her "story."

But it was Abby Campbell who provided the most vehement support of Mary Kay Letourneau. And it was Abby Campbell whose idea of assistance seemed to be enabling Mary Kay Letourneau to do what she pleased. Some would say actions on behalf of the jailed teacher would have dire consequences.

"She was a housewife that was trapped with the boredom of raising kids and was taken with the interest and excitement of the story and the involvement. [She] has hated it, but in the long run has reveled in the excitement, the notoriety," David Gehrke said later.

Mary Kay needed attention at the time. She was sitting in jail with nothing but her own thoughts to keep her company. When the men and women started coming, she agreed to see them. She was literally a captive audience. One man came nearly every day with a rose for the teacher—though jail rules prohibited him from giving it to her. Others phoned the jail just to see if she was all right. It irritated jailers because she wasn't supposed to be getting a fan club going, she was supposed to be paying for her crime.

But as time went on, the danger grew. The groupies supported Mary Kay Letourneau. She was in love and it was nobody's business but hers and Vili's.

"Why are you rolling over?" they'd ask over and over. *"Why are you letting your attorney do this? Why aren't you fighting this?"*

The Fish twins were mystified by all the people who were hanging around the jail. As far as they could tell, none of the hangers-on who had crawled out of the woodwork knew their friend before she was arrested. Before going in to see Mary Kay one time that fall, Amber and

Angie noticed a woman with a stack of notebooks and an attitude.

Who in the hell is she? both wondered.

As the visiting time ended and the phone service between the glass partition of the Visitors alcove was shut off, there was a raucous pounding on the door. Amber and Angie looked over and saw it was the same woman with the notebooks and clipboard hammering away with her fists to get their attention.

As they swung the door open Mary Kay was being led back to her cell, and the woman scolded them sternly for taking up all of *her* time, as if she were their mother.

"Usually if I get here people will let me in to talk to her," she said, pushing past and yelling for Mary through the glass. Mary called over her shoulder that she would phone her later. The woman fumed.

"Like she was so important. But I'd never seen her before," Angie said later, "so I didn't care."

The three exited the building for the parking lot. The woman with the notebooks hurried ahead.

"Well, who are you?" Amber asked when they caught up with her.

"Abby. I'm a friend," she said, turning around.

"I've never seen you before," Angie retorted.

Abby Campbell explained that she was helping with Mary Kay's case. When Angie asked if she knew how they could reach Steve to send a card to the kids, Abby became noticeably bitter.

"We're going to get those kids back," she said. "You can help us campaign."

Campaign? What did she think this was, some election or something? She doesn't even know the Letourneau children.

The girls thought she was odd, a middle-aged woman, caught up in something that made her feel important.

Amber figured Mary Kay had found someone to do her bidding.

"Mary Kay knows how to use people. She knows exactly what to say and do," she said later.

*   *   *

More so than some of the others, Kate Stewart could see the true basis of the bond between Abby Campbell and Mary Kay Letourneau. She could readily dismiss what some had said—that Abby was a groupie living through the stranger in jail, enraptured by a tale of forbidden love. As Kate rationalized it, Abby was a woman in need of a mission in life; a person in search of a purpose. It evidently wasn't enough that she had a lawyer husband and a house full of children to raise.

"Abby was there for whatever Mary Kay needed to do. It's a two-way street, but Mary Kay is the needy one now, so Abby comes," Kate said later.

Errands? Abby could do them. Calls to David Gehrke? Abby could make them—sometimes every day. Running down psychologists for Mary Kay's defense? Abby could do it. Kate and Michelle were glad that someone was in place to do what they couldn't do from a thousand miles away. At times, Kate thought her college friend's troubles had "consumed Abby's life way too much." Abby lived and breathed Mary Kay Letourneau and relentlessly worked the phones and sent e-mails to keep the process moving—even when there was nowhere for it to go. It was almost obsessive and certainly annoying to some.

One time she called Kate when she was hosting a party at her suburban Chicago home. Kate's physician husband picked up the phone and let Abby have it. "What's your problem?" he barked into the receiver. "You've got five kids! Get a life! You're following this Mary Kay thing too much. Let it go," he said.

Appearances were crucial. Anyone who knew Mary Kay Letourneau knew that. Shopping, grooming, saying the right thing at the right time, all were of the utmost importance. During visiting hours at the jail one time, Amber and Angie Fish made the mistake of mentioning to Mary that she was looking thin. They should have known better. Mary Kay was always worried about her weight. After giving birth to her children she went on a protein drink to put weight back on.

"Do I really look bad?" she said from behind the glass partition.

The twins tried to reassure her, but it was too late.

"Do I look sick? You should see the food they give us. I'll start ordering cookies at dinner. I swear."

Mary also obsessed about her hair, which was flyaway and out of control.

"It's the shampoo," she said. "I can only order baby shampoo and no conditioner—that's why my hair looks like this."

The girls laughed along with her.

"You don't ever want to get into trouble, you guys. This is not a place you want to be."

Amber and Angie agreed. *No one wanted to be in a place like jail.*

"Did you see Audrey?" she asked.

The girls said they had.

"Isn't she getting big? A little too big for that outfit?" she asked somewhat conspiratorially.

"Audrey was wearing stretch pants—Mary Kay's worst nightmare," Amber said later. She asked the sisters to go shopping to get her baby something decent to wear. Beth Adair, she said, could give them the money. Amber and Angie promised they would.

"Did you see her hair?" Mary Kay made a disgusted face.

They had.

"What's wrong with her hair?" Amber asked.

"They have that grease on it," Mary Kay said in an exasperated tone. The girls gathered that it was some kind of Samoan style. Soona had used some kind of oil to slick up the hair before twisting it into shape.

Mary Kay was upset about it, but there was nothing she could do. Soona was dressing and grooming that baby the way she would any of her children. When Mary Kay got out of jail and could raise the baby, the grease, the stretch pants, the hideous red dress, would be history.

Mary Kay Letourneau wasn't an overnight sensation, as so many would later claim when her notoriety pushed her into

Lorena Bobbit and Amy Fisher's turf, Tabloid Territory. Hers was a slow-building tawdry story of an inappropriate act by a schoolteacher before it became a media-made tale of a romance gone wrong. The spring that baby Audrey was born saw a steady flow of interest by the local media before the national vultures with moussed hair and journalistic pretense swooped down from Los Angeles, New York, and Chicago. In the beginning, maybe before they knew what they had, before they could take credit for creating Mary Kay Letourneau, victim of love, the story was locals-only and media access was rationed.

One producer from a smaller television show knew that the carrot that had been so freely dangled by Dave Gehrke and Bob Huff had most likely been yanked completely out of reach after the *Dateline* appearance of Mary and Vili. Calls were no longer being returned. The secretary at the law office had a different excuse each time the producer inquired about catching up with Gehrke. "He's in court. He's out of town. He's with a client."

Finally, at wit's end—and knowing full well the concept of being "blown off"—the TV producer made an appointment to make an appointment to set up further discussions to get Mary on his show. It was the secretary, not Gehrke, who telephoned later.

"She called me back an hour before and said, 'David can't make that time,' . . . and I had scheduled it a week in advance!"

This is crap, he thought. The show isn't a big enough player.

In time, the young producer felt a shift coming from Mary Letourneau's legal team. He felt the lawyers had been friendly, even intimate. David Gehrke faxed some material relating to soccer and his son, just like an FYI that a friend might send. Their attitude in the beginning seemed genuine: *"She really needs help. I don't know if we can do the show, but we'll try. We'll really take a look at it."*

But after Karen O'Leary's interview with Vili Fualaau in the park, things changed. The shift was more apparent as Mary Kay Letourneau became a media sensation, a commodity to be brokered, and a ticket to the good life for the lawyers, her friends, and the Fualaaus. National TV. First-class airfare. Theater tickets. A new suit. Four-star hotel accommodations.

"I talked to people back east who said money had changed hands," the producer of the small program said, quickly adding that his program was more honorable and didn't pay for guests. It became clear to members of the media that getting Mary's story out was not as important as "how much can you pay?"

The producer finally accepted that his show was out of the game.

With all the wheeling and dealing, blatant or disguised, the producer felt those around Mary Kay were taking advantage of a person who needed help more than she needed publicity. Mary was her own worst enemy, he thought, because she was so very ill and completely unable to be an effective advocate for herself.

"She was so deranged anyway that I don't know that she could make a conscious decision," the producer said a year later.

SIXTY

FOR MANY OF the Shorewood Elementary teachers, lessons taught in the classroom were different the fall after their colleague was arrested. What had once been so simple now became impossible. Gone were the hugs to comfort a child in need. Gone were any displays of friendly affection. Nothing like that was appropriate. This hurt many teachers, especially those with younger students. *If a child skins her knee and starts to cry, are you supposed to shake her hand?* But there was more to it than that. The scandal also changed what and how things were taught.

One teacher was unsure about comparing the size of a student's hand in a math exercise discussing growth.

"I thought twice about having his hand compared to my hand," she said. "Touch would be involved."

And touching was wrong.

Another time a teacher was discussing how ballads were often written to bring out sad and tragic stories. Some kid thought they should write about Mary Kay Letourneau.

When another teacher discussed Nelson Mandela's incarceration as a political prisoner in South Africa, a kid shouted out an example all the students could understand.

"You mean like Ms. Letourneau?"

The teacher changed the subject.

In fact, she changed her curriculum on the spot. No more of the torn-from-the-headlines approach to current events. There was no newspaper, no magazine, that was a Letourneau-free zone.

For that very reason, some also stopped doing current events.

And there were the smarmy jokes about the "private lessons" Shorewood teachers gave their students. It got so bad that some teachers declined to be specific about the name of the school where they taught and even what district. Whenever Highline or Shorewood was mentioned at a conference it brought chuckles and the remark that they were "from the Mary Kay Letourneau District."

Most teachers don't take up the profession because they want to get rich. They do it because they believe they can help young people grow and learn. Being associated with a breach of professional ethics occurring in their own school was humiliating.

What was a mother to do? Danelle Johnson asked that question of herself over and over. Her kids weren't eggheads, but neither were they retarded. She was convinced that with a little support from the Highline School District or even an interested teacher, her twins Molly and Drew could make it through school. For a time, she thought that Mary Letourneau's interest in Molly and the after-school projects might have been the answer. When Mary dumped Molly from the group and months later when the scandal broke, she knew what false hopes she had harbored.

After she had the twins tested and found they were academically at a third-grade level—not seventh—she played hardball with Highline.

"I went from being a neglectful, nonparenting, nonhomework-guiding mother to an overbearing, pushing bitch in about two and half minutes," she said later.

Seventh grade at Cascade was proving iffy—though Danelle had no idea until later that one of the reasons was that her son and daughter had become so wrapped up with Mrs. Letourneau and Vili Fualaau.

According to her mother, Molly was having the most difficult time in middle school. She was a truant. She was a runaway. A former classmate from Mary Letourneau's sixth-grade class took Molly to Seattle and attempted to sell her virginity to an Asian gang—or so Molly said later. The girl couldn't stay focused on school and the administration notified her mother: She was disruptive and they didn't want her there anymore.

Danelle went to the school to straighten things out.

"I know she has problems," she told an administrator, "but you are going to help her. She's not going to alternative school. She's not going to another school in the district. I'm driving her here every day until hell freezes over. She's going to get out of the eighth grade at Cascade."

"You can't—" the administrator said.

Danelle cut him off with the coldest look she could make.

"Do not make me say the L word. Because I will scream 'Letourneau' until the cows come home if it's the only way that I can help my daughter."

"We don't want that . . ."

Later, when her best efforts at helping her daughter stay in school were still failing, Danelle recalled her threat.

"I don't believe that it is all Ms. Letourneau's fault," she said. "It is unfortunate that my kids got mixed up with that group of kids because they've got a hard enough background. They didn't need this kind of drama to lead them up the wrong way."

She saw the school as somewhat culpable. Why hadn't

someone from Shorewood stepped in to stop the teacher when this were clearly amiss?

"If those kids were really down there until ten o'clock at night, if she was in that school so late—*until ten*—who in the hell is running the place?"

SIXTY-ONE

MARY KAY CALLED Michelle from jail to tell her some extraordinary and welcome news. She was not alone in the effort to remain true with her love for Vili Fualaau. A man from England named Tony Hollick, characterized by Mary Kay as a man of "unquestionable brilliance," offered to lead the charge from the tyranny of her "oppression-based" treatment to a blissful life with her fourteen-year-old lover. Tony Hollick had read about Mary Kay's case on the Internet and contacted her at the end of the summer of 1997.

"Tony's such a great ally for me," Mary Kay said with the same kind of breathless exuberance she once reserved for a new boyfriend. "He has such great connections. He's really going to help me. He's a warrior, a freedom fighter."

Over the next few weeks, Michelle Jarvis conversed with Tony Hollick by phone and through e-mail. He was certain that Mary Kay Letourneau was the victim of a vast conspiracy involving federal, state, and local agencies. Part of it was to destroy her as payback for her disregard of the unconstitutional law. Some of it, he hinted, was even darker. As they chatted and emailed, Michelle found herself agreeing with things that would later seem beyond bizarre, but in her desperation to help her friend seemed so clear at the time. She saw the prosecution as overzealous and bought into Tony's conspiracy theory that eventually had all sides of the law in cahoots to railroad the schoolteacher who crossed the line. An official with the Republican Party, according to Tony Hollick, said that King County was going to "make an example out of Mary

Kay.'' That meant a *demonstration* prosecution. The strict liability statute was also a problem. It took none of the facts of the case into consideration and sent her to the slammer or into a treatment program for which she was not even qualified. Tony Hollick all the way in London could see it. Couldn't anyone else? he asked.

Much of what Tony had to say seemed to make sense to Michelle, especially since she wanted to find a way to get Mary Kay out of jail and back with her children. But there was that little item that always made Michelle cringe. Tony let it be known that he intended to marry Mary Kay Letourneau.

"If she would have me," he said.

For weeks the calls from Tony Hollick to Kate Stewart were almost daily, too. At first, the mother of three didn't mind their frequency or inevitably lengthy duration, though she could not deny the calls from London did tend to eat up more time than she really had—time from her husband and children. Kate considered Tony highly intelligent, eccentric, "a freedom fighter who happens to be totally enamored with Mary Kay." His feelings for Mary Kay, however, harmed the effectiveness of the eight *amicus curiae* legal briefs he "electronically filed" with the courts and other missives he used to attack the enemies of the American woman he'd never met.

Kate delicately advised Tony to "keep the love part and the enamored part out of it, because nobody is going to take you seriously."

But Tony couldn't refrain from letting the world know of his true feelings. He recognized a great injustice and he could not deny that he loved Mary Kay Letourneau. He dispatched e-mails to the FBI, the White House, and the King County prosecutor outlining the ways in which Mary Kay's constitutional rights were violated. If it was obvious that he was in love with Mary Kay, so what? He'd press on.

No matter if he couldn't leave his heart out if it, Kate was glad for what Tony had done for Mary Kay.

"He's exposed people who might have done some un-

derhanded things," she said later. "He's put the limelight
on some that have been against her."

Michael Jarvis, like most of the husbands of the women
who supported Mary Kay, kept out of it for the most part.
But when the conversations with his wife, Michelle, and
Tony Hollick went for hours at a time, the patience of the
pilot-turned-multimedia-developer was stretched to the
limit. When he could hear his wife divulge deeply personal
information about herself, it made him wonder what the
Brit's real intentions were. It seemed weird.

*Who is this guy? What is he getting at? What in the
world could that possibly have to do with helping Mary
Kay? he thought.*

When Michael asked his wife about it, Michelle dismissed his worries.

"He's probing into the character of people that were
close to her," she said. "He's trying to understand more
about her, by understanding the people that were really
close to her such as myself."

Michelle didn't care what her husband thought at the
time. She and Tony shared common ground. Both wanted
to get Mary Kay out of jail and out of the SSOSA program
before it took every shred of life from her soul.

"He's extremely intelligent," she said later. "He's got
these major emotional problems that put this weird slant
into everything he does. Which basically invalidates his
brilliance. Which is really too bad."

But they talked and talked. If he was a little odd, he
could be forgiven for it.

*There's someone out there who cares. We aren't alone,
Michelle thought.*

At about the time Tony Hollick had come forward,
Michelle learned the existence of Abby Campbell, the
woman who had so irritated the Fish twins with her lead-
the-charge attitude at the jail earlier that fall. Mary Kay
praised Abby's support ("she's a wonderful girl and she's
helping me out"), but she told her oldest friend that Abby
was more a gofer than a key player like herself, Kate or
even Tony.

"She's useful for what she's doing," Mary Kay confided in her little girl's voice.

When Michelle suggested that it might be a good idea for her to contact Abby, Mary Kay dissuaded her from doing so.

"You really can't talk to her, Michelle," she said.

Later, when the dust settled and Michelle learned what Abby Campbell had been doing behind the scenes, she figured that Mary Kay specifically hadn't wanted her to compare notes with Abby. Abby was privy to things that Mary Kay had kept from her oldest and dearest friend.

"Mary Kay is the queen of manipulation," Michelle said later.

What was wrong with her? Mary Kay Letourneau's problem wasn't her relationship with Vili Fualaau, but the one with her lawyer, David Gehrke. At least her friends thought so. Few close to Mary Kay had any doubts that David had sympathy for his client and that his tears during interviews were real. It only made their concerns more difficult to reconcile. If David cared so much, why was Mary being labelled a sex offender?

What Would Jesus Do? asked his bracelet.

Jesus, some thought, would get a new lawyer.

Kate Stewart was one from the get-go pushing hard for Mary Kay to get rid of her neighborhood lawyer in favor of someone who could handle the intricacies of the case without selling her out.

"From the very beginning," Kate recalled, "he had all kinds of problems. He wouldn't show up. He lives minutes from the jail. He was MIA two or three weeks at a time, not even calling. *On the biggest case of his career.* That was the writing on the wall right there. She saw it. And he'd go visit her and pacify her. Then he'd send Bob [Huff] in and make her feel better. She's smart. She sees through it. But again, she's needy now, she's there, she's removed from everybody. They kept convincing her. She knew in her heart, she had to get rid of them."

"Get them out," Kate kept advising. Mary Kay was not some nobody who couldn't get a decent lawyer. The attention to her case had brought offers of support and money. "Get rid of them, Mary Kay. You can get another lawyer. There is money all over your name."

Mary Kay said she wanted to sever the ties with her lawyers, but she was afraid. She didn't have any money yet and didn't know how much she could get.

Kate urged her at the very least to hire another legal representative to keep an eye on David Gehrke and Robert Huff.

"Get someone to watch them," she said.

Months later David Gehrke would become misty-eyed at the suggestion that he didn't do his best on Mary Kay's behalf. He wanted to keep her out of prison and the deviancy program was the answer. And though he believed Kate and Michelle hated him, their behind-the-scenes criticism and blame still hurt.

"[They say] I'm responsible for Mary Kay being in prison. I don't know why, but I'm responsible."

SIXTY-TWO

IF ANYTHING, JULIA Moore was a striking presence. The psychiatrist's movements were deliberate and forceful. Glasses were lowered when she spoke. Her gestures commanded attention. There was no doubt that Dr. Moore was a believer in her field, not one of the many psychiatrists embittered by the law and its relationship to the medicine they practice. She was a perfect fit for the Mary Kay Letourneau case. She had attended a Catholic convent boarding school in Pennsylvania, and Marquette University in Milwaukee—the same school where John Schmitz met Mary Suehr.

It was Abby Campbell, through a referral from University of Washington psychologist Elizabeth Loftus, who brought Dr. Moore and Mary Kay Letourneau together. As the new friend explained it, Mary Kay was miserable with her treatment as a deviant, especially the requirement to tell her children that she was a sexual predator. Abby

Campbell wondered if something else was at work, something the other evaluators had missed.

Dr. Moore had followed the Shorewood Elementary teacher's case only marginally, but Mary Letourneau's calm demeanor had struck her whenever she saw her on television. "She was being practically stoned like the Magdalene—by the media and the public—but she came across as being serene in a naïve sort of way. *What is going on here?*"

In early October 1997, Dr. Moore spent her first hour with Mary Kay Letourneau, the most famous prisoner at the King County Jail. For Dr. Moore, the first jail visit was an audition. Mary Kay wanted to make sure she could trust the evaluator—the evaluator that she would allow inside her mind and share the truths that she claimed were in there, deep. She would judge the psychiatrist by her demeanor, by the questions she asked, by the responses to *her* responses. Mary Kay wanted control, the power to pass on to Gehrke the name of the woman or man who could set her free without the label "rapist."

When Julia Moore arrived that first time, the visit was between the glass panels that separate the jailed from the free in the visitors alcove. Mary Kay was an unraveling quilt of emotions. She had lost weight since her incarceration in the summer. Her red jumpsuit hung on her frame.

She was charming and controlling "in a nice way," Dr. Moore recalled later, but she was clearly out of touch. She told the psychiatrist that her children wanted the relationship between their mother and Vili Fualaau. She had deluded herself into thinking that Steven, Mary Claire, Nicky, and Jackie supported her love for Vili.

"Her bipolar condition was so severe that Mary could only focus on the hypersexual object—the boy—and her involvement in him," Dr. Moore said later. "She loves her children, but she cannot see the effect on them of the divorce, their separation from her, their mixed feelings about a boy they knew betraying them, Mom betraying them. She does not understand what her children feel."

Throughout the jail interview, Mary Kay had to use several pieces of paper to keep her thoughts in order and her mind raced from one subject to the next. But it was her emotions that were most revealing. Her laughter would turn to tears, Dr. Moore said later, "with the flip of a switch." The mood swings were not a result of the subject of their conversation. They were driven, the doctor felt, by a mood disorder. Mary Kay said she slept between two and four hours a night. It shocked her how others had given up on Mary Letourneau and supported a course of treatment in a sexual deviancy behavior modification program. The woman in the red jumpsuit didn't need that. She needed medication to stabilize her moods.

Dr. Moore could see clearly that in March when Mary Kay had been diagnosed as bipolar, no one had noted the rapid nature of her thoughts and the scant amount of sleep she needed to function. Mary Kay's bipolar disorder was marked by hypomania followed by mania. It was a pattern that led to the disruption of her social functioning skills. She had been able to hold it together well enough prior to the relationship with the boy. She had had a family life and a successful career and she snapped.

Dr. Moore believed she could help. She considered the troubled woman a basically good person who needed treatment to "get back to who she is." One key was to determine if any of Mary Kay's neurobiological symptoms were present in any other members of the Schmitz family. Though she barely scratched the surface of the family dynamics, and suspected there was much more to learn, she wondered most about John Schmitz.

Steve Letourneau was of no help. He referred Julia Moore's calls to his lawyer. Steve had completely bailed out on Mary Kay, despite the fact that she was the mother of his four children—and always would be. Mary Kay's network of friends seemed to include people who had known her for only a brief time and could offer no verifiable history. The only family member Dr. Moore could reach was Jerry Schmitz, the brother in Tempe, Arizona. Jerry wasn't of much help, either. He was matter-of-fact about what was happening with his sister. He didn't believe she suffered from any mental disorder. His dismissal of any concerns was strange to the psychiatrist.

"This is *her* choice," Jerry said reiterating Mary Kay's position. "She's just like everybody else. It has nothing to do with any disorder."

Dr. Moore didn't know what to make of the brother's reaction. His sister was facing prison and he didn't seem all that engaged. The call lasted only twenty minutes.

Julia Moore also turned her attention to pinpointing the catalyst for the events that led to the relationship with the boy. Why had Mary Kay, who had been functioning at a reasonable level for years, suddenly gone over the edge? The trauma of her childhood could have had an impact, but Dr. Moore discounted Philip's drowning, and the Carla Stuckle affair, as significant. She was instead concerned with more recent events, more recent bouts of depression. She made a list of key events. Mary Kay's father's cancer, her disintegrating marriage, her miscarriage—all within a year leading to the affair with Vili—had sent her into the depression that was followed by the mania.

Dr. Moore could see that the Letourneau marriage was a disaster. Mary Kay and Steve were not a good match in nearly every regard.

"She was more cultural, more into talking, into needing new cultural and social stimulation, had plans for her life, envisioned the future. She saw him as not really interested in having a life that much outside of work. Not interested in work being meaningful. But she was willing to tolerate all that for the sake of the kids, until her father got this prostate cancer and she was devastated and she was very depressed and could barely function, turned to her husband for help, only to hear 'What do you want me to do about it?' "

From what the psychiatrist learned during her consultations with Mary Kay, Steve's lack of understanding about her father's cancer was the crushing blow.

"She took it as utter rejection. He [Steve] was never really the man of her life, her father was. With her father dying, who would be the man of her life? She couldn't depend on him. She had to move on."

Dr. Moore was a caring woman who saw nothing but tragedy in the Mary Kay Letourneau case. She felt that

Mary Kay's situation was a problem that had progressed needlessly from a privately treatable problem to an all-encompassing media feeding frenzy.

"I think this should have been nipped in the bud when she was found in the car with apparently no clothes on. But I wish that instead of calling official attention to it, that could've been dealt with very privately with Mary or with her husband, or with her family. I know this is wishful thinking, because this isn't the way law enforcement works. Law enforcement is not oriented to the cause of the crime. Just the crime."

It was Dr. Moore's conclusion that Mary Kay needed medical help for her bipolar disorder. David Gehrke told the psychiatrist efforts to get her on medication while in jail had thus far proved unsuccessful. A call placed by the doctor to the jail medical staff indicated they didn't buy into the bipolar diagnosis. One doctor said he thought she was merely depressed because she'd been sent to jail. *Who wouldn't be depressed?*

But after determined prodding by Dr. Moore, the jail doctor agreed to give Mary Kay a dosage of Depakote, an antidepressant. Dr. Moore was pleased; though the drug wasn't a first choice for bipolar disorder, it was an effective antidepressant. Lithium was generally considered a better and faster-working medication, but it took a lot of fine-tuning of the dosage to ensure effective therapeutic levels.

When Dr. Moore saw Mary Kay ten days after she started Depakote, she saw a different Mary. She had been sleeping better and her mental focus had improved. She didn't require the scraps of paper to keep track of what she was saying.

"Her attorney said she could get done in ten minutes what took four hours before. Her moods were more even. She was more realistic about sentencing."

Not everyone liked the idea of Mary Kay on Depakote. Tony Hollick considered it another major injustice. He was convinced that the antidepressant would take the very things from her that made her such a free spirit and wonderful and gifted dreamer. He saw her forced medication as an attack on her human rights and worthy of international focus. Ironically, the smitten Englishman was on Lithium himself.

And he e-mailed everyone from Hillary Clinton to Amnesty International and the FBI. In fact, he made calls to the Seattle field office of the FBI on several occasions to alert them of a conspiracy involving Mary Letourneau.

"This case could prove to be one of the greatest political scandals in American history. I fully expect numerous leading Republicans in Washington State to be sent to prison . . ."

SIXTY-THREE

A SECRET MEETING. It was Mary Letourneau's suggestion and psychiatrist Julia Moore agreed it was a good idea. Dr. Moore wanted an opportunity for Mary's friends to hear her side, some explanation about what had happened to her and how bipolar disorder had contributed to her problems. Invitations were mailed to neighbors, friends, and even a few teachers with the admonition to keep the get-together confidential so that no media would show up with notepads and cameras pointed.

The hush-hush meeting in a home of a PTA president near Shorewood Elementary lasted two and a half hours.

The friends in attendance had known for a long time that the Letourneau marriage had been in trouble and, for the most part, they blamed Steve. They characterized Mary Kay's husband as "irritable," "very demanding," and "unappreciative of Mary."

"Some had worried about Mary from time to time," Dr. Moore said later of the group that gathered that November evening. "They loved Mary. They knew something [had] happened to her, some major psychiatric event. They were hurt and angry that she had done this. But they didn't think she was bad."

Dr. Moore carefully sketched out the series of events,

the chain reaction that had led to Mary Letourneau's criminal charges. She said that Mary Kay had probably experienced hypomania since mid-adolescence. She defined that as being marked by rapid thinking, grandiosity, and elation. Hypomania, she explained, in and of itself is a problem, though many people who suffer from it go undiagnosed. In fact, people who exhibit this characteristic are often quite successful, charming, and energetic.

That was Mary Kay Letourneau.

As the psychiatrist explained it to the group, if there was a "safe way to have hypomania, we'd all want it." But it was a roll of the dice, and it frequently led to trouble—sometimes serious trouble.

Although some of Mary Kay's behavior might have suggested a "hypersexual" component—an uncontrollable desire and interest in sex—the psychiatrist was uncertain if that was truly part of her background and her bipolar disorder or not. The hypersexual role was inconclusive based on what she had gathered.

Working with papers and charts, the doctor outlined the sequence of events that she believed caused Mary Kay to fall apart.

She fell into a depression when her marriage began to crumble, according to Dr. Moore. Steve had cheated on her and fathered a baby outside of their marriage. Mary suffered a miscarriage. She had given herself so completely to her role as teacher that she had excluded close relationships with adults who might have seen how devastated she was. She was alone. When her father's cancer resurfaced, it was too much for her to handle.

She flew out of the depression into her hypomanic self, followed by mania. The mania, she said, was marked by pleasure in high-risk activities—for a teacher, having sex with her student couldn't have been more perilous. When Mary Kay lost her grip she found a young boy who was there at the right time. Though he was twelve, Vili became the man in her life. Steve couldn't be that man, and in reality, he never was. Her father, the most important man in her world, was dying.

Ellen Douglas wanted—*needed*—a way to make sense

of what had happened. Why was it that Mary was willing
to set aside everything she had held so dear for the love
of a boy? The very idea that there was a name for it made
it somewhat easier to take.

"I admit I want it to make sense. I need a reason to
understand how you could do this when you loved your
kids, and even if you don't love your husband anymore
and that's breaking up on both parts . . . I think the bipolar
helps us understand."

One face was new to everyone. It was Abby Campbell.
Ellen had heard of Abby for a while, though she didn't
know much about her, except that she hadn't met Mary
until after she became newsworthy.

"My feeling was that she was like a groupie," Ellen
said later.

Outside of Dr. Moore, Abby Campbell appeared to have
the most to contribute during the meeting. Ellen thought
the woman's running commentary was odd, almost inappropriate. At one point, Abby piped up with her take on
Washington State law.

*Where did you come from? Who are you? Ellen
thought.*

The new friend also provided her opinion about the injustice of it all and how the judge might react to Mary
Kay's treatment and what her future might be. Ellen
couldn't understand the new friend's role in the whole
thing.

*You can say all you really want to, Ellen thought. It
doesn't matter. It is up to the lawyers and the judge.*

Mary Kay prepared a two-page handout for her friends.
She had felt used and misunderstood on her appearance on
Seattle's KOMO-Television's *Town Meeting* and wanted
them to hear from her. The media and the law had distorted
the reality of what had transpired between teacher and student. She had originally written it for the media and gave
it to her "media representative," Bob Huff.

She wrote:

*"What is really at the heart of this case is a very per-
sonal and deeply painful story of a couple that tried ear-
nestly year after year to provide an enriched life for their*

children—a home. The family was in need of resources, but proudly private and set on making the best out of every day for them, and their children. The foundation of marriage was not there to endure the complexities of a household, the complexities of life's changes. Boundaries collapsed. The woman here happened to have been a teacher."

Mary Kay told a friend that Bob Huff never gave her written statement to anyone, though she had asked him to. Months later, she surmised the reason why: *"Mary's not allowed to talk. Her voice is worth money. We can't let her give her voice away."*

One Shorewood teacher heard about the bipolar meeting later. What stunned and hurt her was that it was held at a friend's house. She knew she hadn't been on the guest list for obvious reasons—she was angry with Mary for dragging Shorewood and the teaching profession through the mud with her arrest. She had hurt so many.

"There's a secret thing between us that we can't bring out," the teacher said of her friend and colleague. "They've never mentioned they did it; it broke my heart. They could have at least told me."

Mary Kay waited in her cell for the sentencing. She barely slept. Her mind was full of thoughts of Vili, her children, and the treatment that had been prescribed. Drugs to dull her senses and words to turn her children against her. She had told supporters that she had no intention of following the treatment provider's plans. She would never sit down with her children and brainwash them with lies.

She thought of Christmas and how she'd spend it with Steven, Mary Claire, Nicky, Jackie, and Audrey—though terms of her treatment specified no contact for six months. She had missed Halloween with her children and that had hurt. Christmas with all her children at Beth Adair's would make up for it.

"Everything's set out in a box at Beth's. Their stockings, the decorations, the presents . . . everything for Christmas," she told a friend.

But mostly, as had been the case for months, she thought of Vili. *How she missed him.* His voice was deepening and fine black hair made a darkening shadow above his lip. Nothing could keep her from him. Not Steve. Certainly not the police. During the previous spring and summer Mary Kay had been bolder in her disregard of propriety and the law than many were aware—not even Michelle. Her boldness had been vintage Mary Kay. When she was pregnant with Audrey, Vili had accompanied her to her obstetrician's office. They had gone to the movies, even a drive-in theater with her children. She was Rose and he was Jack from *Titanic*. They had kept no real distance from each other during art classes at Highline, and Mary Kay sensed that some of the others in the class thought they were boyfriend and girlfriend. The couple sipped lattes and mochas at Starbucks and walked arm in arm in downtown Seattle. Mary Kay told a friend later how she and Vili had even sneaked off for a Fourth of July getaway to the Oregon Coast.

"*. . . each question we asked,*" she wrote in a poem, "*only strengthened the truth we knew . . .*"

SIXTY-FOUR

STEVE LETOURNEAU HAD something he wanted to show Linda Gardner when he came to Seattle for the sentencing. It was a drawing that Mary Kay had done. He never said how or when his estranged wife had done it. It was a picture of the four Letourneau children in front of the house in Normandy Park. All of the kids were sadly waving good-bye. Steve was in the picture, too.

"It had Steve with a really mean face . . . and then there was me," Linda said later.

The image haunted her and even scared her a little. She knew that Mary Kay had known all along that it was she who had made the phone call that led to her arrest, but since she never heard directly from Mary Kay, she didn't think she had focused much on that little fact.

But in jail she had time and it made Linda nervous.
What if she told one of her little friends where I lived?

The whole world had come to watch Mary Kay Letourneau, the teacher who had sex with her student, when the
oft-delayed sentencing finally took place on November 14,
1997. In reality, there was no genuine drama underlying
the event. Prosecutors and defense lawyers had already
hammered out an agreement and King County Superior
Court Judge Linda Lau was expected to go along with it.
Six months jail, credit for time served, and three years in
a sexual deviancy program. With that, she'd skip the
seven-year prison sentence.

The charges were reviewed; the psychologists mapped
out Mary Kay's mental problems while the defendant
stared ahead, or down at a legal pad. Her hair was up,
makeup just so, and the sleeves of a sweater covered her
spindle-thin arms.

She later told a friend what she was thinking about at
the time. "The truth was that nothing anyone was saying
was about me. It had nothing to do with me and I knew
it. But when [the psychologist] talked about Audrey, my
children, then that was about me."

Soona Fualaau identified herself as a "very private person" and read a lovely statement about Mary and the fact
that it was in the best interests of baby Audrey to keep her
mother out of prison. She did not agree with what Mary
did, but she did not think her son was a *victim* of anything.

Mary Kay stood and read from a prepared statement
and the sound bite was made, the kind of sound bite that
captures a moment and follows a person for the rest of
their lives, or as long as the public cares.

"Help us," she said, her hushed voice cracking, "help
us all."

A crush of cameras and a round of live *Court TV* commentary and it was over. The teacher/rapist with what one
reporter called "soft tendrils" of blond hair faced a few
weeks in jail to fulfill the remainder of the six months'
time required in her guilty plea. With time off for good
behavior, the tearful and seemingly repentant Mary Kay

would be free around Christmas. The freedom, of course, would be hollow. There would be no contact with Vili and no unsupervised visits with her children, including Audrey.

Like just about everyone within close range of a television set, Grandma Nadine sat on the sofa in front of the tube watching the news report of Mary Kay's sentencing that November day. Although most were touched by Mary Kay's pleas for compassion, Steve Letourneau's grandmother thought it was a snow job.

You need help all right, Nadine thought. You need a swift kick in the rear and to be sent to the moon.

It made her angry that Mary Kay hadn't publicly acknowledged the impact the relationship with Vili had had on her family. As far as Nadine knew, she never owned up to that.

The seventy-five-year-old woman's loyalty would remain forever with her grandson. She had heard a few things about him that she didn't care to know, but whatever he had done, he didn't deserve the grief his wife had given him.

"An ordinary man would have had her killed. Even if he had an affair, and was a philanderer, an adulterer, what would give her the right to pick on a sixth-grader?" she asked later.

Michelle Jarvis saw her friend on the news that night, too. And when she had the opportunity, she asked about the wrenching plea for understanding and forgiveness.

"David told me to act sorry," Mary Kay said over the phone. "So I did."

Not long after Mary Kay talked with Michelle, David Gehrke and Bob Huff seized the moment borne of their client's notoriety and arranged a deal with *The Larry King Show* to appear alongside her on the popular CNN show. Mary Kay didn't want to do it, and unhesitatingly told them of her reluctance. It wasn't that she *didn't* want to be heard. Rather, she didn't want the image of her in jail broadcast. She did not want her children to see her looking like a common criminal.

"I was *not* going to do a face-to-face from jail," she confided later. "David and Bob are practically jumping up and down telling me to do it, do it. They kept asking what it would take to make me comfortable. It was almost funny. They were focusing on such superficial things—my hair, and my makeup, what I would wear. They'd even get me a new blouse.''

A producer came to the jail to set things up, but Mary Kay refused to talk to her. She had already said she didn't want to do it. David Gehrke and Bob Huff were in the air flying back east for the broadcast.

"They weren't real happy with me," she said.

The image of Mary Letourneau in tears begging for forgiveness was haunting and would never be erased from the memories of those who loved her. But a question still lingered. What had caused Mary Letourneau to throw everything away? In her office at a Highline elementary school, former Shorewood principal Patricia Watson gave the question serious and heart-wrenching thought, as she had from the first day she'd heard the news of the arrest. She saw Mary's relationship with Vili as the tragic result of a breakdown, "a metabolic imbalance that sent her off the edge."

It wasn't the troubled marriage. It wasn't that her mother had not loved her enough. It wasn't that she had been in the pool when her brother died. Or the miscarriages. It was, Patricia believed, the *sum* of all of those things piling on top of each other.

"Every day was worse," the elementary school principal said. "All the different things that happened to her, there was never any relief. She had a breaking point."

Mary Kay's former principal also wondered what role the third and fourth child might have had in their mother's overloaded psyche. She didn't doubt that she wanted Nicky and Jackie, but perhaps they were more than she could really handle.

"Two kids she could manage, and school and home and keep it together. The third kid might just have been more than she could bear, and the fourth one just rocked it completely."

SIXTY-FIVE

IT STARTED WELL before sentencing, but David Gehrke didn't address it. But as the winter holidays approached, it got to the point where he couldn't ignore it. The groupies surrounding Mary Kay Letourneau were working overtime telling her that the plea, the sentence, her lawyer's strategy, had been a complete and sinister travesty. David was the target of most of their wrath and he knew it.

Mary Kay had been getting the message that by listening to David's advice she had blown it big-time. It was love, not rape. It was unconstitutional and she should have challenged it.

"These were all people who didn't know what the law was. She broke it. They don't know what it meant," David said later. In addition, those bolstering Mary Kay and her fantasy of life-long love with her former student didn't know what strings the lawyer had pulled to keep her out of prison.

"It was not until the day that she pled guilty that I was able to get the prosecutors to agree not to seek an exceptional sentence. They had her pressed that hard and there were several bases to seek an exceptional sentence upward. I felt like I had a good shot to get her a treatment program because of her clean record and who she was. I won. I got her a great deal."

He could see that whatever he accomplished was in jeopardy and he drafted a letter with the lead-off sentence, "Mary K. Letourneau needs your help!!" and mailed it to Kate, Michelle, Tony, Maxwell McNab, and Abby Campbell. He also sent the letter to Mary Kay's father and her brother, Jerry, in Tempe. He wanted those who cared about her to rally around her in the appropriate way. That meant, he wrote, supporting her treatment when she was released. Bolstering her defiance was not helping her one iota.

Don't keep telling her that she got screwed and that it's love, he thought.

Certainly David understood some of the frustration with the statutory rape laws and how penalties varied from state to state and, as Tony Hollick had pointed out, country to country. He knew that what had happened between Mary Kay and Vili would not have been a crime at all in some states.

But it wasn't so cut-and-dried.

"In some states she'd have done a hundred months per each act. In Wisconsin," he said, "I think she'd be doing twenty years."

The letter angered Michelle Jarvis. She called it "scathing" in its tone and content.

How does he presume to know what advice I'm giving her? she wondered.

"Dump him," Michelle had told her friend when the lawyer first pushed the sex deviancy treatment as her only option. "I don't think he's doing well for you."

"I have no choice," Mary Kay told her.

"Who's telling you don't have choices?"

"David."

"You need another attorney and you need other options."

If not SSOSA, what could be the way out of the nightmare? Michelle discussed the ramifications of Mary Kay saying she was mentally incompetent when she offered her plea.

"You were not able to understand what the plea meant at that time," Michelle said, trying it on.

"No," Mary Kay said. "I will not tell people that I was not all there mentally."

The SSOSA program was designed for degenerates, not Mary Kay, and Michelle couldn't bear the thought of how her friend would fare with the program for three court-mandated years. It was brutal.

"He didn't give her any other options. This is the only way you are going to stay out of jail. You plead guilty, you take the lie detector, you go to SSOSA, you tell them what they want, you see the therapist once a week, and take your drugs. What he didn't tell her was that going to SSOSA was worse than prison to her. How do you tell your family and kids that you're a sex offender? She'd rather cut off her arm.''

Treatment was for pedophiles and baby-rapers, not a schoolteacher in love with one of her students. Mary Kay thought she was misunderstood by a legal system that did not have insight into her heart. She told friends like Michelle Jarvis that once in a program, she was certain the so-called counselors would see the truth—there had been no victim. She was hopeful they'd modify treatment for someone who didn't belong there.

"Certainly," Mary Kay admitted later, "I don't deny that there are dangerous people who violate other people. Is there really a place for them in this society? You have a disorder and you cannot be cured. We can help you control your impulsive behavior. But you cannot be cured.''

They wanted her to tell her children that she was a child molester. Mary Kay refused. She wouldn't do it. She worried that by doing so, she'd alter their understanding of what had really happened between their mother and Vili.

"How can you take a child's perception of reality and abuse it? I would lay down my life,'' she said, "before I ever said those things to my children.''

The groupies blamed David and David blamed the groupies. He saw them as enablers who told Mary Letourneau what she wanted to hear—not what she *needed* to hear.

"If your friend comes to you with a horrible haircut, you don't say it's terrible. That's what they were doing with Mary. It takes a special friend to draw the line between commiserating with someone to 'Shut the fuck up, you got a bad haircut, it will grow back.' A real friend has to say, 'Get a grip.' ''

David considered the Seattle ones gofers. The intellectual power and support came from Kate Stewart in Chicago and Michelle Jarvis in Costa Mesa.

"They're the ones whose opinions really mattered,'' he said later. "Abby Campbell saying something meant nothing to Mary.''

When Kate told Mary that she understood how Steve had been a jerk, how unhappy she'd been all these years,

and how alive she felt since she found Vili, it validated
Mary's feelings.

"They didn't say, 'Gee, Mary, I don't care if you love
him or not. He's a kid. *He's your student.* You're married.
Get a grip.' "

The embattled lawyer thought that Mary Kay could
have been brought back to reality if only Kate and Michelle had stepped in and told her that she couldn't love Vili.
*It was not going to work. It was going to mean the kind
of trouble that would ruin her life.* But they didn't.

It was hard for Mary Kay to get through to her children
sequestered up in Anchorage, though she continued to try.
Steve had done a good job of keeping Stevie, Jr., and Mary
Claire away from the telephone whenever it rang. On a
few occasions, the timing would be just so, and mother
and the two oldest children would get a chance to talk.
Their conversations were drenched in emotion and sometimes ended with a sudden click of the receiver.

Mary Kay's friends phoned too, trying to pass along
messages of love from their mother, but Steve put a stop
to those, too. One of the friends pulled an end run and
contacted Stevie, Jr., through his e-mail account on America Online.

According to what Sharon told Nadine, the friend said
the boy " 'didn't have to pay any attention to anyone
about his schoolwork, it doesn't mean nothing. You don't
have to do it.' He was failing! Steven sent him to summer
school. She was a teacher giving him this kind of advice!"

After that, Steve pulled the plug on the AOL address
for his son.

And as mad as she was at Mary Kay, Michelle, like Kate,
didn't give up on the idea that a new lawyer could fix the
mess that David Gehrke had made of everything by the
guilty plea and the acceptance of the sexual deviancy program. She drove up from Costa Mesa to Orange one Sunday morning and met with one of the lawyers who had
defended one of the Los Angeles police officers involved
in the Rodney King beating. Michelle gave the lawyer a

list of legal concerns compiled by Mary Kay while in jail. He seemed impressed and saw potential in an appeal. The lawyer told Michelle to have Mary Kay call him. But she never did.

"It was apparent after she didn't get in touch with him that she was not going to listen to good advice. She was determined to do it her own way. He didn't want to waste his time with an uncooperative, high-profile client."

A referral to a constitutional law specialist reviewing the case brought the same results. Mary Kay Letourneau didn't call him back, either.

Though thousands of miles from Seattle, Tony Hollick continued to be a major player in the Mary Kay Letourneau saga. He e-mailed the day and night away and spent countless hours on the telephone with the zeal of a true believer. He was so persuasive in his arguments, so damn charming and convincing, that whatever he said was rarely challenged by Mary Kay and her close friends. And because he was so staunch, the fact that he also was in love with Mary Kay was somehow overlooked. He held power. Even Tony's assertion of a far-reaching conspiracy rooted in hatred for sixty-seven-year-old John Schmitz and his political beliefs, which stripped Mary Kay of her constitutional rights, was accepted by the inner circle.

Only Michelle Jarvis began to have doubts.

"When I'd pin him to the wall—'Tony, send me an e-mail with the exact issues regarding the Constitution'—he never could do it. He kept pleading Constitution, conspiracy, and Constitution. 'Send me precise information that I can use with an attorney.' He never came up with it. And Mary Kay was hanging on that as a lifeline in her thread of hope that she'd be able to fight this thing and it never came true."

Tony had convinced Michelle, Abby Campbell, and even Mary Kay that their phones were tapped, cars were bugged, or that people were following them.

"Be careful what you say on the phone," he'd tell them.

Perhaps Tony's greatest influence was his suggestion that the antidepressant Depakote would ruin Mary Kay's creative vitality. *It would crush her like a cracker.* She should not take it. It was part of the conspiracy, part of why she was more a political prisoner for daring to love beyond the limits of society.

Free Mary Kay. Do not take the drugs. It is a conspiracy. Mary Kay, listen!

Outside of a paid appearance by Soona ("I'm a very private person") Fualaau on *American Journal* in November, the gravy train the lawyers had sought hadn't come through. Even Mary Kay was disappointed; she wanted an A-list star to play her in a movie, but even a sitcom actress looking to stretch her acting abilities didn't seem as certain as it had. Bob Huff was having a hard time with his negotiations with publishers. According to David Gehrke, publishers said they liked the story of the teacher and the student, but the ending left them flat. There was also something else at work. Some publishers felt a little squeamish over the idea of a grown woman in a sexual relationship with a young boy. That fall a new version of *Lolita* was in the news, too. It was a critical success in Europe, but American distributors were reluctant to touch it because its content suggested to some a kind of acceptance of the sexual exploitation of a child.

Mary Kay and Vili had wanted the story sold as a love story, not a woman-in-jeopardy or a true-crime shocker. If it was a love story, how could it be written so that it would have a happy ending?

SIXTY-SIX

IN THE FIRST week of January 1998, Mary Kay Letourneau was released from jail. She moved into a spare room at the Seward Park home of former Shorewood Elementary colleague Beth Adair. She was angry that she couldn't see her children, still exiled in Alaska and out of her reach for at least another court-ordered six months. *"I don't care what anyone says, I will see my children."* Jacqueline had turned five years old the week before her mother's release. The little blonde, like her three Letourneau siblings, had been without her mom since the spring. Mary Kay was also burdened and upset by a no-contact order with Vili and his mother; and visits with Audrey had to be supervised by a third party. To those who had not seen her for a while, the photograph taken for the registered sex offender's leaflet to hand out to neighbors would have been shocking. Mary Kay wore a teenager's zippered sweatshirt, baggy pants, and T-shirt two sizes too big. Her hair was pinned in back, but unkempt and disheveled. She looked lost and bewildered.

Later, Mary Kay would admit that she knew she blended in with teenagers. In fact, she and Beth Adair's daughter actually hung out with the media while reporters kept a vigil near the house after her return to freedom.

"None of them knew it was me," she said.

What little Michelle Jarvis was hearing from Seattle during the weeks after Mary Kay was released was extremely alarming. The impression she was getting was that Mary Kay wasn't focusing on treatment or repairing her shredded life. The court had ordered sexual deviancy treatment and her acceptance of that as a condition for a suspended sentence was incontrovertible. Michelle didn't like it any more than Mary Kay did, but a flagrant violation of the court's order would send her back to prison and keep her from her children. If she wanted Audrey back, she'd have to do what was required. But she didn't. She wasn't taking her medication; she was using a vitamin regimen instead. She refused to participate with her deviancy counselor.

She was in love and why couldn't anyone see that?

Instead of doing what the law required, Mary Kay was prowling around, up all night, sleeping all day, and spending money she didn't really have.

"She's not dealing in reality at all," Michelle told her husband. "If it was me, I'd be looking at rebuilding my life. I've a second chance here. I don't want to screw this up."

Every time she called Beth Adair's house, she was left

with either no answer or word that Mary Kay was out. Messages were left, but she never returned a phone call. Not once. The change startled Michelle. When she was in jail she had called regularly.

What's going on up there? she wondered.

For Linda and Kyle Gardner, the repercussions of turning Mary Kay in to the police were lasting and excruciating. While they had been invited to the cousin's engagement party back in January 1997—when Steve and Mary Kay's absence got Secret Squirrel to thinking—they were not asked to attend the wedding that spring. Some family members didn't call anymore. Some ignored them at family gatherings. Being ostracized for doing what she thought was the right thing hurt Linda deeply. When he thought she was wallowing in something over which she had no control, her husband told her to knock it off.

"Don't let it consume you," he told her. "You need to go on."

But she couldn't. Not completely. Because even though Mary Kay had done something so reprehensible, the Letourneau side of the family could not find it within their hearts to support Linda.

"I'm the villain," she said later. "I'm the bad person. I shouldn't have turned her in. *You shouldn't have. You shouldn't have.*"

At one family event one of the relatives made it a point to remind Linda that "ignorance is bliss."

But she knew.

"Because they didn't do something right away, I've paid a price," she told a friend.

What stunned Linda even more was that so many knew for so long. Mothers knew. Fathers knew.

"Mary Kay was the golden girl, all right," she said later.

One evening in mid-January Linda Gardner got a call from a girlfriend.

"Linda, you'll never guess who I saw at the Super Mall. Mary Kay Letourneau."

The woman who had started the ball rolling with her

call to Child Protective Services and the school district was all ears when the caller said she actually tailed Mary Kay for a while just to see what she was doing at the mammoth discount mall on the outskirts of Auburn. She was with another woman, whom Linda deduced must have been her good friend Abby, the wife of the lawyer.

According to what the friend said, Mary Kay had been walking around in a cloud "*la la la la,* wanting people to notice her. In fact, she was in one of the designer stores, you know, saying 'I've been out of fashion for about six months, what's in now?' "

For Mary Kay's old Normandy Park neighbors, there had been little contact with the Letourneau children once Steve took them to Alaska for a fresh start, out of the fray. Ellen Douglas and her son, Scott, were among the only neighbors to see the kids in their new household up north. A Boy Scout event brought mother and son to Anchorage, and a visit to the townhouse Steve now shared with flight attendant Kelly Whalen was wanted very much by all sides. It was January 1997, and the television played scenes from the Winter Olympics. The townhouse was immaculate, not a speck of dust anywhere.

"*Sunset* magazine could do a spread," Ellen said later.

She watched Jacqueline run around the off-white carpet carrying an open box of grape Jell-O without a reprimand from anyone.

Don't fall with that mix, Jackie, Ellen thought.

But the place was calm. The kids seemed happy and relaxed. No one talked about Mary Kay and what might happen now that she was free to start her life over. Ellen liked Kelly, she seemed caring and involved and she provided the kind of order that their mother never possessed.

"They seemed okay," she said later. "Maybe they were wrecks, but I don't know. I know it is going to be tough."

She and her son left Alaska feeling hopeful that things would turn out all right after all.

*　　　*　　　*

The Mecca Cafe was one of those authentic restaurants where meat loaf was still served, and waitresses worked there long enough to know almost every customer by name. The cafe at the base of Seattle's Queen Anne Hill was a favorite hangout for one of Mary Kay's chief groupies, and had been so for a decade and a half. The friend thought it would be a wonderful out-of-the-spotlight place for Mary's thirty-fifth birthday. She agreed. The guest list was small, a few regulars from the Mecca, Mary, the friend, and Abby Campbell. By one P.M. on January 30, 1998, everyone was there.

Mary arrived in what had become her signature outfit since her release: full-blown teenage regalia that consisted of pedal pushers and a baggy T-shirt. She was upbeat, happy. Conversation was breezy that afternoon and spirits were high. Abby Campbell pulled a batch of photos from her purse and presented them to Mary. Images of Vili and baby Audrey were fanned over the back booth's surface. Abby invited Mary to keep a sampling—but not all of them. The friend who arranged the birthday lunch thought it was peculiar. Mary didn't ask for the whole lot of them. It was as if she didn't mind being told what to take, what to do.

She's a teenager, he thought.

A little while later, after Abby left, the friend leaned over and pounced. He had one question he'd been dying to ask.

"How the hell do you stay in touch with Vili?" he asked Mary.

Mary looked over her shoulder; her eyes darted over the restaurant, up past the row of stools fronting the counter to the front door.

"Abby Campbell and Bob Huff help me," she said.

The friend had suspected as much, but the answer ate at him. If true, not only were the pair helping Mary to violate a court order prohibiting contact between Mary and Vili, they were putting a fragile woman in a precarious situation. They were adding fuel to a bonfire. Mary Letourneau didn't see it that way. She saw their help as a way to stay close to the man/boy of her dreams.

"I had a bad feeling about it," he said later. "And, of course, I was right."

Later, when he confronted the others about what Mary had told him, they denied it. If Mary had been in contact with Vili, then it hadn't been through gofer Abby or lawyer Bob Huff.

"Believe what you want," the friend said later, "I know what I heard."

Bob Huff stood firm on the subject many months later. He did not, *would not*, facilitate communication between Mary Kay and Vili.

"[Neither] Mary nor Vili ever put me in that position," he said. "They knew I wouldn't do it and they knew it would get me in hot water with the judge and the prosecution. Besides, why would I encourage the relationship between Mary and Vili? I didn't think the relationship was particularly healthy. Let's say that there wasn't equal bargaining power between Mary and Vili. I thought it would be better for him to be without her for a while, anyway. Let him be for a few years . . . so he can move in another direction if he wants to."

On the other hand, Bob Huff couldn't absolve Abby Campbell of possibly keeping what she apparently considered star-crossed lovers in touch.

"Abby did a lot of stuff I wouldn't do," the lawyer said finally.

SIXTY-SEVEN

IT WAS A typical winter's night. The low temperatures were in the forties and the high the next day would only be ten degrees warmer. Dogs barked intermittently down by Lake Washington and porch lights glowed like fireflies in the 4800 block of Forty-ninth Avenue South, the Seward Park neighborhood where Beth Adair lived. One family even had Christmas lights still on, though it was February 3, 1998.

At 2:24 A.M. Seattle Police Officer Todd Harris was

pulling routine neighborhood patrol when he happened across a VW Fox parked in front of the Shorewood Elementary music teacher's home. He could see a woman sitting in the driver's seat, her head turned toward the passenger side. Her blond hair was matted against the glass of the windows painted with condensation. The parking lights of the Fox were on.

The officer ran the plates and drove past the car. Of course, it wasn't against the law to sit outside and talk in a car. Running plates was just something a cop does to pass the time. It was routine. As he passed the car Officer Harris could see that the driver wasn't alone; it appeared there was a passenger with her—though the passenger's seat had been fully reclined. It looked like a young man, a teenager, was with her.

On this night the routine of running the plates brought more than he bargained for. And for the woman inside the car it brought an end to her story.

The car was registered to Mary Katherine Letourneau, a registered sex offender.

The Seattle police officer drove back and pointed his spotlight at the car. In an instant, Mary Kay Letourneau got out and walked toward the beam. In her haste, she left the driver's door open. She was alone, she answered, when the officer asked if she had someone with her. She had no identification; she gave her sister Terry's name when asked who she was. Vili Fualaau emerged from the car and also gave a phony name. Mary Kay said they'd only been in the car six minutes, though the condensation on the glass and on the hood of the car indicated much more time had passed.

"There was great hesitation in both parties in giving their names," the officer later said.

Later, Mary Kay said she had gone to a movie by herself, went to Nordstrom, and when she returned, Vili was waiting for her. He had run away from home.

Vili laid out the story differently. He said that he had paged Mary Kay earlier in the evening and she had picked him up. They went to a movie, bought beer, and sat in the car for an hour and a half.

And though no one will ever know the truth, Mary Kay and Vili have told varying stories of what happened that night and the days before.

Just after three A.M. television reporter Karen O'Leary was awakened by a phone call from KIRO's overnight assignment editor.

"Karen," he said, "you're not going to believe this, but Mary Letourneau's been caught with a sixteen-year-old!"

Karen sat up. "What?"

It must be some other boy. Not Vili, she thought. Vili was fourteen.

The editor filled her in on the arrest and Karen was rocked by the news. She had thought that Mary Letourneau had been fixated on Vili and no other boy.

What? she thought.

And as more information came to her that morning as she prepared for a trip out of town on another scandal story, Karen O'Leary was left feeling sad and duped.

"Everything that had come earlier had been a lie. All of the people that had said Mary Kay Letourneau should go to prison are right. I was wrong. She needed to be in prison. She made no effort to stay away from him. She didn't even wait a reasonable amount of time. She didn't wait a year, two years, five years . . ."

Mary Kay has her own special memory of Karen O'Leary. According to Mary Kay, the TV reporter approached her at the Kent jail just after the lawsuit was filed. According to Mary Kay, the breathless reporter was indignant over the suit Bob Huff had filed.

"Maybe she wanted me to call off the dogs or something, I don't know her purpose in telling me that."

But it was something else Karen said that really stuck in her memory:

"Mary, Vili says he's going to wait for you. Isn't that the saddest thing you've ever heard?"

What is the purpose in saying that? Mary Kay wondered. Out of all the things in the world, what would I want to hear more than that? Why would that be sad? It was Vili's choice and I couldn't have been happier.

The rest of the morning, details were made available. It was the inventory of what was found in the car that provided clues to what might have been going on between the pair and made it clear that whatever Mary Kay and Vili had told police didn't quite mesh with the facts of the case. Under the carpet by the gas pedal, police found Mary Kay's passport. In a little lockbox given to her by pal Abby Campbell were sixty-three hundred-dollar bills. Investigators found books, toys, young men's underwear, shoes, and baby clothing. Receipts for more than $850 from Nordstrom. Two rolls of film and a disposable camera containing more film were sent to the lab for developing. A couple of beer bottles were found, one almost empty, one unopened. Two ticket stubs to *Wag the Dog,* the movie Mary Kay said she'd seen. A letter from Cascade Middle School suspending Vili from the school for smoking was found, too.

When the film was processed it showed pictures of Mary Kay Letourneau, Vili Fualaau, and their daughter, Audrey. Some of the images were taken indoors; others were out in public. Seattle's Pike Place Market was readily identifiable.

They also found a message pager issued just a few days before.

SIXTY-EIGHT

MARY KAY LETOURNEAU broke hearts all over town the morning of her second arrest. Among those who shared the disappointment and the sorrow were the Fish twins. *How could this be? How could she let this happen?* They wondered if she was sick and unable to control herself.

"We thought she was somewhat erratic at times because we knew her personality, but we never put a label on it," Angie said later.

For those closest to Mary Kay, the ones who knew her before she was notorious, it was an excruciating betrayal that spoke of both mental illness and selfishness. Neither of which were attributes those who knew Mary Kay wished ascribed to her.

As practical and logical as Kate Stewart could be, she had put her marriage at a bit of a risk by standing by Mary Kay and running a media command center out of her century-old Chicago two-story. She'd defended her college friend to her husband's family. She explained all that she could to those she allowed to know her connection with the teacher in love with a student. Kate even accepted that it had been love.

But talking to the audacious and unrepentant Mary Kay from prison after the second arrest brought her no real answers for the questions that ran through her mind daily.

How many crazy things can you do? You don't watch your back. You don't care what happens. You feel as if you are on top of the world. I can do anything! So here she is sitting out in front of her house having spent the entire day with him. Going to a movie, getting a six-pack at 7-Eleven. Saying 'Fuck you' to the court!

For Kate, the greatest bond that she and Mary Kay had when they went their separate ways after Arizona State was the fact that they were mothers.

"The thing I find so difficult and so ironic is that she's a mom who is dedicated to her kids. I don't question the dedication. It is definitely there. What I don't understand is how, how can you make the decision to repeat this business when the most important thing in your whole life is your children. Who you live and die for, dressed, bathed, fed, educated, developed. Called the shots. Ran the house. *Everything.* Made sure they had the perfect birthday party. Had the right stuff. Not for other people, to impress them. But for *her.* That was her fulfillment."

But Mary Kay squandered it all for the night in her car with a teenage boy she had been forbidden to see. Kate would try, but she could never fully accept Mary Kay taking that kind of dangerous, irrevocable risk. Not when she knew that Mary Kay really did love her children. She just *had* to.

Abby Campbell phoned Michelle Jarvis with the terrible news. If Abby had done so with the thought that Michelle would commiserate with her over the injustice of it all, she was disappointed.

"She damn well deserves everything she's getting now," Michelle said. "Because she's pissed it all away."

Her remarks caught the mother of five off guard. "I can't believe you're saying that," she said.

Michelle sighed. "That's how I feel."

And she hung up. Michelle had been through good times and bad times, ups and downs, with Mary Kay. Bad times that got her an inch from *big trouble*, but nothing like this. What else could she say? *Her children were without a mother now.* And unless there was some kind of a miracle, Michelle knew Mary Kay was going to prison. There was no arguing it or wiggling her way out of it with tearful brown eyes. She'd broken parole. There was no second chance. Cake had used that one up already.

Michelle bitterly gave Tony Hollick the heave-ho that same day. It was high time, she thought.

"I hold you personally responsible for her being back in jail," she said. "It's your fault. If you had not stirred up all of this crap about how this medication was going to hurt her centers of spirituality, love, blah blah, and all these other side effects, then she would have been on her medication and she probably would have been able to control herself and not be back with Vili again."

Devastated by the news of the arrest, Tony held back. He didn't debate and he didn't charm. He hurt too much. The woman he loved was in serious trouble and Michelle Jarvis and her ranting couldn't change that at all.

It was a given. Indeed there was the look of shock and anger when eyes met throughout the Highline School District the morning Mary Kay Letourneau was arrested. But there was also the look of bitterness. The wound was gaping and bleeding. The jokes would come once more. But even worse, it was Election Day for a school funding levy and voters were coming into the schools with one thing on their minds—the pretty teacher in the steamed-up car with her former student. They weren't thinking about education and how much it should cost and which programs were worthwhile. No, they were thinking Mary Kay.

The levy lost.

"Bad feelings were dredged up again and this did not help. There are many of us who believe that Mary Letourneau cost us the election," said one administrator.

They were all there. The media vultures had descended on Seattle and the King County Courthouse as they always do when they can mix sex, a crime, and a pretty woman into their newspapers and television shows. Producers and cameramen from *48 Hours*, *The Oprah Winfrey Show*, CNN, and the usual local suspects strung cable like Chinese noodles through courthouse hallways to Linda Lau's courtroom.

For a woman who had jailhouse tantrums over her hair and attire, the Mary Letourneau who showed up at her resentencing on February 6, 1998, had let herself go. Her hair was no longer the sun-streaked coif of a woman out of touch with her crime and the public's perception of it. Instead, she was a mess. She could have achieved the same look by using a garden rake and a can of hairspray. But she hadn't, of course. Her red King County issues were long and limp on her skeletal frame, her face ashen and devoid of blush and lipstick. She weighed barely more than a hundred pounds.

"Mary Kay could have used some Mary Kay [cosmetics], if you asked me," said one observer.

Testimony from the police, supposition from the prosecutor about what was happening ["she was going to flee"], and an emotional plea for mercy from David Gehrke because his client was out of touch with reality and functioned like an adolescent had little impact on what Judge Lau could do. Mary Kay's tears would have no bearing on the outcome, either. Nothing anyone could do would stop the judge from sending her to prison.

"This is not about flaws in the system," said Judge

Lau. "It is about an opportunity you foolishly squandered."

Mary Kay Letourneau was led away to face seven and a half years in prison—her original sentence before it was deferred in favor of treatment. But there would be no treatment, now. She had abdicated that in favor of a prison cell. Her home would be the Washington Corrections Center for Women in Gig Harbor, just west of Tacoma. The first thing she did was head for the phone to call her children in Alaska. *Screw the rules of the deviancy program.* She was in prison, but she was free.

Inmate no. 769014 was instantly the superstar of the Washington prison system, if not the most celebrated or notorious female face behind bars in the entire country. Upward of thirty letters flooded her cell each day and filled the mailboxes of the lawyers and friends in support of her case. Some contained money for the defense fund. One man from Ohio sent $200.

"She is innocent because she didn't force the then thirteen-year-old to have a sexual relationship . . . He initiated the sexual part of it," wrote one supporter.

At his home in Des Moines many months after the revocation hearing, David Gehrke blamed the groupies for Mary Kay's downfall.

"I found out that people were covering for her," he said.

And look at what the "help" got her. He blamed Abby Campbell—"this groupie who was trying to help her, encourage her, and cover for her." It was Abby who had provided the pager that ended up with Vili. Her actions, David believed, were paramount in setting the events in motion that led to the parole revocation.

"I don't know what [Abby] wanted but if someone had told me about all this it would have been real obvious to me that it wasn't the right thing to do if you were enabling them [Mary Kay and Vili Fualaau] to be together."

According to David, friends also rushed over to Beth Adair's spare room where Mary had been staying and emptied it out "for fear that there was evidence of Vili" there.

"Then Abby called me on Saturday after the Friday

revocation terrified that she had all this stuff . . . and wanted to know what to do with it.''

David told Abby he'd take care of it and that she should bring Mary Kay's belongings to him. She agreed. She was glad to get rid of the stuff.

The spick-and-span room only made it look like Mary Kay had planned to flee.

It was widely known in the neighborhood that Soona was having a hard time keeping tabs on her youngest son during Mary's month-long release from the Regional Justice Center in Kent. Several times Soona and her oldest children went on Vili hunts, knocking on doors and making phone calls all over White Center.

"His family is very strict and very religious. If he didn't come home, they'd come looking for him, the mom, the brother, and the older sister. They don't stop until they find him," Danelle Johnson said.

It wasn't the fault of the Fualaaus—at least, not completely. At fourteen, Vili was determined to do what he wanted.

"He didn't tell them the truth. He didn't say I'm going to see my girl, Mary. He didn't come home from school when he was supposed to or he'd leave when they were asleep. They didn't let him go do it. They just felt hurt again," Danelle added.

Danelle Johnson remembers how upset Soona had been over her son's running around. She was very worried that the authorities would find out and take Audrey from her.

"She thought that they would think she wasn't a good mother," she said.

Though she could not see it clearly at the time, Danelle Johnson was able to see more clearly with the passage of time. Doesn't everyone? When the smoke of Mary Kay Letourneau's disaster dissipated enough for her to peer through its curtain, she could see that the teacher's legacy was formed from the trust she maintained with her young students.

"They felt like she was one of them. But she knew a little bit more than what they did, so they would do whatever she said. *She wouldn't do anything wrong to them.* She brought them into this thing. I don't know if it was to facilitate her thing with Vili or whatever. She dragged a lot of kids down with her.''

SIXTY-NINE

WITH THE REVOCATION of Mary Kay's parole, all hell had broken loose and the lawyers were busier than ever. Everyone from Oprah Winfrey to Barbara Walters to Connie Chung courted David Gehrke and Robert Huff. David in particular shuttled back and forth from one satellite hookup to the next.

It was a second chance to make the megadeal that had seemed so certain when the story first broke in the summer. Mary Kay Letourneau's incarceration for an early morning tryst with Vili Fualaau was the fade-to-black ending they needed.

"Now you've got a finish. Now you've got the last chapter," David Gehrke told producers who had passed on the project during the first wave of attention. "Now it's goddamn, she got what she deserved, or oh, man, this is really tragic," he said later. "If you just present it in a neutral fashion everybody thinks, yeah, what a story, and you don't have to moralize. Now she's in prison . . . it's a horrible tragedy or justice."

David and Susan Gehrke and Bob Huff and his girl-friend flew to New York to discuss the Letourneau story with media queens Walters, Chung, and Sawyer. When they returned to Seattle, Bob Huff sent Mary Kay a packet of information about an interview with ABC ("the only thing he's ever sent me here in prison"). Mary Kay already knew she preferred Barbara Walters and would not consider Connie Chung at all. But Susan Gehrke urged Mary Kay to talk with Diane Sawyer, too. But Mary Kay had already talked with Barbara and committed to her, so *20/20*'s anchor would have the exclusive interview.

The prisoner in the spotlight wasn't in a hurry, however.

She was sick, upset about being in prison, and didn't want anyone to see her in such a miserable state. When she said yes to the interview, she didn't know that she had to do it immediately. She thought she'd have a few weeks to get her head together.

But the next thing she heard was that Barbara Walters had cancelled the interview. "Then they [Bob Huff and David Gehrke] got all upset. 'You blew it with Barbara Walters, Mary! You've really messed up now! You made Barbara Walters wait! You made Larry King's producer wait for five hours for nothing!' "

Behind the scenes things were coming to a head insofar as David Gehrke and his representation of Mary Kay Letourneau was concerned.

The group of supporters cringed nearly every time he opened his mouth and the groundswell against him grew. When he told a national magazine that his client was "obsessed" with the boy, the outrage deepened.

It seemed that whenever a camera was around, David Gehrke was there. But whenever she needed him, Mary Kay complained to her friends that he couldn't be reached.

"You know after she got sentenced that he didn't go see her?" a friend asked. "How could he not go see her?"

Once two weeks went by without a visit to his client in prison.

"He was in New York having dinner and doing press and other things," the friend said.

David Gehrke took exception to Mary Kay's friend's characterization of a starstruck lawyer, indifferent to his client's needs. It was true that he didn't see her every day and it was also true that he did let a couple of weeks lapse between face-to-face visits. But he was within reach.

"I've always allowed collect calls from jail or prison and I can almost always be reached by telephone, at home or at the office. But I don't charge enough to babysit clients and hold their hands two or three times a week. Not even the best retained—*most expensive*—lawyer can afford to do that."

A week after Mary Kay was sent to prison, Soona Fualaau appeared in "disguise" on *American Journal*. Mary

Kay had what she thought was a better venue: *Oprah*.

"I can say with all certainty that this young man is the love of my life. Otherwise I would not have put my children through this," she said during a phone interview. She called back after her time on the prison phone was cut off. She seemed out of touch and the audience was out for blood. David Gehrke and Robert Huff sat onstage looking ridiculous and helpless. Following Oprah's lead that she didn't buy the bipolar excuse, the audience sneered, too.

"Bipolar, fourpolar, or nopolar," said one from the gallery of mostly women.

The *Oprah* experience was proof that there was great risk no matter whose show you went on.

"The *Oprah* people were pretty good," Kate Stewart said later. "But Oprah slammed her. I don't think it was personal. I think Oprah was stressed because of her own litigation in Texas."

Kate Stewart didn't run from one talk show to another. She didn't appear in the pages of national magazines to fight for her friend. She stayed behind the scenes and pressed on with the campaign for support and understanding. It was a lonely gig. When it became better known among her Chicago circle of friends that she and Mary Kay Letourneau had been college roommates, she found herself in the awkward position of defending Mary Kay to those who had been poisoned by the negative media. Some were embarrassed and dismissive. It hurt.

"You know her," she told a friend. "You met her at the wedding. You know she's a friend of mine. She's sitting in jail."

Often she'd be asked if she would feel differently if her son had been involved with his teacher. Of course, she told people, she wouldn't want her son to become intimate with his teacher. No mother would. But on the other hand, if her son was a boy at complete risk as Kate believed Vili had been, and she could not do anything to save him, then maybe the love of his teacher wouldn't be so bad.

She reminded her friends, her husband, and others who didn't get it that it was about two people. *Not just any boy*

and any woman. It had been about two people who found
each other and fell in love.

"The mistake she made was breaking the law. She's
helped that boy. She's given him the best of life. That boy
would be one of the teenagers who commits suicide," Kate
explained.

Sometimes they softened and said they understood.

"She had consensual sex with a teenager. So what?"
Kate would repeat sometimes, driving the point home that
Vili was not the only teen having sex. "All the other teenagers are out there doing it anyway at thirteen and fourteen, which Vili was doing. They don't go to prison. It's
taboo, but should she go to jail for seven years?"

One thing surprised Kate Stewart more than any aspect
during the months of the second wave of the media war
against her college friend: *Why didn't her family and its
prestige play a role in creating support for Mary Kay?*

Kate expected headlines with more understanding.

"If I read a story in the newspaper and it told me
Rockefeller's daughter . . . well educated, raised conservative Catholic, in a good home. I would think, 'Wait a
minute, why would this girl do this?' I wouldn't automat-
ically think she's a nut or pedophile," she said later.

Kate just didn't get it. *Why didn't Mary Kay's background give her credibility?*

It wasn't *Time* magazine or even *People*. The big exclusive
that so many had sought had been given to a rock magazine, *Spin*. Maxwell McNab also had an assignment to
write an article for *Mirabella*, but it was expected to be a
rehash of what had happened during the months he was
hanging out with the Mary Club at the jail in Kent.

It was Seattle novelist and journalist Matthew Stadler,
sympathetic to Mary Letourneau's plight, who took the
Spin assignment and managed to actually speak with the
subject of the article. Not long after it was known that he'd
gathered access and taped interviews, the supermarket tabloid the *Globe* called offering to pay for his notes, photos,
documents, and any interview tapes that he had accumu-

lated. The writer didn't have to think twice. He turned down the *Globe*.

KIRO-TV's pursuit was a bit dicier. Since Matthew's brother worked at the Seattle station, several people there assumed they'd have the edge. Karen O'Leary was one.

"Do you have the tapes?" Karen asked.

The writer hedged. "I don't know where they are."

That didn't seem to suit the TV reporter. Later he learned that Karen had told his brother that he in fact had the tapes and that he'd find them.

"Karen is waiting for the tapes," the brother said.

Matthew Stadler was furious. "I told her I didn't know where they are and I'm not going to find them."

Another staffer called next.

"[He] said they'd pay me money if I would find the tapes."

Not in this lifetime. Stadler got rid of everything. Making quick money by betraying Mary Kay Letourneau wasn't his style. There had already been enough of that.

And deep down, he knew there would be a whole lot more.

SEVENTY

THE BOY WAS Samoan, and, in 1998, people began to focus on that aspect. Was it cultural? Was he some man-child from the island? Lima Skillion, executive director of the Seattle Samoan Center, a social services agency serving the four thousand Samoans and Pacific Islanders in the area, wanted to help, she said, not ridicule. The mother of two put the word out. She wanted to know who the family was. And did they need support?

No one came forward right away. But in time, word sifted throughout the community that the Samoan boy was from White Center and was the son of a single mother. Though KIRO-TV's interview in the park had showed his hands and ring, his face had been obscured. No one knew

exactly which Samoan kid had the fling—or was raped—
by his pretty, blond teacher.

Not long after Lima's outreach, a local social worker
came to inquire about the resources available in the Samoan community.

"[Social Services] had a meeting finding out about how
the Samoan community was looking toward this particular
situation, case. Nobody knew then who these people
were," Lima Skillion recalled.

She advocated a slow approach, no "jumping into conclusions."

"They were discussing taking the child—the boy's
baby—from these people. What would Samoan people do
with this baby?"

She understood through overtures made to the social
service agents that the Samoan senior center offered to
help take care of the baby. But they really didn't know
what could be done. No one knew who the boy was. Or,
if they did, they weren't talking.

It was a nudge from a staff member in the parking lot
of the White Center Albertson's grocery store that finally
clued in Seattle Samoan Center Executive Director Lima
Skillion.

"That's the boy's aunt," the staff member said.

Lima Skillion couldn't believe her eyes and ears. She
didn't need to ask *which boy*. She knew her companion
meant the boy who had become the talk of the Samoan
community—the boy who was involved with his teacher.
She also knew his family. The father of the clan had been
a minister. She knew what kind of people they were. From
what she had seen over the years, Lima Skillion could not
have imagined that that particular family could be involved
in such a scandal.

"That mother was always with this family, putting her
family together. Telling her children that this is not right
and this is right and blah, blah, blah. And how they turn
out . . . we've done our part. You can only do so much. I
know he was from a very disciplinary family."

It couldn't be a boy from that family. "No," she said
that early evening in the parking lot. "That's not right."

Her staff member nodded. "Yeah. Yeah," she said.

Lima Skillion put her shopping aside and walked over to Soona Fualaau's sister's car and stood by the driver's window, while the occupant rolled it down.

"Is this true?" she asked.

"About?" the woman asked.

"Is the boy in the news your nephew?"

The woman was surprised and not all that happy about the intrusion, the question. But she admitted that it was Vili, her nephew. It bothered her that it was known among the people of the community.

The aunt was in shock, Lima said later.

"She had just found out that the citizens and people had discussed the case. They were more private people. There was too many people into their business."

Lima offered to help in any way that she and the center could. She passed a business card through the open window.

The aunt was much happier. Maybe relieved. She left with words that the Samoan leader would never forget. It was a rebuttal to some things said by others in the Samoan community.

"Lima," the aunt said, "we didn't teach our boy to go do what he did."

Not long after running into Vili's aunt in the grocery's parking lot, Lima made the same offer of help to the pastor of the Fualaaus' church. She didn't discuss the case, she just told the minister that she understood what tremendous pain the family was going through and that she and all of her resources were there for them. Soona's mother called later to thank Lima for her concern and for the offer of help. Yes, she said, they had a lawyer.

Some thought the whole affair reeked of the exploitation of a young boy, but Lima Skillion viewed it differently. Though Mary should have known better, she was in love. So was the boy.

"I looked at their feelings," Lima said later. "They got strong for one another. You know those emotional feelings—right or wrong. You've got to fight with your inner person there, where she acted it out. I know that the feeling was mutual for both of them. I believe it was a love deeper than we can really look at it. It meant a lot to her, this whole thing here with this boy.''

She felt sadness for Mary Letourneau and how things would turn out for her. The boy's family was strong, she thought, and they'd make the best for him. But Mary, Mary was a tragic figure.

"She truly loved him for her to risk a whole lot of her heart, her life. She lost a lot more than he did. It is a sad price to pay if there was true love.''

SEVENTY-ONE

IT WAS ALWAYS the same song and dance and Mary Kay Letourneau's lawyers learned the steps and the lyrics quickly. The Hollywood crowd still seeking the rights to Mary Kay's story wanted to secure it by putting a small amount of money down with the promise that when they placed it "with a major production company and major network," they'd all get a giant payday. But David Gehrke didn't want promises of more later. He wanted it now. So did Bob Huff. They wanted an offer of cash up front.

"We like your connections," David said more than once. "Your proposal sounds great. Put the figure down on paper and we'll consider it.''

But the producers never did.

"One guy said he had a cashier's check for two hundred thousand and we told him we'd meet him at the airport. Be sure to bring the check. Call us when you're there.''

That hot-to-trot producer never showed up at SeaTac.

As David Gehrke and Bob Huff entertained offers from mainstream American television and film companies, a unique opportunity presented itself when James Kent, a producer from the British Broadcasting Corporation, contacted the lawyers in the early spring of 1998. A veteran of more than two decades of producing documentaries, James Kent had seen a story about Mary Letourneau in

November 1997 and was intrigued. When the teacher was arrested for the second time, his interest grew. The Brit booked a flight from London to Seattle. He didn't know it at the time, but things were about to become increasingly difficult for the legitimate press, and the BBC could certainly be considered one of the premier media outlets in the world.

James Kent did not see her during that visit, but Mary Kay told him over the phone that she and her lawyers were very interested in participating in a film produced by the BBC. With that understanding, James Kent returned to London and arranged for financing.

When he returned to Seattle a short time later things had changed dramatically. By that time, messages weren't being returned by either David Gehrke or Robert Huff. Mary Kay, however, still seemed supportive of the BBC production, to the extent that she made repeated calls to the producer providing background and details that would constitute the basis for the on-camera interview that they agreed to record at the prison later in the summer.

By that time, several media deals were hammered out. Sonny Grosso, a New York producer, negotiated the rights for a television movie that eventually found a home at cable's USA Network. A book was also in the works. The publishing company was French—Fixot, headquartered in Paris. The publisher was Robert Laffont.

The rumored deal for the French book alone was a quarter of a million dollars.

"It was much more than that," David Gehrke said later of the deal that gave Bob Huff a fifteen to twenty percent agent's fee and united both convicted rapist and victim in a mutual business deal. How much Mary Kay was getting from both deals was unclear. She told friends that a trust fund with proceeds from the book was being set up for "all of my children." She had no profit participation with the movie.

"They [Bob Huff and David Gehrke] didn't want my name on anything," she said later. "My involvement in any deal could be used against me by the prosecution."

There was no contract for the TV movie and no direct

promise of money, though at one time a lump sum was discussed in lieu of a percentage of the gross.

"I'm not getting anything, but I hope that there is some gift for my children. I haven't asked Susan [Gehrke] about it, but I'm hoping."

James Kent rented a house and planned to stay for six weeks—four weeks researching and two filming.

"I was caught up in a kind of media legal tangle that I had never experienced before. It clearly was a story that involved legal participants and those in the media circle around the story in a way they themselves got entangled in it. I think there was money to be made from this story and I think that did complicate clear lines of command. Mary couldn't, ideally, represent herself. She was caught between her legal team and the media."

The British producer knew a book deal was in the offing, but he didn't know exactly how wrapped up into the whole affair Mary Letourneau and her two Seattle lawyers were. The publishing company had big plans for the story, including a documentary and possibly even a theatrical release. What no one knew for the first few weeks of the spring of 1998 was what that all meant to members of the media seeking access to Mary Kay.

"I think they [the lawyers] themselves, to be fair, didn't realize that the publishers of the book, who had their own intended documentary planned, would have reacted so negatively to a BBC film being made."

James Kent would become less charitable in his assessment of the Letourneau legal team. In the beginning he found sympathy for their position. He sensed David Gehrke and Bob Huff were in over their heads, unused to a story of the magnitude of the Letourneau case.

"They found themselves, let me put it this way, caught between the devil and the deep blue sea—the media, the book publishers in France, and the BBC in London," he said later.

Sometimes Kate Stewart would wonder how it got so strange. There she was, darkness all around, with time to think about nothing but Mary Kay Letourneau. Kate was up at two A.M. waiting for a messenger to come from *People* magazine to take photos from Chicago to New York. She had spent half the night carefully identifying the images of Mary Kay and Steve, mostly from her 1988 wedding.

"They were a happy little family," she said later while reviewing the images remaining in her album. Empty pages provided silent testimony to the demand for pictures from her wedding.

Mary Kay had loathed the jailhouse photos, the mug shots that had been plastered in the media. She wanted something decent out and Kate agreed not only because she was her friend, but also because she had a treasure trove of Mary Kay photos.

That early morning as she waited, firemen were flushing the hydrants and a spray of water hit the edge of the Stewarts' charming front porch. She kept an eye on the family dog to make sure no one woke up. But mostly she worried about the water ruining the photos in an envelope on the porch and the bizarre turn of events of the past months.

How did I get involved with this crazy story? she asked herself.

SEVENTY-TWO

MARY KAY LETOURNEAU was pregnant. It was the topper of all toppers and when it was discovered in mid-March it pushed Mary Kay Letourneau back on the front pages of newspapers and into world headlines—though there had barely been a lull since her arrest in February. Newsgroups chattered about her on the Internet. Talk shows geared up. *American Journal* came calling again. After she arrived in prison, a sonogram was performed and it detected the heartbeat of a six-week-old fetus. The fact that she was pregnant again moved her story into the category of the unbelievable, but true. For Mary Kay, it gave her something on which to focus while she appealed her case and sought a new lawyer. She was overjoyed at the life growing within her.

It was further proof of her love for Vili Fualaau.

When the second-pregnancy story made the news, it was attributed to Kate Stewart, "a good friend from the Midwest."

But she had never confirmed anything.

"That was a reporter's trick," she said later. "They were only saying that because they got inside information from the prison and they needed a second confirmation. They just used me. They couldn't say they got it from the prison . . . that was illegal. They tried to get me to confirm it but they couldn't."

Abby Campbell called Michelle Jarvis to recount Vili's words when the teenager found out he was going to be a father again.

"Oh, fuck!" he had said.

"What do you think of his reaction?" Abby asked.

What could Michelle say? She figured it could be one of two things. Vili might have been horrified that he was going to be a father again, or it might have dawned on him instantly that her pregnancy could provide proof that they had sex again.

For Bob Huff and David Gehrke, the pregnancy meant Mary Kay had made her story worth all that much more money. And some believed that was all that mattered. As spring marched forward, Michelle Jarvis began to feel that no one really cared about Mary Kay. All they cared about was making money off her.

"She's nothing but a commodity . . . her story is something that is fodder for the media. They own it and it's just money making," she said later.

Bob Huff, for one, would have no part of Michelle's allegations. He had been given a job to do—to sell her story, but he insisted that didn't mean he didn't care about her. He said when visiting her in prison, at times, he was depressed for her.

"Whatever she is . . . in love with Vili or some sick monster . . . whatever anyone thinks, prison is not the place for Mary Kay. She's quick-witted. She's charming. She's funny. And I was more concerned about what was happening to her than *she* was. She'd try to cheer *me* up."

One of the most tragic aspects of her friend's life, Michelle believed, was that Mary Kay was so wrapped up in herself and her love story that she couldn't see what was happening.

"She's so narcissistic that she thinks that she is so important to all those other people, she doesn't see herself for what she is—just a way for them to make money, that's all. I don't think that anybody really gives a damn about her. Does Vili?"

SEVENTY-THREE

IN THE LAST week in April 1998, Michelle Jarvis boarded a flight to Seattle to honor the request of her best friend. Mary Kay had asked Michelle to be Audrey's godmother. She didn't want to go and considered trying to get out of it. She had been worn down by the pressure and the hopelessness of everything that swirled around her childhood friend. Mary Kay had been mad at her for some of the things she had said on the *Sally Jessy Raphael* show.

"I never said Vili was twenty-some years old . . ." Mary Kay protested.

Michelle had processed so much her head was spinning. She thought of excuses, but her sense of duty won out. Among the items she carried onboard was a copy of *People* magazine with Mary Kay and baby Audrey on the cover and a note from her husband, Michael.

"Read it when you get onboard," he said when he kissed her good-bye.

She and Michael had argued over the whole affair and whether it really was a good idea for Michelle to be a part of what was happening in Seattle. They had anguished over it for months. There had even been tears the morning of the flight. From where the Jarvises sat, Audrey's baptism looked more crafted for the camera than for God. Michael wondered if Michelle was simply being used.

"A lot of times," Michael Jarvis said later, "Mary Kay wasn't really there for Michelle, but whenever she needed something or help with her problems, Michelle was there."

Michelle got to her seat and unfolded her husband's note. No words ever rang more true:

"Mary Kay being the fine manipulator that she is, look where you're sitting right now. I know you love your girl-friend regardless [of] how she feels about you—I know you are going to be there, because that's the kind of person that you are."

Tears rolled down her cheeks and she stared out the little oval window, not focusing on anything but her thoughts. It was such a terrible mess and Michelle knew it was far from over. She knew that because she knew her friend better than anyone else in the world. She doubted that Mary Kay still loved Vili, but she had been boxed into such a corner that she had no choice but to continue the charade.

"Regardless of what she thinks about Vili," she said later, "she's going to have to make the world believe that she's a victim, because that's the kind of person she is. She manipulates things to that extent. It doesn't matter what she thinks of Vili, she's going to let the world believe that she's in love with him until it is convenient for her to let go."

Michelle flipped through the pages of the magazine and turned her thoughts to the baby, the reason for her two-hour flight north.

What will become of Audrey? she asked herself.

It was to be the perfect baptism of Audrey Lokelani. Nothing short of perfect would do, because Mary Kay Letourneau expected nothing less for any of her children. She had instructed both Kate and Michelle from her prison cell to be sure the details were just so. The ceremony was set for the chapel at Seattle University. Officials from Seattle's St. James Cathedral had refused to allow the baptism to take place there because of concerns over publicity. Mary Kay was disappointed, but that the Jesuit priest who had worked with her and Steve on their "peaceful coexistence'' contract was officiating lessened the blow. She had ordered a beautiful lace christening gown from an exclusive boutique in Redmond, Washington, during her weeks out with Vili in January.

She thought, of course, that she'd be able to be there.

That morning, Mary Kay looked out the window from the prison clinic where she was being monitored for some spotting during her ninth pregnancy and held the image of the spring sky in her mind. She wrote of the day in a journal that she kept for Audrey. Though she wasn't there, she wanted her daughter to know that she was a part of the sacred day in her heart, and spirit. She made out a list so that Audrey would know who had been present. She made special mention of Michelle, of course, as her baby's godmother; Favaae Fualaau, Vili's older brother, was the godfather.

The ceremony was lovely; Kate had seen to it. Mary Kay saw her friend as a stand-in for her taste and sensibilities.

"She is me as far as aesthetics go," Mary Kay later said. "Making sure the crown for Audrey was perfect, the roses for the top of the cake, the details at the brunch."

It was the brunch at the Marriott Hotel near SeaTac, however, that was not so perfect. Mary Kay had selected the venue because she thought that the garden theme of the dining area would be pretty, given the time of year and the love she had for flowers. Had she been there, she would have cringed at the scene.

It was not a typical baptism brunch, nor could it be. But the way the Fualaaus and representatives of their lawyers were acting, it was clear that the focus was not on the baby, but on the business deal that had become Audrey, Vili, and Mary Kay. Attendees had been sworn to secrecy so the media wouldn't intrude. A different name was used for the reservations at the Marriott.

Bodyguards in dark glasses ran around looking in bushes, setting ground rules for photography, reminding people to keep their mouths shut to protect the Fualaaus' reported $50,000 deal with the *Globe*. It was assumed that the whole world would converge on the hotel if someone leaked news of it. And with all the money beginning to change hands, there was the incentive to keep a lid on it.

What is this? Kate Stewart thought, put off by the whole attitude. This is like having lunch with the Mafia.

Kate brought her camera and had only needed one good shot. She had promised Mary Kay that she would get one to James Kent, the BBC producer. She ended up taking fourteen rolls of film.

"Soona took the negatives from me," she said later. "So in fear that they might get out somehow and jeopardize her deal, or to protect the baby, I don't know."

A bodyguard took the film to a nearby photo processor and waited in the back while the prints were being made to make sure that nobody stole any pictures.

Michelle was dumbfounded by the whole thing as she watched a few attendees knock back drinks in the bar. *This is a baptism, for God's sake.* When their eyes met, she could see that Kate was feeling the same way. *What was going on here?*

"It's all about money," Michelle concluded later. "When it comes down to it, nothing else mattered in this whole scenario. Not the kids, not Mary Kay, not Vili, nothing, but for the money that could be made."

Oddly—considering their roles in the case—the lawyers had not been invited. Susan Gehrke, David's wife, however, was present. When she saw Michelle Jarvis she went up to her to tell her that she and her husband had admired the way she stood her ground during an appearance on the *Sally Jessy Raphael* show.

"David and I were impressed with how well you did," the schoolteacher said.

Michelle turned her back on Susan. "Well, if your husband hadn't done such a bad job that wouldn't have been necessary."

"It almost reduced her to tears," David Gehrke said later of his wife's reaction to the remark.

Paranoia and blame had settled in and a baby's baptism was somehow lost in the mire.

As David Gehrke saw it later: "The *Globe* article had just come out and the *Globe* representative was bird-dogging Soona to protect her and protect *Globe*'s rights. BBC was around and there was talk that they had been invited in by the Chicago faction to surreptitiously videotape it. The Boston attorney was in town and was talking that it [the fact Mary Kay was in prison] was all my fault.''

Kate had, in fact, also promised to videotape Audrey's baptism with the idea that Mary Kay's parents and the BBC would get copies. One for love; one for money. But according to Kate and others, the video was confiscated moments after she shot it. The *Globe* was in town and had an exclusive on the story. That meant sentiments were shoved aside. No one was to take anything from the event. Nothing but memories.

"It felt like nothing must come in the way of the money that was being made from the Mary Kay Letourneau story," James Kent said later. "There were people who saw this as a chance to make a lot of money, and I felt very disappointed by that."

Lawyer Huff didn't deny that cash was being collected from the Letourneau story or from Audrey's baptism in particular. And, he said, if the air was tinged with paranoia at the blessed ceremony, there was good reason for it.

"I think Soona was worried about the pictures getting out," Bob Huff said later. "Soona was trying to cool it on the baby pictures because she got reamed by the judge in selling photos. Also, I think she wanted to keep the photos because they were worth money. I think Mary's friend's sold some of those that Soona gave them later. Soona was real pissed about that.''

Meeting Vili and his family was eye-opening for Michelle. She and Mary Kay had spent hours in her Spyglass Hill bedroom dreaming of their lives and the men they would marry. Michelle had realized her dreams of a loving husband and three children. Sure, it wasn't exactly as she had planned, but it was close. But Mary Kay and this boy and his family seemed so far off the mark. It wasn't that Michelle didn't like or accept Vili. There was a side to him that she could see Mary Kay might have found appealing in her loneliness. Michelle's heart was touched when the fourteen-year-old put a white rose on a chair to symbolize Mary Kay's presence at what was to be a holy gathering. The three rings he had also moved her: one from Mary to him, his to her, and one for their baby, Audrey.

Michelle looked at his artwork back at the house, and like Kate, thought he was a talented artist, and some of his writings were "quite deep." She could see how a woman falling apart might romanticize the boy and his abilities and what it all could mean to her.

But in reality, she knew, the boy with the stubby ponytail and shaved sides of his head was also a typical teenager.

"Then he turns on rap music where every other word is rap music with the F word."

Michelle could see the family was doing the best that they could, or at least they seemed to be trying. Audrey was getting a lot of attention, a lot of love. But what common ground did Mary Kay share with those people? None that Michelle could see.

"They weren't raised at the same social level as Mary Kay was. We're talking poor people. There is a huge difference. This is not against the family. It is just the facts."

A shopping trip for Doc Martens at the mall became a kind of bonding experience for Kate and Vili. But he was still so young, so awkward, that Kate could never find the right moment to ask the question that lingered in the back of her mind.

Will you wait for Mary Kay?

Finally, she broached the subject to Soona.

"I want him to be happy," Vili's mother said with great conviction. "I want whatever is right for my son. Just because he has two children with Mary does not obligate him to marry her."

Kate understood. If it had been her son who had been caught up in the turmoil of such an affair, she'd have felt the same way. She might have hoped for a more positive response from Soona Fualaau, but Kate knew that only time would tell anyway. And there was a lot of time. Seven years, to be sure.

Vili's grandmother was less "let's wait and see."

"Don't you look at another girl," she said to Vili as Kate looked on. "You've got those babies . . . you marry that girl. You wait for her."

Even before there was a second baby on the way, Mary Kay and her friends worried about whether she'd ever get Audrey back from Soona. It wasn't that she thought Soona was unfit, but simply that Mary Kay wanted to raise her own daughter herself. She had lost her first four to Steve and it would be a battle on the order of a world war to get them back. For a woman who often defined herself by the children she bore, Mary Kay was desperate to retain the bond that she had tried to forge between herself, her infant daughter, and Vili.

"Mary's parental rights are definitely at stake here," said a close friend. "As more time goes by, the more attached Soona is to Audrey. And there ain't no parting of the ways with that woman and that child, I'll tell you now."

When Soona referred to Audrey, it wasn't as her granddaughter, but her own infant.

"She says that's 'my baby.' *My baby*."

But there was also another possible reason. By keeping Audrey, they kept the tabloid and book money, too.

"She's like the little Vanderbilt child in that family," claimed the friend.

SEVENTY-FOUR

THE DAY OF Audrey's baptism, April 26, four women made the drive from south Seattle to Tacoma and across the Narrows Bridge to the women's prison near Gig Harbor. They came with the hope they could see Mary Kay Letourneau. Abby Campbell drove, and Kate Stewart, Michelle Jarvis, and a TV tabloid reporter for *American Journal* accompanied her. The reporter was along "doing background," but at least Michelle suspected that she was still after a Mary Kay interview and knew that hanging out with her three best friends couldn't hurt her chances. By then, the three women were old hands at the tabloid game. Abby and Kate had been interviewed, but they'd kept their names and faces out of the news. Only Michelle had gone on camera.

The women met with disappointment when, after filling out the requisite forms, they were denied the opportunity to see Mary Kay. The guards said Mary Kay was in the infirmary and could not have any visitors. One of the friends asked if they could have a tour of the prison, but that was also denied.

"For security reasons," the guard said. "And no picture-taking on prison grounds, either."

When they got outside, one of the women suggested taking a group picture in front of the prison flagpole.

"Let's just stand together and hold hands and send Mary Kay our energy and hope that she knows that we've been here."

The television tabloid reporter took the photograph and the four started to walk over to their car when a voice called out.

"Hey! Hey!"

"Run!" Abby started to yell and the other three sprinted for the car. Michelle was unclear why they were running, but like a member of some kind of herd her feet started to move.

What's going on? she thought.

Just as Michelle jumped into the backseat, Abby Campbell pushed the gas pedal to the floor and threw the car into reverse. The dark blur of a uniformed officer moved in their direction and a little meter-maid-type cart was also revved up and headed their way.

"What do you think you are going to do?" Michelle asked the panicked driver. "Outrun them?"

"Pull over," the voice said.

Abby looked blankly at a guard. "What did we do?" she asked.

"We specifically told you not to take pictures on the prison grounds."

"But we were in the parking lot," Abby said.

The guard pointed out that the entire property was considered a secure area and the instructions for no photography applied throughout—parking lot included.

"We won't take any more."

Later the four laughed it off, but what they didn't know was that their parking lot escapade and Abby's getaway-car antics had cost them something very dear. A few weeks later each would get a letter from the prison superintendent, Alice Payne.

"When staff learned of your actions and attempted to make contact with you, you attempted to elude them unsuccessfully."

The prison put Mary Kay's friends on notice: They were no longer eligible to visit any inmate at the women's prison. They were banned from prison grounds. For good.

"I was so crushed when I got that letter," Michelle Jarvis said later. "It was just another way they are trying to destroy Mary Kay by cutting off access from people who are closest to her. Their whole mission in life is to completely crush her. They hate her. They hate her. This was an easy way to put the screws to her again."

Having lost faith in David Gehrke, Mary Kay's friends wanted very much to meet his partner, Robert Huff. But just as had been the experience of most of the media, the younger of the two attorneys was extremely elusive. Again, as always, no return calls.

The baptism was an opportunity to see him and both Michelle Jarvis and Kate Stewart knew it. When they finally reached him, he promised he'd either get back to them or meet them after the baptism. Though they talked that one time—mostly about money matters—he never did show for a meeting.

"He told Kate that he thought money could go to Mary Kay's defense fund as long as it didn't come from us," Michelle recalled. "If it came from Vili's family then it would be okay. But we're guessing he's telling Vili's family that they can't give any money to the defense fund because it might be a problem. I'm guessing he's playing two ends against the middle. He's controlling the money totally.''

And as the bank account from the Letourneau story grew fatter and fatter, the friends wondered where the money was going and when it would help Mary Kay get out of prison.

That first *Globe* article made Mary Kay's real friends wince. They knew instantly it would make their positions as defenders of a great cause even tougher than ever. Michelle and Kate saw it for the first time when they were up in Seattle for the baptism. *Such good timing.* An *American Journal* reporter told the women that she thought, as Vili's agent, Bob Huff had been paid for the photographs and interviews with Vili and Soona.

Certainly the money concerned Michelle. It wasn't that someone shouldn't be paid, it was where the money was going that distressed her. As far as she knew the defense fund had not received a penny from the selling of Mary Kay.

The article's description of the to-the-moon sex, anytime and everywhere, disturbed her greatly and gave her doubt about what had really happened between Vili and Mary Kay.

''Kate and I thought at one point the affair she had with Vili was nothing more than sexual obsession. Maybe that's all it was. Really. [She said it was] this incredibly spiritual, passionate thing, when it was nothing more than this heightened sexual state that she goes into.''

Shorewood teachers and students got a quick lesson in the reality of the supermarket tabloids around that time. A pair of Shorewood teachers was shopping at an area Wal-Mart when one told the other she needed to get a *Globe*. The teacher cluelessly searched the shelf while the other grabbed the tabloid and put it in her basket.

''And I'm looking for a model of the Earth,'' she said.

It was a mistake she'd never make again. Nearly from the beginning, *Globe* was not a planet, but a source of Mary Kay Letourneau news.

One student looked at the spiffed-up pictures of Vili Fualaau staged for his daughter's baptism.

The girl shook her head and pointed at the demure photographs.

"This is not him. He dresses gangster style in the large shirt and baggy pants. They made him look all so neat."

Puhleez, the mother of the Shorewood student thought.

As the world beat a path to Soona's front door to learn more about her son who had been raped by his teacher, the other Fualaau children were shoved aside, leaving the attention focused on the youngest. *The star of the story.* He was not courted for his artistic talents, but for the fact that he had been sexually involved with a teacher.

It could not have been a proud moment for any mother.

Kate was certain David Gehrke was either directly or through Susan Gehrke's mysterious entertainment contract—*television, film, literary?*—reaping some kind of windfall from his representation of his now-famous client. The "haven't made a penny" proclamation didn't wash with her. Kate was adamant that whatever deals Bob Huff was engineering with the tabloid media and book publishers, David Gehrke was getting a piece of the pie, too.

"Huff was the front man on the media deals. David was in the shadows, but he was a part of everything. He doesn't want anyone to know," she insisted later. "How many attorneys do you know who profit from this kind of stuff? Not many."

David Gehrke shrugged off Kate's charges. He admitted his wife's story of being Mary Kay's friend could lead to big payday—if the TV movie was produced—but it was Susan's deal, not his. Besides, he said, "Mary wanted Susan to be a paid consultant on the project because she trusts her to do it right."

Instead of getting rich, David told Kate and others that when it came to his legal fees he gave Mary Kay a deal.

"I gave her my neighbor's-charged-with-rape-friend-in-need-easy-plea-discount," he explained later. "I've joked to colleagues how little I got paid for all the work I did. I basically got a few trips out of it, and that's about it."

In April 1998, a no-nonsense lawyer from Boston named Susan Howards joined Camp Mary Kay as the appellate attorney. She'd made much of her career and reputation by winning appeals for women who had been abused by boyfriends and husbands. Though she didn't publicly make a statement about Mary Kay's appellate efforts, it was considered a good bet that the alleged abuse by Steve Letourneau was going to factor into the case, too. It was the appearance by Michelle Jarvis on the *Sally Jessy Raphael* show in New York that led to the new lawyer.

"It was the one good thing that has come out of doing any media," Michelle said later.

David Gehrke and Bob Huff were out and the women and men devoted to Mary Kay Letourneau could not have been happier. But the break wasn't as clean and complete as some would have liked. Bob Huff was still involved with the media deals. Somehow they'd retained that responsibility. And though he had no connection to Mary Kay other than as the broker for her story, Bob Huff sometimes called Kate after weeks of being out of reach and would say he was tired of being kept out of the loop.

"Like it's *our* fault," an exasperated Kate Stewart told a friend. "Like it was Susan's fault. Like it's someone's fault."

Kate couldn't figure out what Bob Huff was doing half the time, he was so elusive. He seldom got back to anyone.

"I don't know what kind of law he practices," she said. "I don't even know if he has any other clients."

"She's washed her hands of David," Kate said.

Cutting all ties to Bob Huff proved more difficult.

"I think Bob's her link to Vili and she's afraid to hurt that," Kate said.

In prison, isolated from her children, virtually ignored by her siblings, Mary Kay Letourneau saw the lawyers as her family.

"You know how you have members of your family and you might not agree with everything they've done or said, but you still accept them because they are family."

When she heard a particular photo had appeared in a magazine that she hadn't authorized, she suspected it had been taken from her storage locker. She was both disappointed and exasperated. But she knew who was responsible.

"I kept asking them [the lawyers] for a copy of the article," she told a friend later, "but they never sent it to me."

They were family and she could almost forgive them.

Bob Huff maintained there had never been any theft from Mary Kay's storage locker or anywhere else. He recalled how in the summer of 1998 he and ghostwriter Bob Graham accompanied Vili to retrieve some of Mary Kay's belongings from a mini-storage unit.

"She would say Vili should make decisions, then he would go and do stuff and she'd get mad. You couldn't win with her," he said.

According to the lawyer, Mary Kay was upset because a cheerleading photograph showing her spread-eagled in midair turned up in the media.

"She was mad because she said it was the wrong shot. It showed her in some kind of flawed position," he said. "She told me, 'Anyone who knows anything about cheerleading can see it . . . it is so obvious!' "

SEVENTY-FIVE

REPORTERS LIVE AND die by the tips that come their way. On the morning of a legal conference with lawyers to discuss their next move in the lawsuit, the television reporter at the center of the legal storm got a tip that Vili Fualaau and Mary Kay Letourneau were on the front cover of the *Globe*. A few calls later, the grainy image from a fax machine spit out the pages from the May 5, 1998, issue.

JAILED TEACHER'S 6TH GRADE LOVER TELLS ALL!

The four-page "special report" detailed how Vili and his teacher had had sex in every room of the Letourneau home, on the deck, even on a yard swing. The boy who Bob Huff had said wanted nothing but to be left alone was blabbing about the most intimate details of his life. And his mother, who had wrung her hands with worry over the impact of the KIRO interview, was spilling her guts, too. As if she hadn't even paid attention to the sexual escapades described by her son, Soona told the world how Vili's "romance with his teacher was based on true love, not lust."

Karen O'Leary waved the fax in front of the lawyers. She knew the law. Her estranged husband was a lawyer. So were her father and her brother. Everyone in the room was aware that the article had been of the type where money had changed hands. But just how much? They knew Soona had been paid a few thousand for the *American Journal* interview, but this was a bigger deal. Twenty-five thousand dollars? Fifty thousand? Maybe more?

One thing was certain. Bob Huff's lawsuit was toast.

"It was a bombshell that totally undermined their case about violating this boy's privacy, with the boy plastered all over this tabloid about losing his virginity," Karen said later. "This was manna from heaven. It just showed the lies that was their case."

Michelle Jarvis couldn't bear the sight of Steve Letourneau on television. She refused to watch Oprah Winfrey's talk show earlier in the year because she knew that Steve was appearing on the program. She saw him as a man whose primary purpose was to destroy his wife, to make her pay. She remembered what Mary Kay had told her he said when their battle turned ugly: *"I will win."*

"He hasn't finished with her yet," Michelle told a friend. "Every minute that he torments her he's happy. That's his motivation to go on living. She says that he's a good father. I don't know that he cares about those kids. I don't know that *she* does."

If Michelle couldn't face watching Steve Letourneau on television, Kate Stewart stayed up late one night to catch

Steve and his girlfriend Kelly Whalen on one of the tabloid shows that had claimed them as their "exclusive" prize.

The whole idea of Kelly appearing on TV sent Kate reeling.

"Why would she ever put her face out here? Standing by her man, like Hillary. He's going through a divorce and has a live-in lover!"

As time passed and the media frenzy continued, Steve's comments in the newspapers and appearances on television not only irritated Kate, but she felt they gave the world a true and unflattering glimpse at the man behind the woman and the boy.

"Look what he's done to his family," she told a friend, her voice rising to stress the importance of what she had to say. "Why did he have to try his wife in the press at his children's expense? Let's have the world look at that one. That's the one thing from a religious standpoint that he's going to come down and die on that one. He could have handled it in private. *They were going to*. His ego couldn't take it."

Steve Letourneau's media appearances were as dangerous as a baby crawling on broken glass. By putting himself out there in front of America—and the world—he was risking having his own behavior made public. It wouldn't be hard for the disclosure of his affairs, and the fact that he had fathered another woman's baby, to give the sympathetic and the fence-sitters a reason to believe in Mary Kay.

Steve, with his deer-in-the-headlights gaze, was a tragic figure and most could rally around him, but the more he said, the more he tried to compete with his wife's relentless media assault, the greater the chance that a reporter would ask: *What were you doing when your wife was sleeping with a sixth-grader?*

Secret Squirrel Linda Gardner confronted Steve after another of the endless waves of media interest.

"Steve, you might think it is kind of neat having these people wanting to interview you. Someone is going to dig out all of it. And you are going to be made out to look like the bad guy."

Steve pooh-poohed her worries.

"We need the money," he said. "We're broke. I've got four kids to raise."

But it was the children who were precisely the reason Linda advised against the media blitz.

"Your kids are seeing it," she said.

Even Kelly weighed in with a defense. They were, in fact, doing it for the children. There was no child support from their mother.

"We're not getting any money from Mary Kay," she told Linda.

Steve's cousin's wife Linda was incredulous. "She's in *prison*," she reminded them. "What does she get, ten dollars a month?"

As time passed and Steve's face became a bit more familiar in magazines and on television, Linda calculated what kind of money the effort was bringing to the Alaska coffers. The figures she heard from Steve and other family members put it at $30,000 or more. But the money didn't seem to go far enough.

"I know the money is gone," she said later. "To pay bills, buy a computer. Go to Nordstrom to go shopping. Eddie Bauer."

She made another stab at getting Steve to see the light and confronted him.

"Steve, you are a fool. Get off of the TV. What are you doing? People know you're getting paid. Don't talk to those trashy magazines. Don't talk to *American Journal*. You might as well talk to the *Globe*."

He didn't listen. Not when his wife was a superstar and he was known as the man who had been pushed out of his marital bed by a kid who didn't even shave yet.

SEVENTY-SIX

WHILE THE FALLEN schoolteacher recounted her love story to Bob Graham, the Irish ghostwriter assigned to help her write the French book, it seemed no one was counseling Mary Kay on what she should and shouldn't say to the man. He kept pushing her during their interviews to give up the most intimate details of her relationship with Vili Fualaau. Mary Kay was reluctant to do so. It wasn't the kind of book she wanted her name on. She wanted the focus to be on her love for Vili, not their sex life.

"You're not trusting me enough," she recalled the Fixot ghostwriter telling her.

Mary Kay later said she felt awkward about it. She was sitting there in a visiting room with a guard right next to her listening to every intimate detail that the ghostwriter could pull from her.

"Every time he asked a very personal question, she [the prison employee] would stare at me and listen," Mary Kay told a friend later.

Mary Kay had been promised she'd have a chance to edit the book before publication, so there was at least that safeguard. But it really wasn't enough protection for a client who, whenever she opened her mouth, dug herself in deeper and deeper.

Lawyer Susan Howards had no say over the deal made between Bob Huff and the French publisher. The book deal, friends like Kate Stewart believed, was the pot of gold the lawyers had sought from the beginning. They believed the deal wasn't about getting Mary Kay out of prison or even presenting a more positive image to the world.

"The only thing Bob Huff and David were concerned about was making a million-dollar book deal. The only concern they've had that they've said outwardly to me is the book deal," Kate said later.

Kate and others had been worried about the deal from

the beginning. She didn't know if it was really in the best
interest of her friend to do it. She knew it would make
money. But would it really help Mary Kay's cause? It was
about getting her freedom. Kate begged her friend to get
another lawyer to look at the book contract.

"I don't care if it's a fly-by-night attorney, have someone else look at it. You sit on it."

Mary Kay did not take her advice. She signed the agreement without a second opinion.

"They pressured her," Kate recalled.

The money the Fualaaus received was problematic for
Steve Letourneau's supporters. Though Steve cashed in
also, some felt he didn't do so in a way that would make
his children love their mother any less. Steve was careful
about what he said. So careful, some assumed that he was
some kind of a doofus who didn't have anything to say.

Further, the four children in Alaska were not benefiting
from any of the big money deals made by the Fualaaus.
They were out in the cold, left with the tales of their
mother having sex with Vili in "every room in the house"
and on the swing in their yard in Normandy Park. Steve's
lawyer, Greg Grahn, considered the whole moneymaking
effort "unfortunate." Not because Soona and Vili didn't
have the right to do so, but because of what he worried
would happen later.

"I think them doing it is going to have repercussions
on other innocent people, mainly the Letourneau children,
later. It's not that I'm pissed off that they are doing it. I
think it would be a lot more dignified if they wouldn't do
it," he said.

Driving home from work, Steve's divorce lawyer would
listen to talk radio as an endless stream of callers weighed
in on the Letourneau story. A number of times, he reached
for his phone and dialed all but one of the numbers. He
wanted to defend his client to the ninety percent of the
listeners who thought Steve was the problem, not his
wife's obsession with the boy.

Mary Kay is not a victim, he thought. Steve is. The kids are. Vili is.

He never dialed the last digit. Better not to vent. There had been too much of that already.

SEVENTY-SEVEN

HER FRIENDS DIDN'T see it coming, and neither did Mary Kay Letourneau. But within a few months of her prison incarceration she crossed over from person to commodity. Ten books were purportedly in the works, including her own and the one announced by her legal team. Steve talked about a book. So did Tony Hollick. She was reminded that her voice was *worth* something, her image could mean money. And she listened and accepted the idea as though it would do *her* some good. But the fact was that none of the deals made in her name were moving her any closer to being released to be with the "young man" she loved or her older children, whom she'd seen only once in the past year. Whether she could fully comprehend it in her isolation—those who had the most contact with her were the ones making the deals in her name—will never be known. Because for all of the things Mary Letourneau was and would be, loyal was at the top of the list of her personal attributes.

A week after Vili Fualaau unmasked himself for money on the front page of the *Globe,* discussions heated up at a Chicago-based production company called Towers Productions. The company had been looking at the Letourneau story as a possible show for several weeks. Jeff Tarkington and other producers there had pitched the idea to the A&E cable channel's *American Justice* in the fall of 1997, but it was rejected. The *Globe* article six months later brought new life to their plans.

In mid-May, Jeff Tarkington started the research process that eventually included conversations with Mary Kay Letourneau and David Gehrke. Both lawyer and former client seemed excited about the project—especially the lawyer. He said he'd be available for interviews when the producer came to Seattle the next month. Mary indicated that she had used A&E's programs in her classroom and thought the vehicle would offer her a positive, fair representation. She had one caveat, however. Nothing she told Jeff could be used in the program. *Everything was off the record.*

"She was really interested in what we had to do and what we thought. I told her we were interested in what she had to say, too, but I told her I didn't know how we were going to work together if everything we talked about was off the record," Jeff Tarkington said later.

Interviews lined up with David Gehrke and the Letourneaus' Normandy Park neighbor Tina Bernstein brought Jeff Tarkington to Seattle the second week in June 1998. When he arrived at the rental-car counter in the baggage-claim area at SeaTac Airport, he got the shock of his career after dialing David Gehrke's law office.

"I got a message through Dave's assistant that he was withdrawing his interview and he would not cooperate with us at any time. *Thank you very much.*"

That was it. Jeff Tarkington couldn't believe it. He wrote letters, faxed them from Chicago to David Gerhke's Seattle office. No reply. Phone messages went unreturned. Not a single word of explanation. *What had happened?* When he left Chicago everything was one big green light. When he landed in Seattle, zip.

"I had no idea where it came from or why," he said later. "I still don't. I never talked to Dave Gehrke again. I can't even speculate on it. There was such an enthusiasm for what we were trying to do and for our program."

And it suddenly got worse when next-door neighbor Tina Bernstein reneged on her interview. A trip to the old neighborhood to see if Tina could be persuaded was a bust.

"I won't talk to you," she said, standing in her doorway. "I *can't* talk to you."

The out-of-town producer explained how badly he needed her input. How she'd be the voice of concern for a neighbor and friend. Would she please reconsider?

"Absolutely not." Her firmness was undeniable. "Please get off my property."

Jeff Tarkington scrambled with the show, talking with Highline School District's Nick Latham and Susan Murphy, Dr. Julia Moore and several other psychiatrists. The show went on as scheduled, but the experience left a bitter taste.

"I was struck by the many brick walls I continually ran into on trying to get answers. It seemed like there was a lock-tight grip on many of the people who were closest to this case."

The carrots had been dangled and yanked away. With none of the principals available—Kate wouldn't go on camera, Michelle never returned phone calls, Steve wanted to put the television stuff behind him—Jeff Tarkington was left without any insiders. Except one—would-be writer Maxwell McNab. Maxwell, whose own ambitions for a book deal or a screenplay had stalled inexplicably, promised that he could deliver all kinds of materials relating to the case. Plus, he told the cable guy, if he played his cards right, Maxwell could deliver an interview with head groupie Abby Campbell. He knew all the principals—he'd visited with Mary Kay in jail and had her blessing as one of the "chosen writers" to tell her story.

Jeff Tarkington was interested at first. *Very interested.* But his enthusiasm waned as Maxwell became more aggressive about remuneration.

"He made it abundantly clear he wanted to be paid," Jeff Tarkington remembered.

At one point, the producer, a little desperate for sources, trial-ballooned an offer to have Maxwell serve as a consultant. He jerked the offer before Maxwell signed on.

"I thought better of it almost immediately, and thought, no. So the offer was never really truly made to [Maxwell]. But he really decided that that was the bandwagon that he should sort of hop on."

They didn't speak again.

"I never returned any of his messages after I returned

from Seattle. It didn't seem right to me. We don't pay for interviews and we never have.''

When Boston attorney Susan Howards first came into the picture in late spring, early summer of 1998, members of the media rejoiced. Many hoped the see-sawing of interviews granted and taken away would end. But there wasn't any improvement. In fact, for the BBC producer, it appeared to go from bad to worse when he learned it was David Gehrke—the affable and media-loving lawyer—not Bob Huff who had been replaced.

James Kent was bewildered and phoned Susan Howards to sort out the mess. According to the BBC producer, the Boston lawyer was in the dark, too.

"What wasn't made clear to Susan Howards was that Robert Huff would retain under his contract all media liaison between subjects and the media. All contractual deals, any money all went through Robert Huff. Susan Howards wasn't aware of that until it became clear that he did have those rights and again the BBC had a little problem," James Kent said later.

It was the modern version of an age-old tabloid story. Lawyers and members of the media tripped over each other in pursuit of who would talk and who would broadcast or write about what was said. In this case, James Kent felt great sympathy for the subject of his film. She said she wanted to do the BBC film, but her hands were tied, though to what degree she was uncertain.

It was frustrating and a complete waste of time for many of those who had come to Seattle to tell the story and head back home. Home to New York, Santa Monica, or London. If someone had only made the terms clear, some like the BBC producer Kent would have backed off. But no one could. And sadly for the BBC—and ultimately Mary Kay Letourneau—James Kent was under the pressure of a deadline. With money already spent and no conclusive hope that Mary would face his camera, he had to move on and look for another way to tell the story.

"But of course within the contract there were also things, I assume, that were not to be made public, and even when she asked for the contract at least to be given to her new lawyer Susan Howards, this seemed to be so long in coming that we had to proceed on the basis in the end that we wouldn't get her."

James Kent was very disappointed. He had come to Seattle with the promise and understanding that an interview with Mary would be forthcoming. He had wanted to be fair to the woman embroiled in the story her handlers were making more unseemly every day. He had wanted to look into her eyes and make an assessment based upon the hours he had spent on the case and the years he had spent interviewing people. He wanted to provide his audience with the complete, true picture of the American teacher who said she fell in love with her student.

The way he viewed it, Mary Letourneau had a media battle to win and he was just the producer to lead the charge. But as the days and weeks passed none of what he could do for her mattered. And in the end, he just couldn't fathom the way it had turned out and the role of those around her. He was the uninvited guest at everyone's dinner table.

"I couldn't believe the BBC having been treated like this. Having the doors been opened, invite us in, take our coat, sit us down at the table and say, 'You aren't expecting any food, are you?' "

At one point, James Kent recalled Susan Howards telling him in a phone conversation that he had "progressed this film prematurely—before having all the consents."

He found the statement outrageous.

"Hold on," he said he told the Boston attorney, "I have a go-ahead from her lawyer. I have a go-ahead from the subject of the film. I've spoken to the subject of the film repeatedly who told me an interview would happen, but to just be patient. I've got access to her good friends. At what point does one embark on a film?"

James Kent had a thought that he knew was as true as anything he learned about the Letourneau case: *She was let down by those around her.*

*   *   *

Within the group of "friends" who became enmeshed
with Mary Kay Letourneau, cause célèbre, there was one
whom the others would consider a traitor—Maxwell
McNab. As Kate saw the situation, Max was a "starving
writer" who ingratiated himself, won the confidence of
Mary Kay and her supporters, and burned them with a tell-
all article in *Mirabella*. Mary Kay felt that she and her
friends had been used and betrayed. Max had said he was
writing a screenplay.

"He got close to her and sold his soul for seven grand
to *Mirabella* and wrote an article that he never acknowledged he would write," Kate said later, still bitter.

But Maxwell went further, an irritation that outraged
her friends and harmed the convicted teacher's "fund-
raising" efforts. Kate heard from other media sources how
Maxwell had continued to peddle his so-called inside information to other shows. A&E producer Jeff Tarkington
called Kate in Chicago about McNab and his offer of material for money.

"Do I need him?" he asked.

"No," Kate said firmly. "He's an outsider and he's
trying to get back inside. He was on the inside and he
twisted the knife. I'll give you all the information you
need."

Articles about Mary Kay Letourneau were translated into
German, French, Spanish, and Dutch. Outside of America
it was seen as a love story, pure and simple. The idea that
Americans passed judgment on it had more to do with a
gut reaction springing from antiquated, deep-in-the-culture,
puritanical roots than whether it was really wrong.

It seemed to Mary Kay that the lack of understanding
surrounding her story was driven by the media. Whenever
information about her love for Vili came out, it brought
knowing snickers.

She and Vili had a secret code, a way to say "I love
you" without others knowing. It was through a look or
things they did—anything at all—with their left hands.

"I know some think that sounds juvenile, but I don't
care. It is quite pathetic that people take everything, dissect

it, and pronounce its worth by calling it juvenile. It was a way for us to say we loved each other, and we'll use the same ways when I'm a hundred years old," Mary Kay said later.

SEVENTY-EIGHT

THE SEATTLE FREELANCER for *Spin* magazine, Matthew Stadler, had been a friendly contact for many of the journalists stopping off in Seattle to court Mary Letourneau, and more critically it seemed, her lawyers. Among those he met with was James Kent, whom he found very straightforward and ethical, nearly an island in the sea of garbage that had accumulated around the story since it went worldwide with the second arrest and the disclosure of her second pregnancy.

James Kent later refused to say much about his Seattle meeting with book ghostwriter Bob Graham, other than to say the tabloid reporter was "very dismissive of the BBC and said, 'Go home, boy.' "

Matthew Stadler called it a setup arranged by Bob Huff. "It was dinner at the 'OK Corral.' He literally told James to get out of town, this was his. It was humiliating and horrible and he hated not only Graham, but Huff for setting the whole thing up."

Bob Huff later admitted that it was important to send a message that the Letourneau story was not for the taking.

"I remember Bob Graham and I getting pissed off at the other guys. We wanted to protect our interests. There were all these people buzzing around our pile a crap and we wanted them out of here."

After the kiss-off from Bob Graham, ostensibly the author of the French book about Mary Kay Letourneau, James Kent's resolve became even stronger. He'd press on with the story. He flew to Chicago to see Kate, the college friend, whose frequent collect calls from Mary had been one of the chief means of information concerning Mary's support of various projects that involved her.

According to James Kent, through Kate Stewart, Mary had indicated that she still supported the BBC film and wanted to remain involved.

"I don't think I've signed away my rights," she told Kate, who passed along the information.

After that Chicago visit, things improved considerably. Mary called James Kent "fifteen or twenty" times.

Bob Graham and the Fixot project be damned. It didn't seem to matter, not when the BBC had Mary Kay Letourneau calling the shots from prison herself—or so James Kent had believed. But just as others found out, with the Mary Kay Letourneau story, nothing lasts forever.

Bob Graham employed tabloid tactics to ensure that his story was protected. James Kent was appalled when he learned that the ghostwriter had told principals in the Letourneau story that *Inside Story* was tabloid trash akin to *Inside Edition.* Nothing could be further from the truth. *Inside Story* was a documentary series of which there was probably no American counterpart in terms of quality. It got back to him that Bob Graham had told sources that the BBC "did hatchet jobs" on people.

Another time, James Kent received a disturbing call from the author.

"I did receive a very threatening phone call from him, telling me that I had gone around telling interviewees that it was all right for them to talk to me, the BBC, because Laffont had no objections. I never told one interviewee that. He said if that continued, he'd sue me and the BBC."

At the same time, Bob Graham made it clear that *he— not Mary*—was running the show.

Mary Letourneau kept James Kent and the BBC on a string for as long as she could. No one could confirm her motives, other than that she wanted to keep her options open; she wanted to control something in which she could not fully participate. But she pulled back, away from the one producer who seemed sympathetic and genuinely concerned about her.

"That was to me a broken promise," he said.

Something else crossed James Kent's mind. He wondered if the love affair had run its course and that was the real reason for Mary Kay's silence, and indeed the silence of others close to the case. Maybe people were keeping mum because Vili Fualaau was no longer pining for his teacher, the mother of one baby, with another on the way.

If Vili Fualaau has already found someone else, it is a bit of a mockery, isn't it? It undermines Mary Kay's case that there was a deep and meaningful love relationship, James Kent thought.

The manner in which those closest to Mary Kay doled out their attentions made many feel they were doing reporters and producers a personal favor by even entertaining the possibility of an interview. The distrust and animosity from those who were speaking on Mary Kay's behalf was uncalled for and undoubtedly detrimental to her position.

"You are so lucky! The BBC is so lucky! You are going to get the chance to speak to Mary Kay Letourneau."

"Mary Kay needs the media more than the media needs Mary Kay," James Kent said later. "This is something her attorneys fail to recognize, apart from David. She's the one in jail. No one seems interested in getting her out."

SEVENTY-NINE

A FUNNY THING had happened to Mary Kay Letourneau on the way to prison. She had become the center of a freak show, *Globe's* favorite cover girl, an editor's antidote for flagging sales, a producer's favorite incarcerated "Get." Mary Kay Letourneau went from person to property. *Moneymaker.* All she had wanted to do was get her message out. Bipolar or not, she wanted the world to know that she loved a boy and he returned that love. No matter what people thought the story was, she said, it was about two families and it was about love. She was hopeful that the French book would change the way some viewed her.

Lawyers Bob Huff and David Gehrke had repeatedly insisted Paris-based Fixot was a publishing company without peer in the entire world and there'd be no selling Mary Kay's story short. Bob Graham, they also said, was the right writer for the job of taking her words and formatting them into a book. But when the ghostwriter left the women's prison after a pair of interviews in 1998, she had been left holding the bag.

"I remember when Bob Graham was leaving and I told him," she told a friend later, " 'we haven't touched on a big part of the story.' " According to Mary Kay, he never returned.

Mary Kay recalled how her biographer said he didn't feel she "trusted" him enough. It was true that she did have an uncomfortable feeling about the writer, but the publisher chose him. She'd had no choice. There had been no interview to see if he was compatible or even if he was a writer worthy of her story from a literary point of view.

"I was reluctant," she said. "I have to follow my heart on some things, and I have a good sense about people . . . and I didn't feel good about Bob Graham from the beginning."

As the weeks passed, Mary Kay's pregnancy brought a fullness to the gaunt features seen when she was arrested in January. Mary Kay told friends she was grateful for the baby. The pregnancy was a diversion from her own troubles as she waited for the writer to return. She had ideas; things that she wanted to say.

The summer ran into the fall, and an upbeat Mary Kay told other prisoners that she would be getting out just after the baby came. She'd be given a pardon or a trial. *Something would free her.* She saw that something as the French memoir.

As the due date of her second baby with Vili grew closer, Mary Kay began to worry and maybe even *accept* that freedom wouldn't come as quickly as hoped. She was suspicious that her stubble-bearded lawyer Bob Huff was not forthcoming about the French book and its publication schedule. When the lawyer visited her a day or two before leaving Seattle for Paris in the fall of 1998, Mary Kay would later say he was evasive. He told her he was *thinking* about going to France to determine what was going on with the book. His remarks were so casual, so off-handed. What he didn't tell her was that the book was already finished, and he had a copy.

"I had no idea he was going the next day! He made it sound vague, like he was only considering going to clear up some business matters with Fixot. He didn't say he was going on a book tour with his teenage daughter, David Gehrke, and Vili. I didn't know the book was even printed. As far as I was concerned we hadn't even finished it yet."

But it was. *Un Seul Crime, L'Amour (Only One Crime, Love)* was a hastily assembled volume of interviews of Vili, Soona and Mary Kay. Mary Kay told friends that chunks of text were simply not true. Disclosures of sex in cars and around every corner of the block were not the words of a soulful and loving young man like Vili. Having sex *two or three hundred times was not the message that she had wanted out!* Blanks were filled in in the rush to get the book out while the story was still hot.

"I know what happened," she said, bitterness creeping into her normally sweet voice. "Bob Huff got impatient and instead of waiting for the writer he drove Vili around Seattle talking into a tape recorder. They filled in the blanks with David and Bob. You can hear David's voice in the book, too."

She didn't blame Vili for what he had put into print. She saw Vili as a bit of a chameleon when it came to interacting with others.

"Put him in a car with a lawyer like Robert Huff and how do you think he's going to respond? He's going to act just like Bob because he wants to be liked, to fit in. Bob's like a surrogate father to him."

Bob Huff later refuted Mary Kay's allegations. He had been working around the clock with the book and didn't know that he was headed to Paris until a few days before he left. There wasn't time to reach Mary Kay. He admitted that he helped to "adapt" the English manuscript to French. He was fluent in French and the publishing crunch was on to get it out while the interest in the story was still high. He did not fabricate any of the content.

"I couldn't make any of this up," he explained. "It's too wild."

But Vili Fualaau's lawyer suggested that perhaps, the teacher's young lover did have a tendency to stretch the truth. Bob recalled one time when he "and the boys"— writer Bob Graham and Vili—were hanging out at Bob Graham's rented place in the Belltown section of Seattle discussing the book's content. Vili's details of conquests with his teacher grew more and more outrageous.

"You know how it goes," Bob Huff said later of the locker room banter. "But I did learn later that Vili did make up some stories. But we didn't need any bullshit. There was enough of a good story there."

Even if inaccurate, the book made headlines, as did nearly everything associated with the former teacher. But if she had hoped the book would help her—there was a postcard in the back pre-addressed to Washington State Governor Gary Locke, with a plea for clemency—it only made matters worse. While she wrote of her undying and spiritual love for Vili, the teen wrote of waiting to have sex with her and betting a friend $20 bucks that he could nail his teacher, and living in her car while she was re-leased from the King County jail. Mary Kay and Vili also wrote how they had disregarded the law and continued to see each other after her arrest at Shorewood Elementary. When she went into labor, it was Vili who drove her to the hospital—though, at 13, he didn't have a license and couldn't manage a stick shift. Mary took over and drove the rest of the way.

Other details were revealed, from the ridiculous (Mary Kay wore Mickey Mouse underwear at her sentencing) to the shocking (the sex). Vili wrote of a life in a violent home in the "hood," of sex with other girls, of influencing pre-teen Steven Letourneau to abandon his "preppy" ways for a gangster style—while he was sleeping with the boy's mother. He had no respect for Steve Letourneau, as a man or a husband.

Before they consummated their relationship, Mary Kay

had even told Vili that when two-year-old Jacqueline was of age, Vili should marry the girl. Mary Claire, she said, was too much like her father to be worthy of Vili's love. And while Vili struck a tough kid pose, Mary Kay's chapters, for the most part, were sweeter than a Hallmark card.

The book also described Mary Kay's month of freedom in January 1998 as one sexual escapade after another. She wrote how she even sneaked Vili into music teacher Beth Adair's Seattle house for nights of sex. When Mary was arrested the second time "in the car with the steamed up windows" Vili wrote how she had threatened suicide and how they had devised a "Romeo and Juliet" pact.

Mary later said there had never been any thought of suicide. She had read a biography of Virginia Woolf and learned how the author had loaded stones in her pockets before walking into a lake. She joked, she said, that she could do the same thing.

"The lake was right there. . . . It was not serious. 'Maybe I could put some rocks in my pockets and walk into Lake Washington'. It was not a threat. It was a joke."

Soona Fualaau lambasted the Highline School District when spokesman Nick Latham told a TV reporter that her son had lied about going on a promotional trip to France to market a book. According to Nick Latham, the boy had said he said he was going to Europe "to study art."

"She told us that we had no right to say anything about her son. Nothing whatsoever," the district spokesman said later.

EIGHTY

VILI FUALAAU WAS in Paris with his lawyers while Mary Kay went into labor and was rushed from the prison in an ambulance driven by Gig Harbor Fire Department paramedics on October 16, 1998. She was taken to St. Joseph's Medical Center in downtown Tacoma while the troop of media, groupies, and friends began to assemble to keep the vigil. A rumor circulated that the *Globe* had offered up to $50,000 for the first photograph of mother and baby. Nurses were put on notice to keep a wary eye for the media. At 36, Mary Kay became a mother for the sixth time when she gave birth to Alexis Georgia Fualaau. But this was not the blissful birth of a baby born to a woman who would take her home and placed her in the family's bassinet lined with the beautiful fabric from Duchamps. It was about a prisoner who handed her baby over to the infant girl's grandmother before being carted back to her cell.

The babies' names remained a point of contention between Soona and Mary Kay. Mary Kay had wanted to name her first baby with Vili "Audrey-Anna", but Soona nixed it as being too similar to the name of another family member. When the second baby was born, Soona refused to call the infant Georgia. In time, Mary Kay and her friends were the only ones who did.

"I'm getting used to these little fussy battles," Mary Kay said later, choosing her words carefully. "Soona and I don't always agree."

The big question after his second baby was born was not how Vili Fualaau felt about being a father for the second time, but whether his "soulmate" would be charged with a second count of rape. Prosecutors had said they considered filing a third-degree rape charge against her, but had decided enough was enough. No more charges would be filed.

"There's no legal barrier to prosecution of Mary Kay Letourneau," King County Prosecutor Norm Maleng said. "It is instead a question of justice. . . . seven and a half years is a substantial punishment for the conduct involved."

And poof . . . if was over. Or some had thought—and hoped—it would be. Few worked the media like the teacher and student.

Vili appeared on TV for money and Mary Kay called in to give her side of the story. She was hurt when Vili went off to France with Bob Huff's teenaged daughter and pictures of the pair appeared in the *Globe*. The tabloid even reported that Vili had several flings with neighborhood girls, though his heart still belonged to Mary Kay.

"I'm still in love with Mary and I still wear her ring. I'm not going to sit around and wait and cry my eyes out. I'm going to keep busy," he told *Inside Edition*.

Things were tough for the "toast of Paris" [as David Gehrke called Vili] when he returned to Seattle after the book tour. Vili was booted out of school for openly smoking pot on school grounds. Bob Huff showed up with his client to argue the boy's case before the school district. "It was the first time I've ever heard of a suspended kid bringing a lawyer to defend him on a routine suspension. Her son could have taken drug abuse counseling and enrolled back into class. Instead, they fought it," said a district employee.

TV reporter Karen O'Leary and others who followed the case knew that the whole sad Letourneau affair would never really be over. It would rear up once more and remind the world that the teacher and the student were still around. On the afternoon of November 9, the cracking voice on a police scanner indicated a shooting, a self-inflicted gunshot at a home in White Center. The address seemed familiar and Karen confirmed it for the news crew headed out with a camera: It was the home of Soona Fualaau.

"I was hoping that it wasn't Vili, that it wasn't some suicide. I thought of the love story he and Mary had tried to promote, and I wondered if the final chapter for the teenager had been written," Karen O'Leary said.

In the middle of the afternoon, Vili's brother, Perry, had been shot in the abdomen while reportedly fooling around with a gun with a cousin. The seventeen-year-old's injuries were severe and he was hospitalized for several weeks, reportedly with the loss of a kidney, damage to his spleen and other serious injuries. Vili, his children, and Soona were not home at the time. Family members said they were living in a hotel paid for by *Inside Edition*.

When KIRO News crews got there, David Gehrke told them the family had no comment.

Later, Karen O'Leary wondered why David would have been there at all. Mary Kay had fired him after she hired the Boston lawyer Susan Howards and filed her appeal in the spring. And, as far as she knew, he never directly handled anything for the Fualaaus.

"He just doesn't want to be left out, that's all," Karen suggested.

Mary Kay went ballistic at the news of the shooting. Her daughters were living in an unsafe environment. She told a friend that she even phoned in a complaint to the authorities to have her kids removed from Soona's care, but nothing happened.

She also worried about Vili.

"I'm hurting for Vili, the lack of support he is getting. I don't expect Soona and the others to support Vili *and* me. Why would they do that? But they should support who he is and what he should be doing with his life. Vili deserves the recognition for his talent, his genius. I'm struggling with my loyalty to them, when they show none to me," she told a friend.

Though it wasn't fast enough for her lawyer and the Fualaaus, Mary Kay spent most nights during the first part of 1999 working on the English language translation of the Fixot book. She told friends she was distressed by the gross inaccuracies she found in the manuscript. At night, she pulled out a little aqua trunk as a table and slid a reading lamp close to her bed and worked into the early morning, revising, commenting, and even laughing. A few times she read the passages out loud to her cellmate and the two would nearly roll on the floor in hysterics. It was ludicrous. The last line was the topper. Bob Graham had written a scene that smacked of an old Susan Hayward movie. She was calling out through the bars for understanding. "I beg of you . . . this is love . . . *I beg of you* . . ."

From her prison phone—her lifeline to the world— Mary Kay told a friend perhaps the most shocking aspect of her story. Her children were being kept from her, she claimed, because she hadn't finished the revisions for the English version of *Only One Crime, Love*.

Bob Huff bristled at the idea that anyone was keeping the children away from Mary Kay. He remembered seeing paperwork associated with arranging prison visitation with Mary and her babies. It was proof, he believed, of Soona's desire to allow Mary Kay to see Audrey and Georgia Alexis.

"I don't think Soona is that diabolical to pull off this big scam of creating the letters and acting like she's trying if it wasn't really true."

Mary Kay also feared that they'd release the book without her input. "I will say it's not me . . . if they step over the line like that. I'll call every news media person I know and they'll put me on the air. I will go down the line on this and Bob and David know it."

Ghostwriter Bob Graham used his interviews with Mary Kay Letourneau one more time in the winter of 1999 when he wrote a pair of pieces for the London *Sunday Times Magazine* and a London tabloid. The article quoted Bob Huff as saying that Mary Kay had threatened to say Vili had raped her, if he didn't do the right thing and marry her. "That's Mary for you," Bob Huff reportedly said, "She wants her way, no matter what happens."

Mary Kay said she wanted to call Bob Huff to ask why he would say such a thing.

"But I can't. He doesn't have a phone that works . . . at least one that I know of. Can you imagine having a lawyer who doesn't have a phone number?" she asked.

In January 1999, Mary Kay spoke on a Seattle radio show hosted by a DJ known as the "T-man." A few days after she told the world how much she loved Vili, a letter was dispatched to the station. The prison considered the radio interview third-party contact with the victim, a violation of Mary Kay's sentence. Vili hadn't been on the show at the same time—not even on the same day—but the prison saw it as Mary using the media to get her message of love and hope for marriage out to the teenage father of two.

According to Mary, Bob Huff was livid. "Any time you speak to any sector of the media, the less value your name has," she recalled him telling her in a fit after the radio broadcast.

The TV movie announced by USA Network also occupied Mary Kay's time and though she didn't have a direct financial interest in it, she was ever hopeful that money would be funneled to her children. Casting was a source of amusement. Tatum O'Neal, Darryl Hannah, Gail O'Grady, even Calista Flockart were mentioned as possible Mary Kays. They were too old, not pretty enough, or too unknown to play the role, but Mary Kay acted as though she didn't care one way or another. It was New York producer Sonny Grosso's and loyal friend Susan Gehrke's project and whatever it was, would be out of her control anyway.

"I very much trust Sonny Grosso. He's like a favorite uncle," she said. "He would make sure it was true, whatever the movie is . . . it will be true."

Mary Kay spent five hours a day in the clinic expressing milk for her baby and storing it in a freezer that the prison bought for her use. "I know other nursing mothers could use it, too. But I feel like it's mine, my own little freezer." Susan Gehrke made several trips a week to pick up frozen breast milk for baby Georgia. Baby Alexis. Whatever name she was called.

According to what Mary Kay told a friend, after the first of the year, the Fualaaus had found a video of her teaching class and wanted to sell it to *Inside Edition*. They needed the money. For a family who had once lived on next to nothing, who had been on welfare and made do, they needed the cash that Mary Kay's name could bring. Mary was upset about the suggestion of airing the video and said it could not be used. There were students of hers in the video and it was out of the question to get them involved in something like that.

The turning point, if there could be one for Mary Kay, came during the February 1999 television broadcast "sweeps" when Vili Fualaau went before the cameras on

Inside Edition with a fistful of letters written to him by the mother of his two children. It was an appearance for money.

It was also evident that the rift between Mary Kay and Soona had widened. In one of the five letters, Mary Kay accused Audrey and Georgia's grandmother of "stealing our babies and not caring enough" about Vili.

She also sounded like a girl obsessed with her boyfriend.

"The only kids you're having are mine . . . I'll give you 18 if that's what you want, but your babies are mine . . ." she wrote.

Eighteen was the number of children that Vili's imprisoned father had sired—the man Vili had once told sixth-grade classmate Katie Hogden he had never wanted to emulate.

But it was the letter with the heading "Test Time" that brought the most attention. She wrote how she threatened "automatic castration" if he even looked at another girl. He thought she sounded a little "crazy," but he liked the fact that she wanted him to be true to her. After the *Inside Edition* show aired, Mary Kay told friends she was shocked and appalled about the betrayal.

"I told them no and I guess they had to find something else to sell. It is okay for Vili to sell me out," she said shortly after the program aired. Her voice caught in her throat a bit, indicating that maybe it wasn't so okay after all. "I guess they needed the income," she said.

Steve Letourneau also found dollars as reason to weigh in and slam his wife once more during the sweeps-rating period. He appeared on the low-rated *Extra* telling the world that Mary Kay had to take responsibility for what she did before he could forgive her. During the tumultuous last two years of Steve and Mary Kay Letourneau's marriage, a total of *four* children were born of their extramarital relationships.

But what of Mary Kay's children, her six "angels"? The four in Alaska were off-limits because baggage handler Steve Letourneau had decided that was best. But what of the youngest? Even during her long summer of waiting for

the sentencing, Mary Kay had been allowed to have baby
Audrey. She had also seen Audrey in the King County
Regional Justice Center. But not at the prison. Mary Kay
told friends that the paperwork for which Soona was responsible was the big hold-up in arranging visits with Audrey and Georgia. When the weeks melted into months,
through a "third party" Mary Kay confronted the "Samoan Queen."

"Why is it taking you [Soona] nearly three months for
to comply?" Mary Kay had asked.

The purported response from the forty-year-old grandmother was chilling: "Have you finished the English manuscript?"

"Those were her exact words. I almost didn't believe
it," Mary Kay later said. "But others have said the same
thing."

Tensions between Mary, her lawyers, and the Fualaaus
escalated in the months since Georgia's birth. Mary told
friends that she certainly understood where Vili's mother
stood when it came to caring for the two babies. Soona
Fualaau deserved respect for taking the children in and,
more importantly, for standing up and saying that Mary
Kay Letourneau wasn't an evil predator, but a part of their
family. *But why wasn't she getting the babies down to the
prison?*

Though for most, Mary Kay kept a brave face and a
smile so indelible a Sharpie could have drawn it, there
were times when it seemed things were sinking in.

"Where are my babies?" she asked. "All I hear is, 'Are
you done with the book?' But I have to play along. What
choice do I have?"

But she couldn't finish it. The book was such a shambles, such a farce, that she couldn't fix it fast enough. It
was her life, not theirs, after all.

"At best I think I can make it a C+, but doesn't our
story deserve better than that?"

Even a year after she traded her baggy jeans and layers of
oversize T-shirts for prison garb, Mary Kay Letourneau
wasn't "over" insofar as the media was concerned. Per-

sonally, however, she was running out of steam despite the fact that the public was still interested. She was still news. She appeared over the phone on *Oprah* during the winter 1999 television advertising "Sweeps".

"I didn't know what *Sweeps* was," she told a friend with an exaggerated sigh, "now I know that when they want to boost their ratings it means putting me on the air."

According to Mary Kay, Bob Huff sent a letter in early 1999 stating that he found her entirely responsible for the delay of the American edition of the book. Nothing, Mary Kay believed from everyone around her, but the book mattered.

"You seem to be totally out of touch with the reality with the ... book ... in completing your part. You have a million and one excuses ..."

According to Mary Kay's interpretation of the missive, Bob Huff was going to demand Vili's share of the advance and cut her out because she was in violation of the contract.

"Vili is the golden egg to Huff," Mary Kay told a friend not long after the ultimatum was made. "Through my name he gets that title, he gets the money because of it. If Vili and I were married, Bob doesn't get his twenty-percent because we don't need him."

All she could do was dial phone numbers and wait for a jaded world to right a wrong, for her lawyers to drop off the face of the earth, for Vili to make good on his promise to love her forever. The problem was that Vili was still a boy, unable to make adult decisions for himself. His mother and his lawyer Bob Huff needed him. And as Mary saw it, it was better for those players that she was confined to a cell at the Washington Corrections Center for Women.

"For a while she kept thinking that she was getting out of here any day now," a fellow prisoner said a year after Mary Kay became an inmate there. "She kept saying that Vili was working on getting her out of here. I felt sorry for her. I wouldn't count on Vili for anything. He's just a kid. He's not working on getting her out. As long as she's

in here, she's worth something to them. Sad, isn't it? Isn't
she something more than a way to make money?''

Yes, she was more. This teenager in a woman's body was
a friend, a teacher, a mother, a felon. To some she was
also a predator, a child rapist. To Mary Kay herself, when
soaring with manic enthusiasm, she was a goddess. Among
the notes Steve Letourneau turned over to King County
Detective Pat Maley was a list of attributes that Mary Kay
had once written about herself. It was crafted in a diagram
format, with circles and arrows leading from one word to
the next as she raced to reach the definition of who and
what she was.

   *"Strong, smart, passion in life, beautiful, look young,
loving, faithful . . . sunsets, a family, giver . . . sunny days,
kissing and lots of sex-love.''*
   "Me.''

Vili Fualaau, on the other hand, is still trying to figure
out who he is and how he fits into the world. His body
has morphed from a boy's to a young man's since he first
kissed his sixth-grade teacher. His mustache has grown
from a shaky C to a solid B. He's taller. He smokes. He
attends school sporadically and girls flock to him in greater
numbers than they might have before all of this happened.
He alternates between seemingly shy and push-the-enve-
lope outrageous. A father of two, he's a teenager trapped
with a grown man's responsibility. He's seen the world's
highs and lows and is connecting the dots in between.

Lawyer Bob Huff isn't sure about the kid's prospects;
he's only sure of what might have been. The whirlwind of
the Mary Kay Letourneau story both lifted Vili up and
pulled him down.

   "Besides a trip to Paris, a little money in a trust—
which ain't that much—he's not better off. When we were
promoting the story in France, there was the brush with
celebrity, the world of art, maybe some scholarships would
come his way, then the big bubble burst. And nothing. The
English version of the book didn't happen. It *could have*
happened. I wanted that for Vili. I wanted him to be able

to make the rounds here to tell his story. But Mary Kay ruined that.''

In the end, neither got what they wanted. Mary Kay had wanted her book to reach out and drain the venom from all the naysayers who dismissed her love for the boy and tagged her a rapist. Caught up in the heady mirage of media dollars, Vili and his family had simply wanted a better future, a piece of the pie.

Depressed over the outcome—a cancelled American edition of the French book, a stalled TV movie because the subject matter made television executives queasy—the lawyer charged with spinning the scandal into gold felt sorriest for the Fualaaus.

"It's like people who win the lottery and are penniless the next year. That's what happened to Vili and his family," Bob Huff said. "Pretty unbelievable. Pretty sad story.''

AUTHOR'S ACKNOWLEDGMENTS AND NOTES

ALTHOUGH THERE WOULD be hours upon hours spent on the telephone, a face-to-face meeting with Mary Kay Letourneau would come only weeks before *If Loving You Is Wrong* was sent to the publisher in New York. The chance to see Mary arrived in the first week in February 1999—in fact, on the first anniversary of the night when she was found in her car with the steamed-up windows.

In that year's time, so much had happened to her, and to my view of her story.

I arrived at the Washington Corrections Center for Women around 6:30 P.M., filled out the forms, had my photo taken, and stood in line with another fellow who was there to see his someone: his wife, his girlfriend, his mother. I didn't know who.

"First time in?" the young man asked. I nodded. "Lots of famous people in there," he said as we walked outside into the damp February air, chain link and razor wire as far as the eye could see, on our way to the building where visits were conducted.

"Really?" I said.

He smiled. "Yeah, I saw at the desk that someone is going to be seeing Mary Letourneau tonight."

I sat down in a cafeterialike visiting room and waited with the others for the visit to start. And I waited. As she always was, according to just about everyone who knew her, Mary was running late. I looked around and saw the women and their men, their children, playing cards and laughing. An old man set up a place for his daughter with all of her vending machine favorites: a Coke, a bag of chips, Reese's Peanut Butter Cups, a Hershey bar, and three napkins fanned out in a place-setting.

When Mary finally arrived, I had been there for a half hour.

The voice on the phone all those weeks was now a person. She was small, so thin, and her childlike demeanor startled me. She had come from the kitchen where she worked folding napkins. It was a job, she said, she didn't mind because she was still expressing milk for her baby. "I need to eat a little extra," she said.

We talked about her life in prison and she told me that it had been difficult, but she knew it wasn't forever. She chatted with a kind of exuberance that didn't fit her circumstances. I asked her about it and she told me that she never gets depressed, she's an "up" person and always had been. What had happened to her after she fell in love with her student was an inconvenience, but not the end of her world.

I noticed her silver ring and I asked to see the inscription. She tugged on the band for a second, then stopped herself because it might be a violation of the rules, she wasn't sure. It was inscribed with "I'll Be There," she said. She told me how she and Vili had searched the Seattle area over in hopes of finding the perfect ring. Vili had even sketched out a design he had in mind; he also sketched the letters for the inscription. Everything, Mary said, was created for their perfect union.

"I didn't know you could wear jewelry here," I said.

"Only a wedding band," she answered. Her smile was coy.

"Then you are married to Vili?" I asked.

"Yes, and it is blessed," she said.

I asked for details, but she didn't feel like giving any. I didn't want to bring up the fact that she was already married to Steve and marrying Vili was another crime. She told me they had exchanged vows of eternal love on Mercer Island, an affluent suburb just east of Seattle—a world from White Center.

She told me she could make it in prison another year, but she was fearful that she could not really survive her full sentence. "I'm willing to do a fair amount of time," she said, "but I don't think I really can make it here much longer than a year more."

She wanted to be out so she could be with Vili. The teenager, the father of her youngest children, was not an enigma to Mary, but a masterful warrior who had captured her heart. He was younger than she by more than twenty years, but in some ways, he was her superior.

"It blows my mind," she said of the boy's character. "He's truly amazing. He dominated me in the most masculine way that any man, any leader could do. I trusted him and believed in him and in our future."

Interestingly, while she talked about Vili at length, she barely mentioned her four oldest children, except to blame Steve for keeping them from her as they battled over custody issues in their divorce.

Mary had given up everything—her family, her freedom, and her profession for the love of a thirteen-year-old. He was an artistic genius, the old soul. He was the leader; she followed him. He was the master. He was the adoring object of her affections. That's how she saw it. The roles they embodied, she said, were from another era. He dominated her.

"I am *with* Vili. If you are truly in love, the roles are natural."

She never felt that way with Steve because he was not, she said, her equal.

Like a teenager who refuses to do the dishes, Mary had been unyielding in her defiance and did nothing to bend to the rules of prison life. Inmates who had befriended her watched her dig herself in deeper. She didn't seem to realize going with the flow gets you out sooner. Pissing off the guards only leads to trouble; trouble leads to a loss of good time. She learned how to do a few things—"to bend, twist, and turn to do my little dance"—when guards demanded a strip search.

She also learned how to blow smoke rings and sometimes, like a lovesick teenager, would blow them into the sky with a wish they'd waft over the razor wire and find their way to White Center and Vili. Vili, she thought, was standing by her. He was Zeus. He was the man of her dreams, a godlike boy-man whose love would hold them together no matter the bars between them. Or so she repeatedly said to inmates, guards, and visitors.

She was younger than her years in nearly every way. She was charming, wide-eyed, and prone to a quick laugh. It struck me that she seemed so happy. No matter that she was in prison and away from the love of her life and her children and she would never teach school again. At times she spoke in the exaggerated manner of a schoolteacher reciting a story, in which she was the main character. Of course, others had told me that she acted "young." Some were convinced that she was so good at teaching grade school because she identified with her students. Others had been harsh in their assessments. They saw her as a case of arrested development—stuck as an adolescent. I know Mary (no one but those who knew her in childhood or through media exposure calls her Mary *Kay*) would argue that nothing could be more beautiful than seeing the world through the eyes of a child. What is wrong with the giddy enthusiasm of youth?

I left the prison that night with more questions than answers. Oddly, the questions had little to do with Mary. Instead, I wondered about those who knew her in the years and months before she became involved with her student. If her manner had not changed dramatically from those days to what I saw in prison, why hadn't anyone helped her? I recalled one of the psychiatrists saying that she had liked Mary a great deal, but was exasperated by her actions and words. She wanted to reach out and "shake some sense" into her. I understood that completely.

Why hadn't Steve Letourneau, who knew her better than anyone, stepped in to help his wife before her meltdown led to disaster?

Didn't friends, co-workers, her principal, see what I saw in that prison visiting room?

And what of all this media coverage? Why had so many people felt the need to get on television to exploit her? Steve Letourneau turned up on a television tabloid show telling the world how he was getting along and how he hoped for a divorce from his infamous wife sooner, rather than later. His flight attendant girlfriend Kelly Whalen was pregnant with his child. The idea that Steve felt compelled to be heard bothered Mary Kay, and she told me so. It was *her* story, not his, that was of worldwide interest. His hawking of family photos and comments about her love for Vili was detrimental to the healing Steven, Mary Claire, Nicholas, and Jacqueline so desperately needed.

"What benefit can there be for the children in his selling the story, the lies? For the sole purpose of making money?" she asked.

When the subject of old friends came up, Mary Kay tried to dismiss those outside of her tight circle as people who didn't really know her. Michelle Jarvis went from close friend to outsider when the Californian cried her eyes out on TV's *Leeza* when the show featured the contents of the French book. Michelle thought Mary Kay was sick, and said so.

For her part, Michelle told friends that she still loved Mary Kay and hoped that one day she'd be able to rise above the travesty that she'd made of her life by getting treatment.

"Not a day passes that I don't think of her and pray for her . . . I don't want her rationalizations ringing in my ears, my heart wanting to believe them while my brain tells me precisely what they really are," she said.

Of course close friends and the Letourneau children have been devastated by what happened in the wake of what happened between Mary Kay and Vili. There were enough tears to fill Puget Sound. Students, teachers, neighbors, friends—all had been left heartbroken. In time, most know, the impact will fade and soften for some.

But for some the legacy of the story will endure. Danelle Johnson's daughter became pregnant at fourteen.

GREGG OLSEN

"She wasn't the only girl in Mrs. Letourneau's class that had ended up like that. When [my daughter] told me she was pregnant—by a man older than eighteen, though I'm not sure how much older—she said her pregnancy was just like Mrs. Letourneau's with Vili. It was *love*. The age difference. The whole Romeo and Juliet thing. Some lesson she learned in that sixth-grade class."

The best true crime books are built on a solid foundation of original research. I always measure the quality of a book in this genre by the information that the author has unearthed. Who wants a rehash of what is already in the public domain? I want to know more. Accomplishing that is not always easy. In fact in these days of tabloid and checkbook journalism, it has become increasingly difficult. Money is now in the mix. Just as a reporter will not pay for information (paying could induce sources into creating false information or even exaggerating legitimate information in order to make the buyer feel as though he is getting his money's worth), I do not offer money for interviews. In this case, more than any I have tackled, the request for cash for information was played out with numbing regularity. Directly or indirectly it was suggested to me that cash would lead to interviews. Those with hands held outward included everyone from a police officer to friends and associates of Mary Letourneau. One individual asked for $70,000. At no time during my phone conversations and visits did Mary Letourneau request remuneration.

Given such a climate, it must be stated here that I could not have overcome all of the obstacles and all of the closed doors without the talents of crime writer and researcher Gary Boynton. Not only did Gary hang in there with the dogged determination of a private eye, he did so with a polite and professional attitude about which several sources—friendly *and* hostile—remarked. Thanks, Gary.

As always, I appreciated the support of my literary agent, Susan Raihofer of Black, Inc., New York; editor Charles Spicer and his assistant Dorsey Mills of St. Martin's Press, New York; and my faithful advance readers,

June Wolfe and Tina Marie Schwichtenberg. Special appreciation goes to Kathrine Beck, who encouraged me when it looked as if the story would be impossible to crack.

Finally, I was not able to secure interviews with Steve Letourneau, Patricia Maley, Vili Fualaau, Soona Fualaau, Sharon Hume, or the Letourneau children for this book, though I made efforts to do so. I spoke to Robert Huff just as this book was being prepared for printing.

—Gregg Olsen
Spring 1999
e-mail: greggolsen@msn.com